IMAGES
of America

TYBEE ISLAND

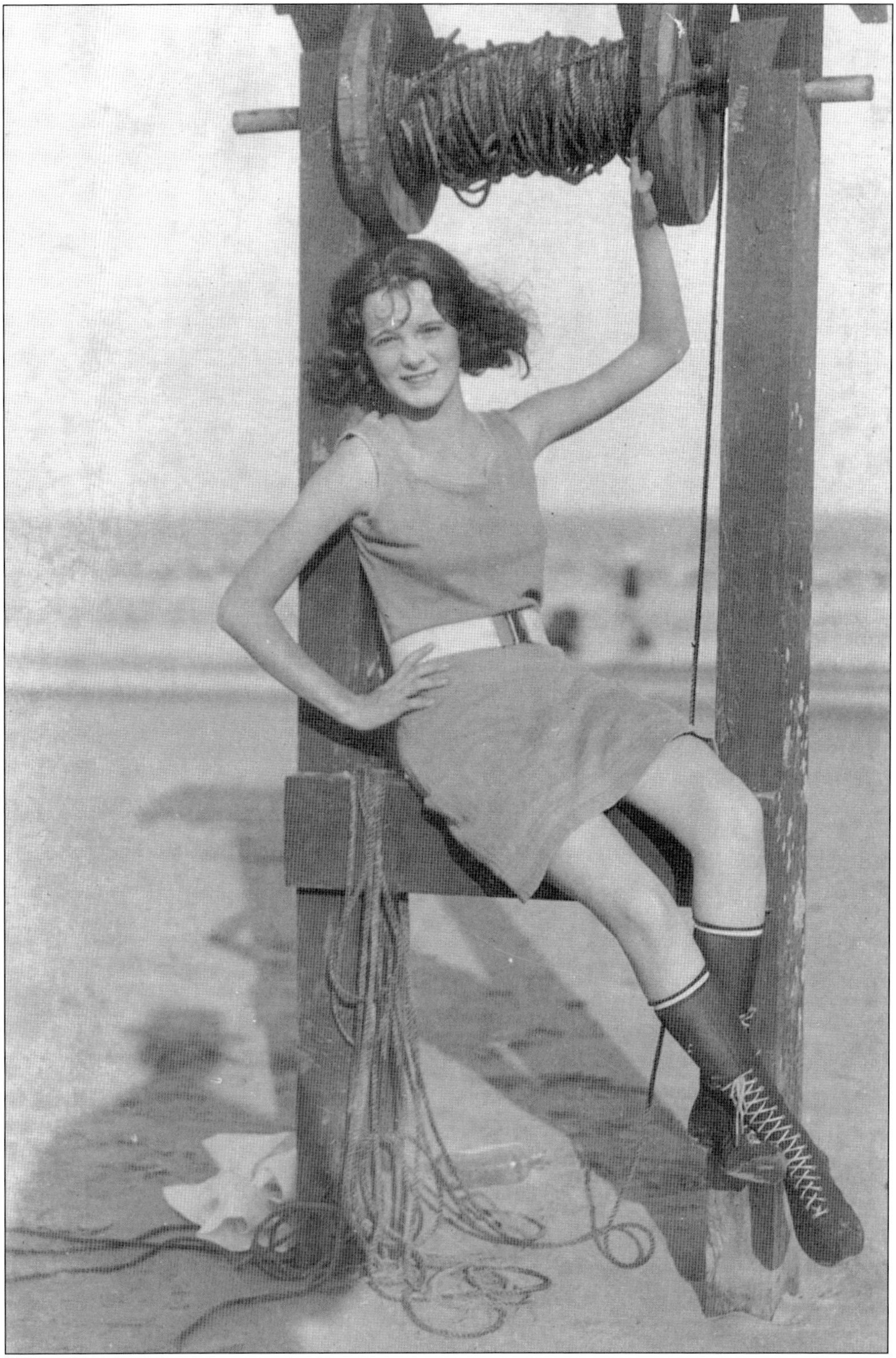

This young lady was an early 1900s visitor to Tybee Island's beaches.

IMAGES
of America

TYBEE ISLAND

James Mack Adams

ARCADIA
PUBLISHING

ISBN 978-0-7385-0576-3

Published by Arcadia Publishing
Charleston, South Carolina

Printed in the United States of America

Library of Congress Catalog Card Number: 00-103177

For all general information contact Arcadia Publishing at:
Telephone 843-853-2070
Fax 843-853-0044
E-Mail sales@arcadiapublishing.com
For customer service and orders:
Toll-Free 1-888-313-2665

Visit us on the Internet at www.arcadiapublishing.com

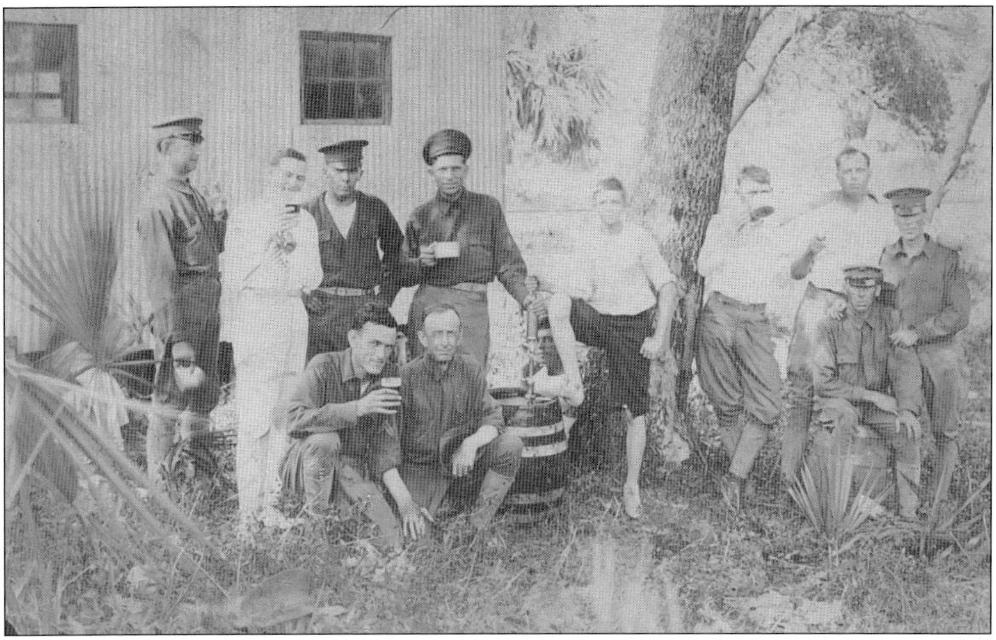

Fort Screven on Tybee Island was an active military post for almost 50 years (1897–1945). Soldiers in this photograph from the turn of the 20th century are enjoying some leisure time after a hard duty day.

Contents

Acknowledgments

A book such as this is never a one-person project. The writer's work would never see print without the help and support of the many people who contribute toward the end product. This book is therefore dedicated to those people, past and present, who have been a part of Tybee Island's history and have contributed to its uniqueness.

The author cannot adequately express his appreciation to Director Cullen Chambers and the staff of the Tybee Island Historical Society for their invaluable assistance, support, and encouragement throughout the production of this work. The society opened its history files and entrusted its collection of rare photographs to the author.

A special thank you is also appropriate to the Georgia Historical Society, the National Park Service, Fort Pulaski National Monument, J.R. Roseberry, Louise White, Carl Looper, and Jane South Lindner for supplying additional photographs.

Much of the text material comes from the author's research for the writing of his "Historically Speaking" column published weekly in the *Closeup* editions of the *Savannah Morning News*, and from his previously published book, *A History of Fort Screven, Georgia*. Also used as reference was *Historic Tybee Island* by Margaret Godley.

Writing has been described as a very personal and a very lonely profession. It can be just as lonely for the writer's loved ones. I also dedicate this work to my wife, Jeanne, who spends many hours without my company while I retreat into the private world of writing.

And, it would be an unforgivable omission not to express gratitude to the many people whose images appear in this book. Without them, there would not be a book.

Introduction

Tybee Island is a small coastal barrier island 17 miles east of Savannah, the Georgia colony's first permanent settlement and now one of the country's largest urban national landmark historic districts. Much of the history of Tybee Island is tied to Savannah. However, the island is singular among Georgia's coastal islands and has a history that is uniquely its own.

This small island is home to approximately 3,500 permanent residents, but the population grows to 8,000 or more during the height of the spring and summer tourist season. Visitors come from all over the country and the world to enjoy the beach, museum, lighthouse, and nearby Fort Pulaski, a Civil War–era fort operated by the National Park Service. Adding to the island's reputation as a tourist destination is its close proximity to historic Savannah.

Centuries before British settlers arrived to carve the Georgia colony out of a wilderness between South Carolina and Florida, Tybee Island was visited by Spanish and French explorers, and served as a food and water stop for pirates who sailed the southeast coast. Native Americans who came to the island to hunt and fish gave it the name Tybee, a Euchee Indian word meaning "salt." It is presumed the name was derived from the ocean and the salt mashes that border the island.

Tybee has had two other names during its history. When the town was incorporated in 1887, it was given the name Ocean City. That name was short lived and was changed back to Tybee a year later.

By the turn of the 20th century, Savannahians were traveling by train and later by automobile to Tybee to enjoy a day at the beach. The "day trippers," as they were called, began to think of Tybee as Savannah's beach. It was during this time the town's name was changed to Savannah Beach.

The number of full-time island residents began to increase during the first half of the 20th century. In the late 1970s, a group of Savannah Beach residents desired to reclaim the town's identity and petitioned for the name to be changed once again back to Tybee. They were successful in their endeavor and the island has been called Tybee from that time on.

In 1736, three years after the Savannah colony was established, its founder, Gen. James Edward Oglethorpe, ordered the building of a lighthouse on Tybee. It was the first major structure in the colony, and there has been a lighthouse on Tybee since that time. The present recently restored Tybee Lighthouse dates from 1773 and is the oldest and tallest in Georgia. The site is visited by over 70,000 tourists a year. A major goal of the Tybee Island Historical Society is to restore the Tybee Lighthouse and Light Station in order to qualify for National Historic Landmark status.

It was during the colonial period that a quarantine hospital was built on Tybee's west end. It was one of a chain of lazarettos, or pest houses, built for the quarantine and medical treatment of persons carrying highly contagious diseases. Vessels entering the mouth of the Savannah River were stopped and inspected for evidence of disease. Passengers or crew found to be ill were hospitalized in the lazaretto for 40 days and the vessel was not allowed to enter the Port of Savannah during the same quarantine period. Those who died were buried on the site in unmarked graves. Tybee Island's western boundary, Lazaretto Creek, got its name from the pest hospital that once set on its bank.

During the first year of America's Civil War, Union Army cannoneers bombarded Confederate-held Fort Pulaski from Tybee's western shore. Historians say this was the first major test for rifled cannon.

During the late 1800s and early 1900s, Tybee Island was considered the premier resort beach on the Georgia coast. This prominence preceded the development and growing popularity of Georgia's "Golden Isles." Thousands of people from Savannah and further away visited the popular coastal retreat to stay in its luxury beach hotels, enjoy the sun and surf, and dance in the Tybrisa Pavilion to the smooth rhythms of the popular big bands of the day.

It was during this resort era that two Miss Georgia pageants were held at Tybee's Tybrisa. In the first pageant, bathing suits were forbidden, even though they were permitted at the time in the Miss America contest. It was also during this era that many of Tybee's architecturally unique beach cottages were built. This style of beach cottage architecture now exists nowhere else on the East Coast.

For the better part of 50 years, from 1897 to 1945, there was a military reservation on the island's north end. Fort Screven served as a coast artillery battery, infantry post, and training base. It was the Army's only underwater diving school in the continental United States during World War II. Fort Screven's most famous commander was Lt. Col. George Catlett Marshall. General Marshall later became Army chief of staff, secretary of defense, secretary of state, and authored the Marshall Plan for the rebuilding of a war-ravaged Europe following World War II.

Tybee seemed to sleep during much of the last half of the 20th century and was referred to by some as "the best kept secret on the east coast." This is no longer the case. The well-kept secret is out. The small island, with its easygoing, laid-back, small-town atmosphere, has been discovered by retirees and by others just trying to escape the big-city scene. The changing demographics have triggered a development boom. As a result, much of the island's historic fabric has either been lost or is endangered.

Realizing what is happening to their island, several residents have worked to spark an interest in preserving as much as possible of the "Old Tybee." The author hopes this book will promote this interest and act as a source for readers to either learn about or to recall the Tybee Island that once was.

One

Tybee's Guiding Lights

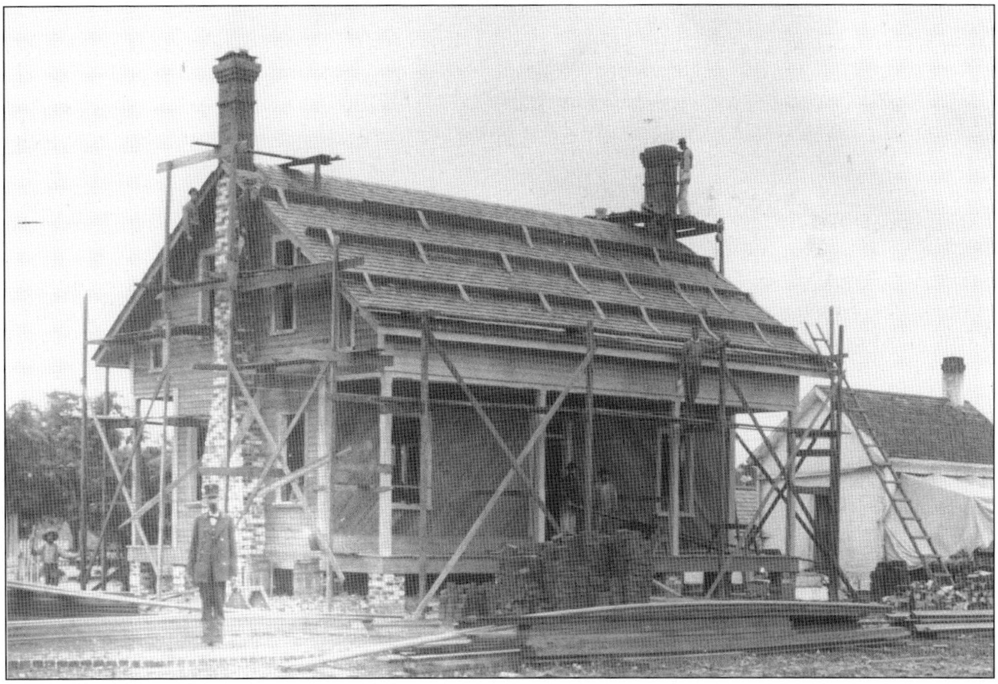

The first assistant keeper's house constructed at the Tybee Light Station in 1885 exhibited the "stick style" architecture that was popular at the time. The man in uniform is First Assistant Keeper Patrick Eagan. The house is now used as the residence of the director of the Tybee Island Historical Society. Workers are also doing some renovation on the c. 1812 summer kitchen.

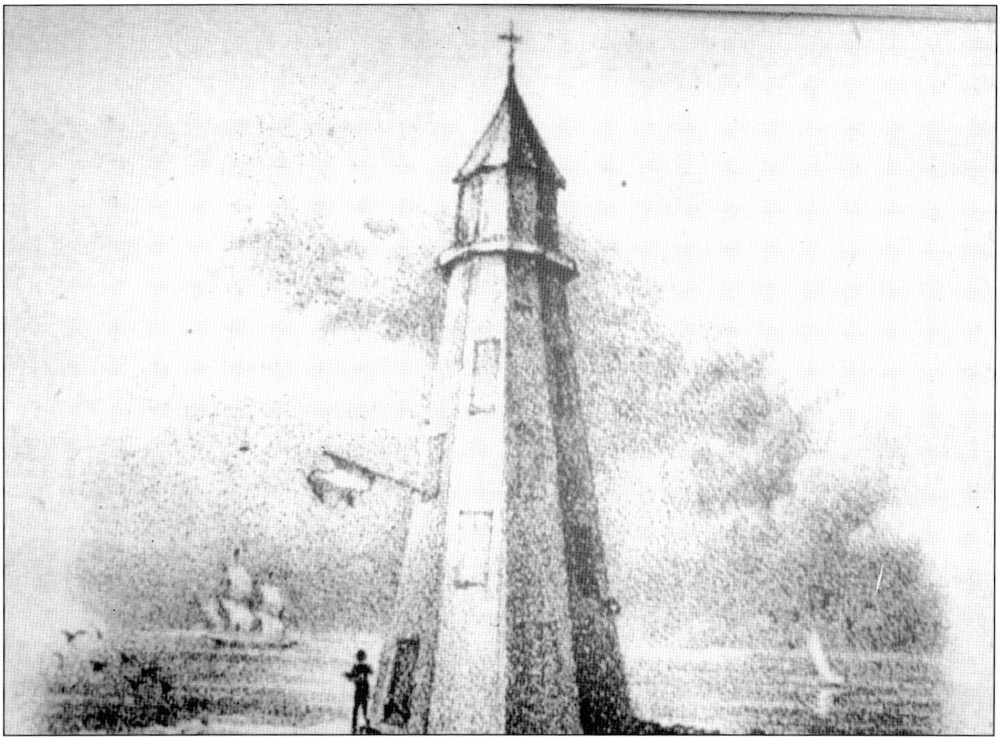

In 1733, Gen. James Oglethorpe, Georgia's founder, inspected Tybee Island to choose a site for a lighthouse to mark the entrance to the Savannah River. The tower completed in 1736 was constructed of wood with a brick foundation. At a height of 90 feet, it was the tallest building of its kind in America. Tybee's first lighthouse was built too close to the shore and fell during a 1741 storm.

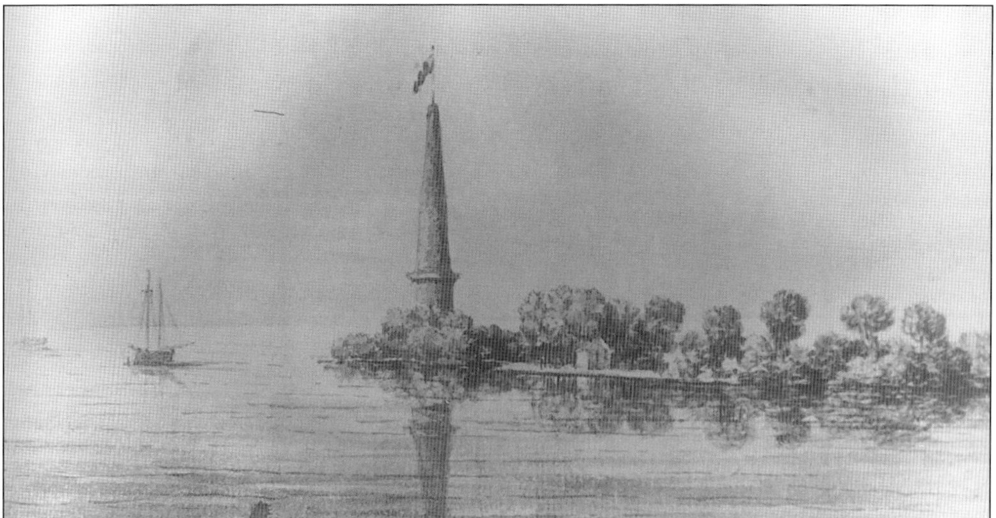

Thomas Sumner built the second Tybee Light over a 10-month period in 1742. The material used was wood and stone. This tower was 90 feet tall and topped by a 30-foot flag pole. Gen. James Oglethorpe wrote that the tower was "much the best building of its kind in America." It also was improperly positioned too close to shore and was toppled in a 1768 storm.

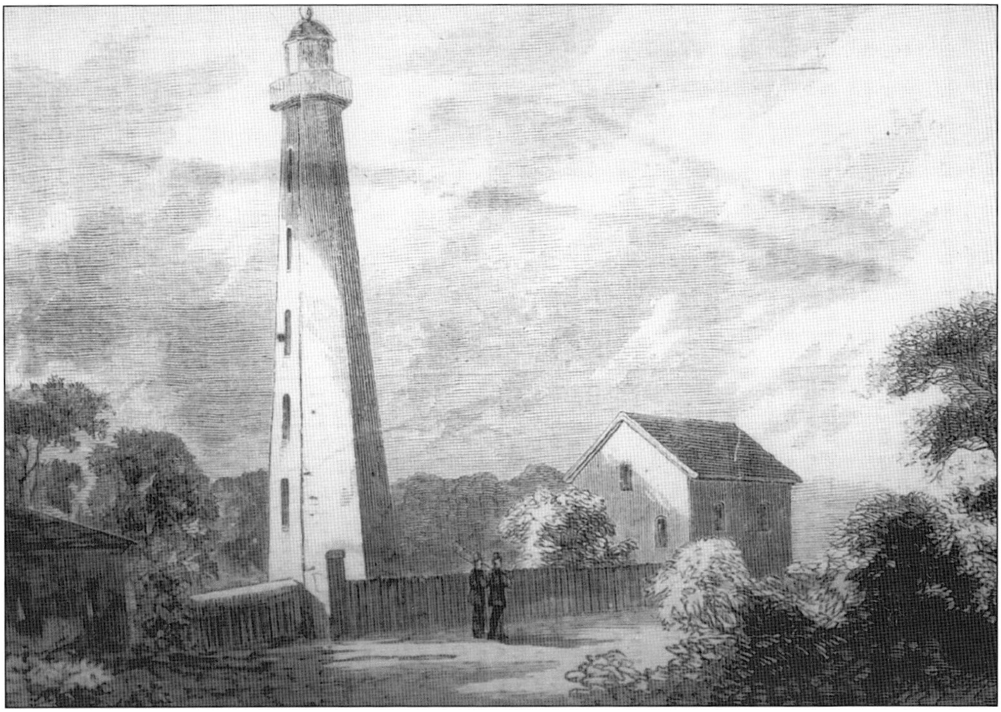

In February 1769, Georgia's royal governor, James Wright, recommended the rebuilding of the lighthouse. Learning from past experience, builders constructed Tybee's third lighthouse in 1773 and placed it well inland from storm tides. This tower was 100 feet tall and had 12-foot-thick lower walls. Sixteen lanterns backed by polished metal disks produced the light. Only one keeper was needed to maintain the light.

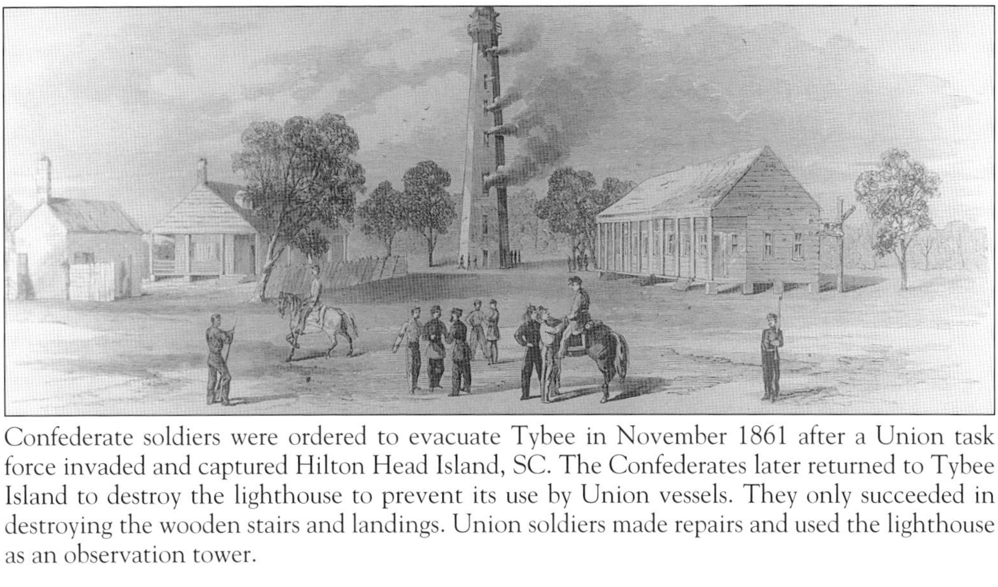

Confederate soldiers were ordered to evacuate Tybee in November 1861 after a Union task force invaded and captured Hilton Head Island, SC. The Confederates later returned to Tybee Island to destroy the lighthouse to prevent its use by Union vessels. They only succeeded in destroying the wooden stairs and landings. Union soldiers made repairs and used the lighthouse as an observation tower.

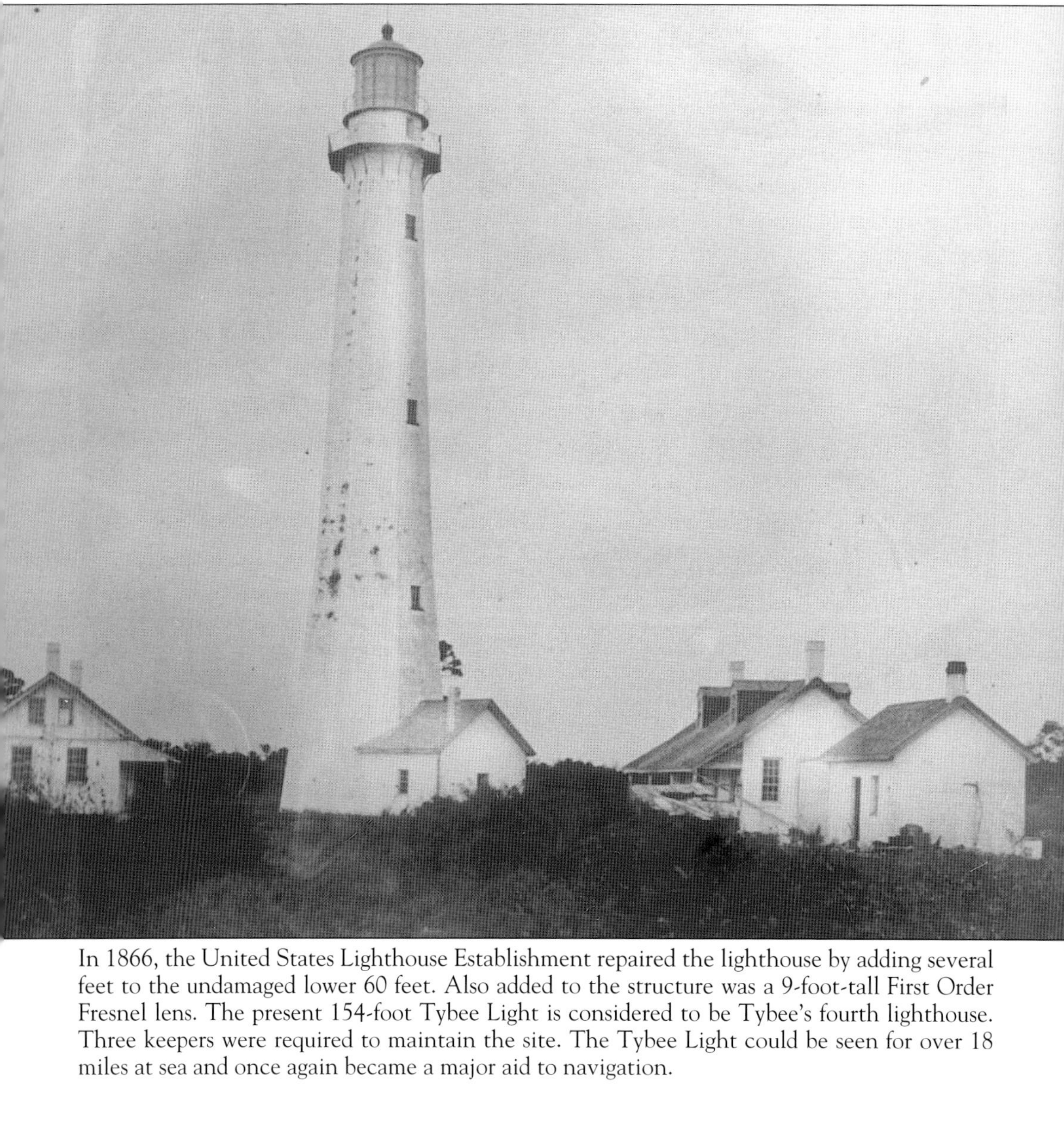

In 1866, the United States Lighthouse Establishment repaired the lighthouse by adding several feet to the undamaged lower 60 feet. Also added to the structure was a 9-foot-tall First Order Fresnel lens. The present 154-foot Tybee Light is considered to be Tybee's fourth lighthouse. Three keepers were required to maintain the site. The Tybee Light could be seen for over 18 miles at sea and once again became a major aid to navigation.

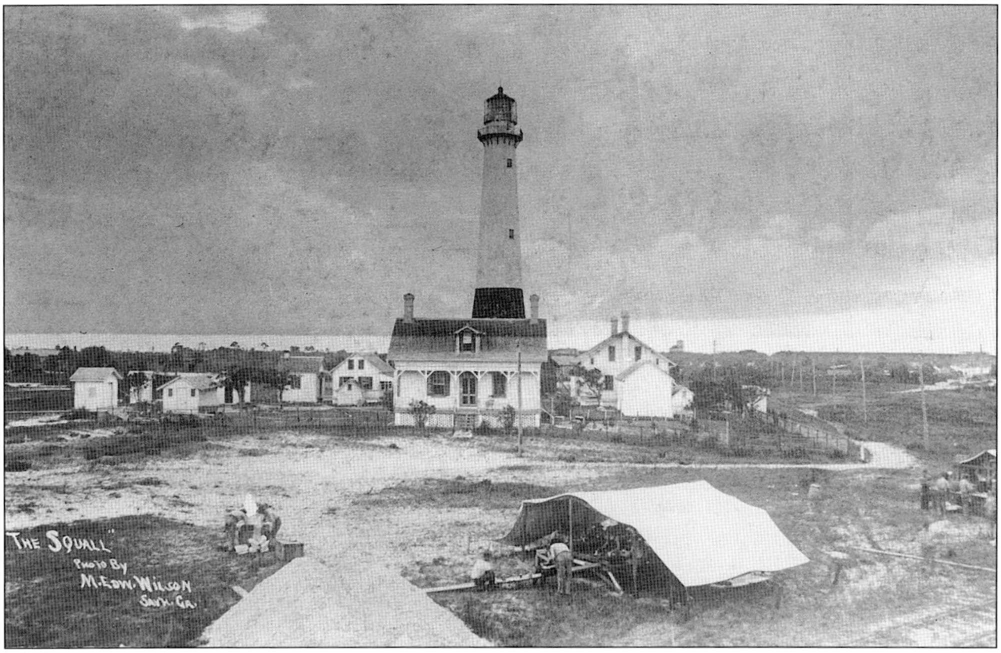

For many years, few people other than the lighthouse keepers and their families lived on Tybee Island. This changed in 1896 when construction began on Fort Screven. In the years that followed, hundreds of workers and soldiers came to the island. The picture above shows workmen beginning construction on Fort Screven's Battery Brumby. It seems a storm is brewing. The photographer named this shot "The Squall."

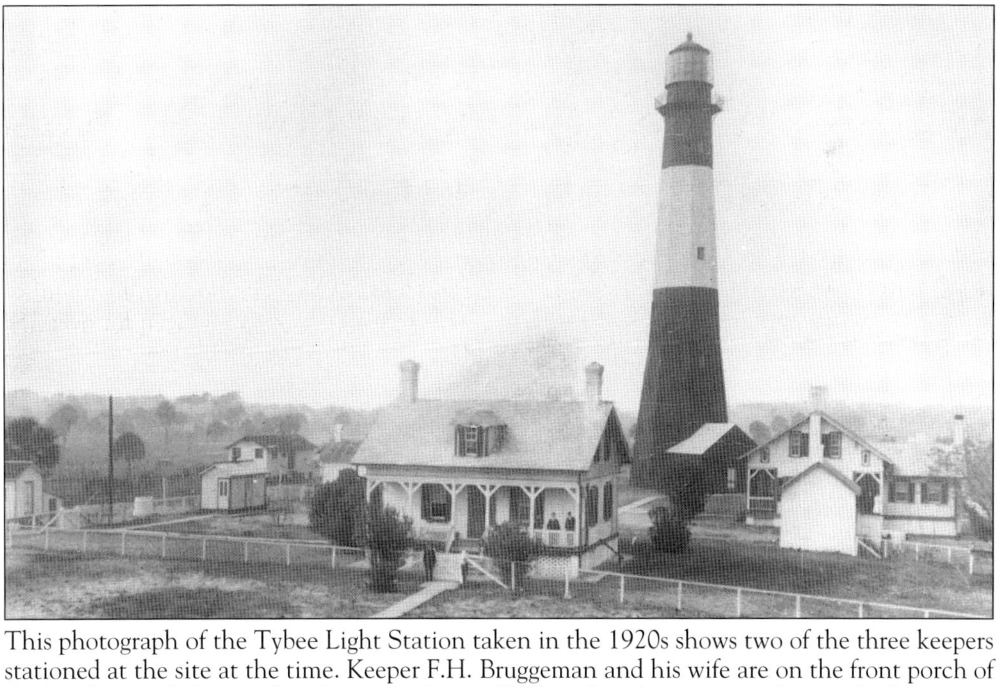

This photograph of the Tybee Light Station taken in the 1920s shows two of the three keepers stationed at the site at the time. Keeper F.H. Bruggeman and his wife are on the front porch of the head keeper's house. First Assistant Keeper William Lundquest is standing at the front gate. Lundquest was promoted to head keeper in 1931 and served until 1933.

HEAD KEEPERS OF TYBEE ISLAND LIGHTSTATION
(Source: Journal of Lighthouse Station at Tybee Island, Savannah River, Ga.)

Mr. Higgins	(1791-Unknown)
A. Cullen	(1865-Unknown)
M. Luge	(1868-Unknown)
George Sickle	(1871-March 31, 1873)
Patrick Comer	(April 1, 1873-Sept. 12, 1873)
H. William Reed	(Sept 3, 1873-Oct. 28, 1874)
Thomas Bergen	(Oct. 28, 1874-July 22, 1875)
Fred W. Symons	(July 22,1875-Oct. 1, 1876)
James McBride	(Oct. 27, 1876-Aug. 3, 1877)
Patrick Eagan	(Aug. 3, 1877-April 1881)
Andrew Anderson	(June 1, 1881-Nov. 1882)
William O'Reilly	(Nov. 22, 1882-Jan. 20, 1888)
Peter Jacob(s)	(Feb. 16, 1888-April 1900)
John S. Evans	(April 1900- Aug.28-1901)
Hans Thorkildsen	(1901-1902)
Theodore S. Johansen	(1902-1905)
Mr. Swan	(1905-1906)
Thorwald Danielson	(March 1906-July 1907)
Franz Traugott	(Aug. 1907-Feb. 1914)
F. H. Bruggeman	(March 1914-1931)
William Lundquest	(1931-1933)
George B. Jackson	(1933-1945)

Listed are the head keepers of the Tybee Island Lightstation from 1791 to 1945.

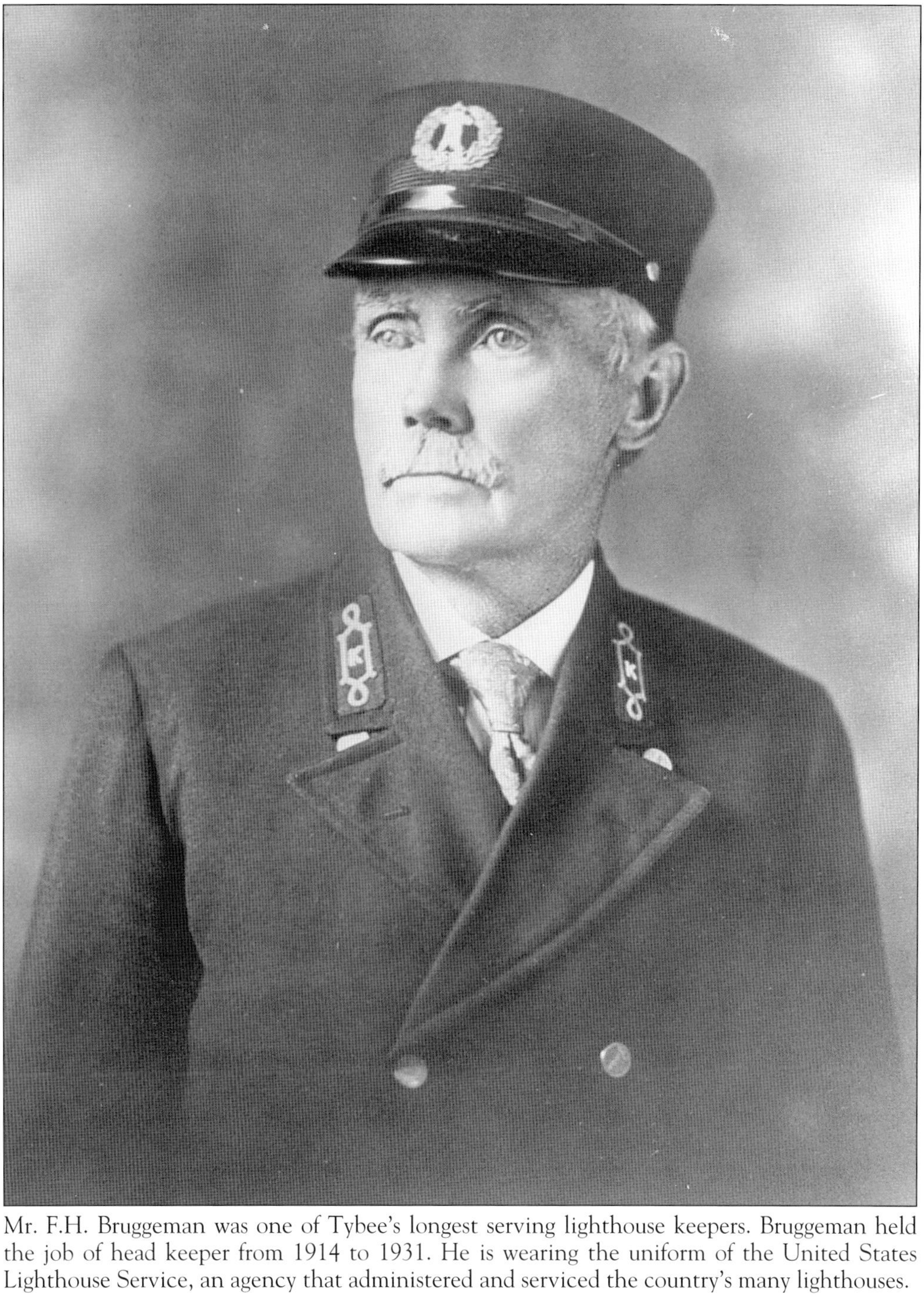

Mr. F.H. Bruggeman was one of Tybee's longest serving lighthouse keepers. Bruggeman held the job of head keeper from 1914 to 1931. He is wearing the uniform of the United States Lighthouse Service, an agency that administered and serviced the country's many lighthouses.

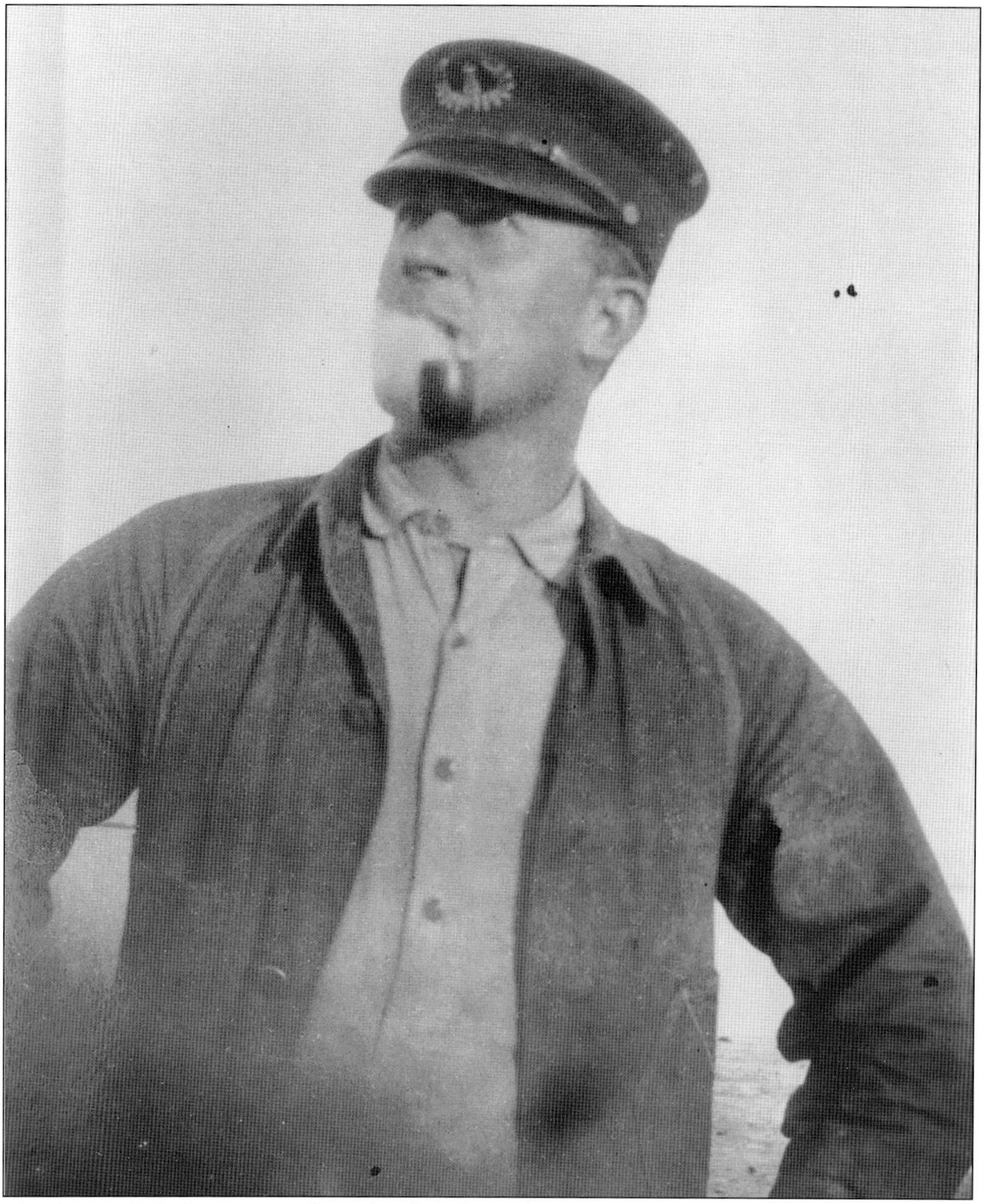

Mr. George B. Jackson was Tybee's last lighthouse keeper under the United States Lighthouse Service. Jackson served from 1933 until 1945. After lighthouses were converted from kerosene fuel to electricity in 1933, only one keeper was required.

Two

The Civil War

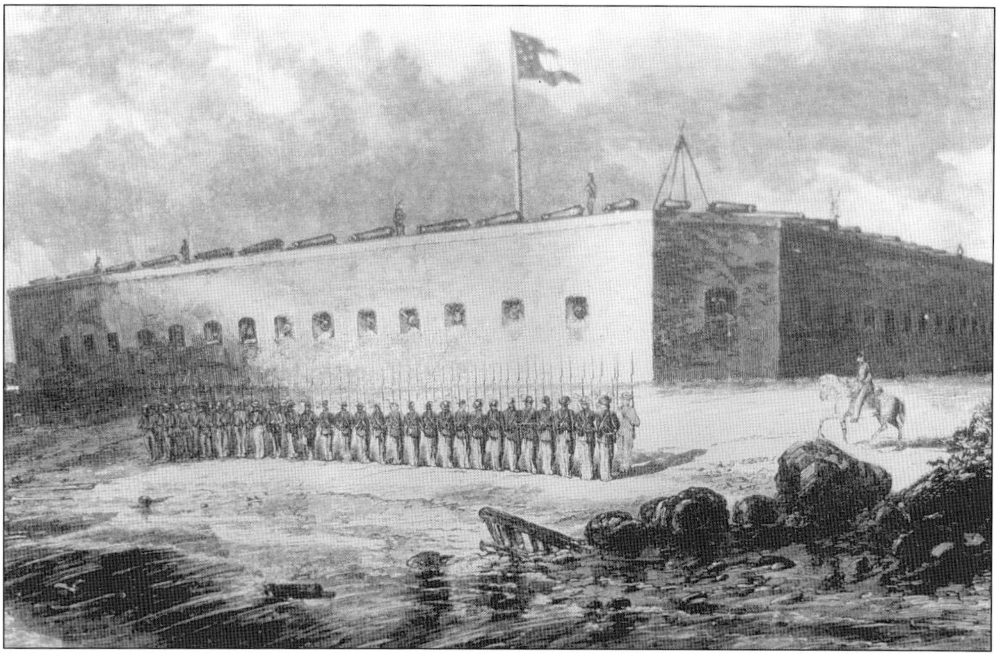

On January 2, 1861, under orders from Georgia Governor Joseph E. Brown, state militia troops from Savannah seized Fort Pulaski, a federal fortification across the river channel from Tybee. Since this event took place prior to the firing on Fort Sumter, some historians have named it the first hostile military action of the Civil War. The image above shows Confederate troops in formation outside the fort's walls.

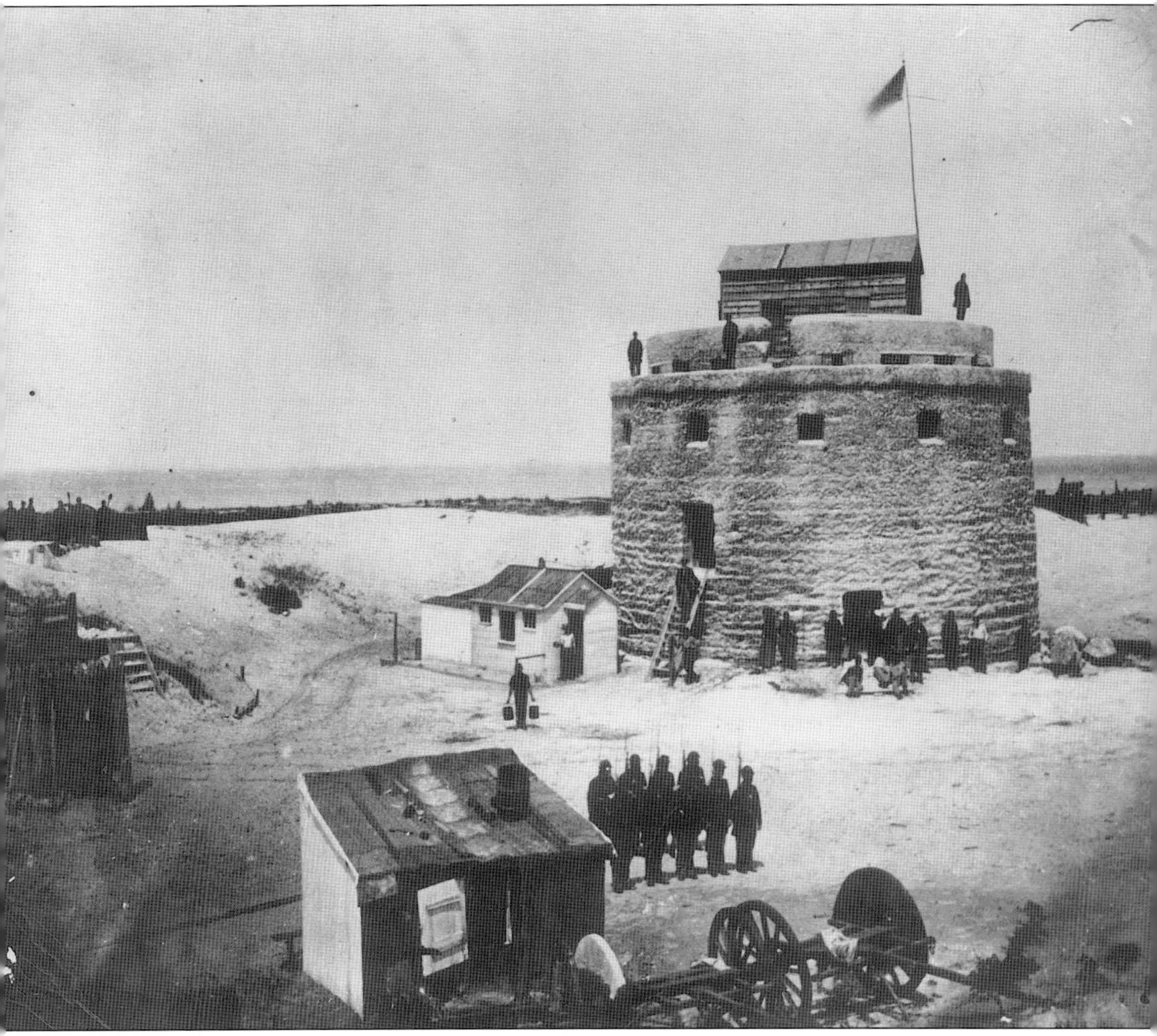

The above photograph from either late 1861 or early 1862 shows Union Army troops stationed around the old Martello Tower that once stood near the lighthouse on Tybee's north beach. Construction of the fort and lookout tower began in 1815 under supervision of prominent Savannah builder and architect Isaiah Davenport. The 50-foot tower was built of tabby, a combination of lime and oyster shells, and had 10-foot-thick walls. The tower was abandoned after the Civil War. In 1882, it was used as an office and employee's quarters for the Southern Bell Telephone Company. The Martello Tower was blown up by the U.S. Army in 1914 because it obstructed the fire of Fort Screven's big guns.

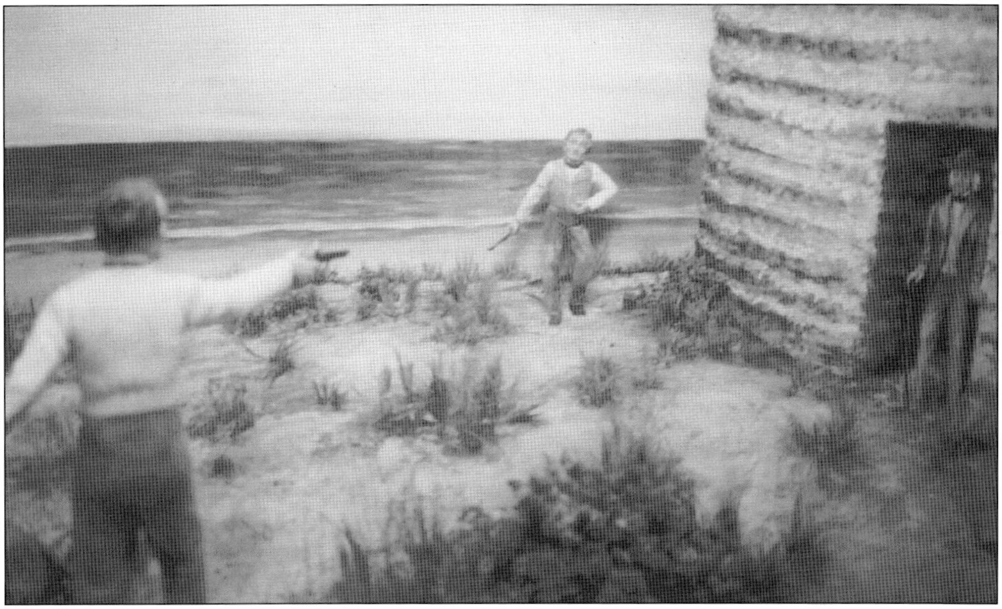

During the plantation era that preceded the Civil War, Tybee's Martello Tower was a favorite location for the settling of disagreements with dueling pistols. The lighthouse keeper was often the only witness. Because dueling was outlawed in South Carolina, many Southern gentleman crossed the river to Tybee to settle matters of honor. It is said the blood of many Carolinians was absorbed into the sands surrounding the Martello Tower and lighthouse.

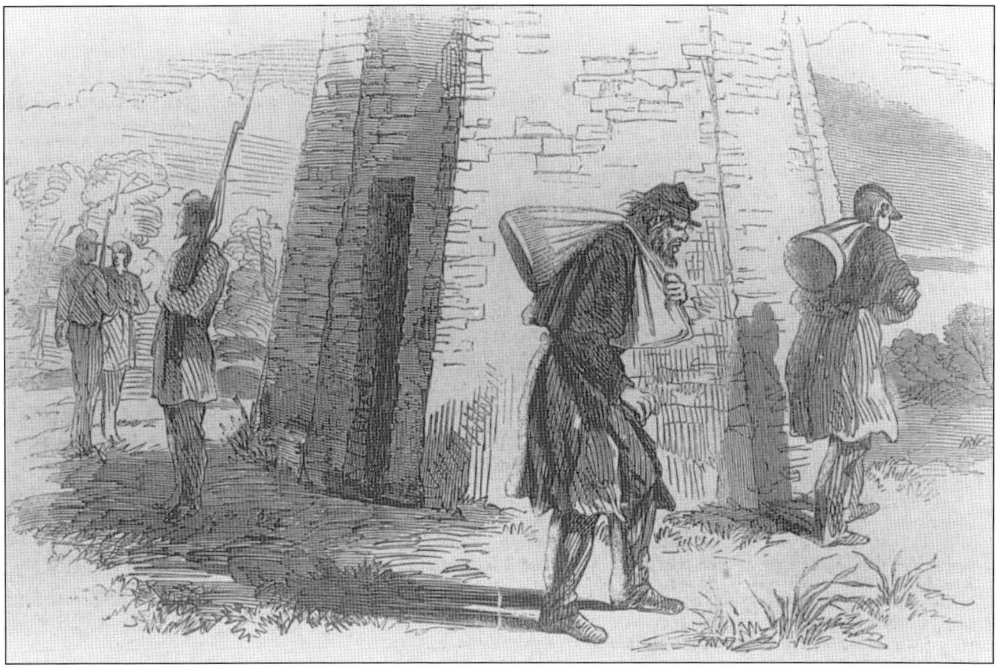

The isolation and boredom that often accompanied garrison duty on the small barrier islands sometimes led to breaches in military discipline. Some rather imaginative means of administering punishments were devised. This illustration shows soldiers being punished for drunkenness by being forced to walk around the base of the Tybee Lighthouse while carrying weighted sacks.

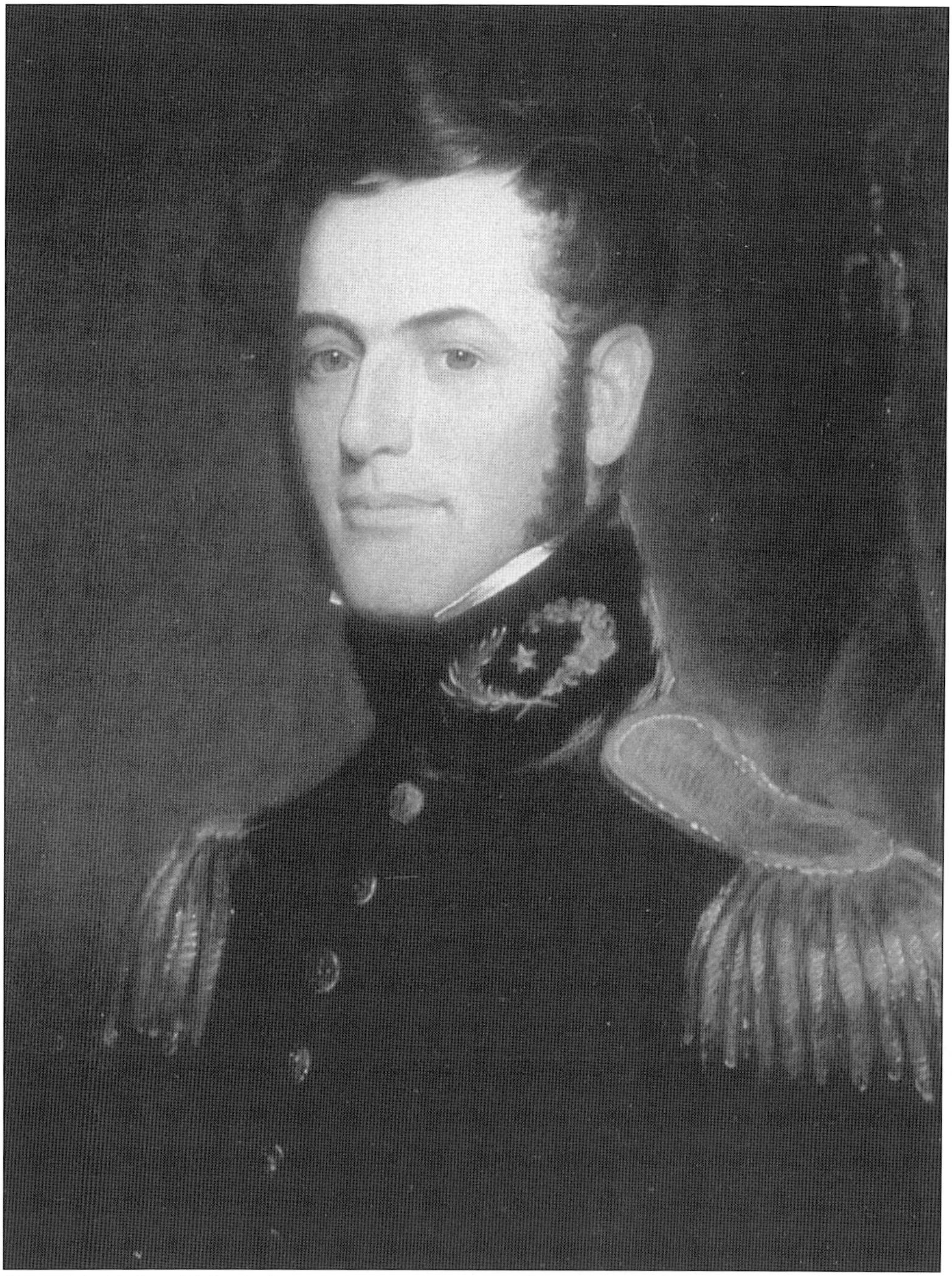

One of Lt. Robert E. Lee's first assignments upon graduating with the West Point class of 1829 brought him to Cockspur Island in the Savannah River. As an officer in the U.S. Army Corps of Engineers, his duty involved doing preliminary engineering and drainage work to begin the construction of what later became Fort Pulaski. Confederate Gen. Robert E. Lee returned to the southeast coast in 1861 as commander of the Department of South Carolina, Georgia, and Florida. Under his leadership, the Savannah River became known as one of the most highly fortified areas of the Confederacy. (Portrait by William E. West.)

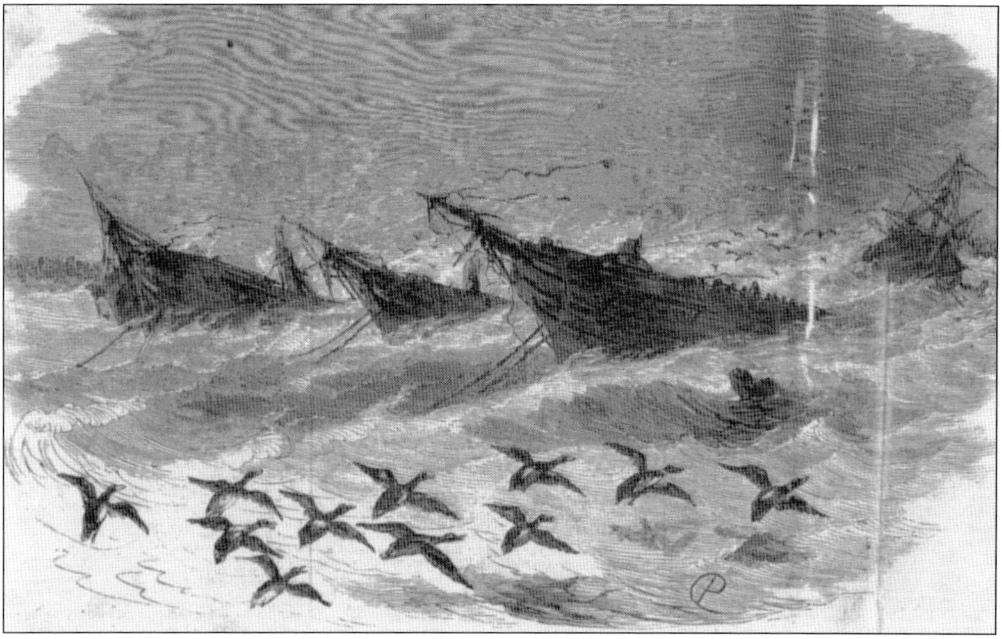

One tactic used by Confederate defenders to prevent Union vessels from sailing down the Savannah River to attack the city of Savannah was to bar the channel with derelict ships. The above sketch from Frank Leslie's *Illustrated Newspaper* shows sunken hulks in the channel opposite Fort Pulaski and Tybee Island.

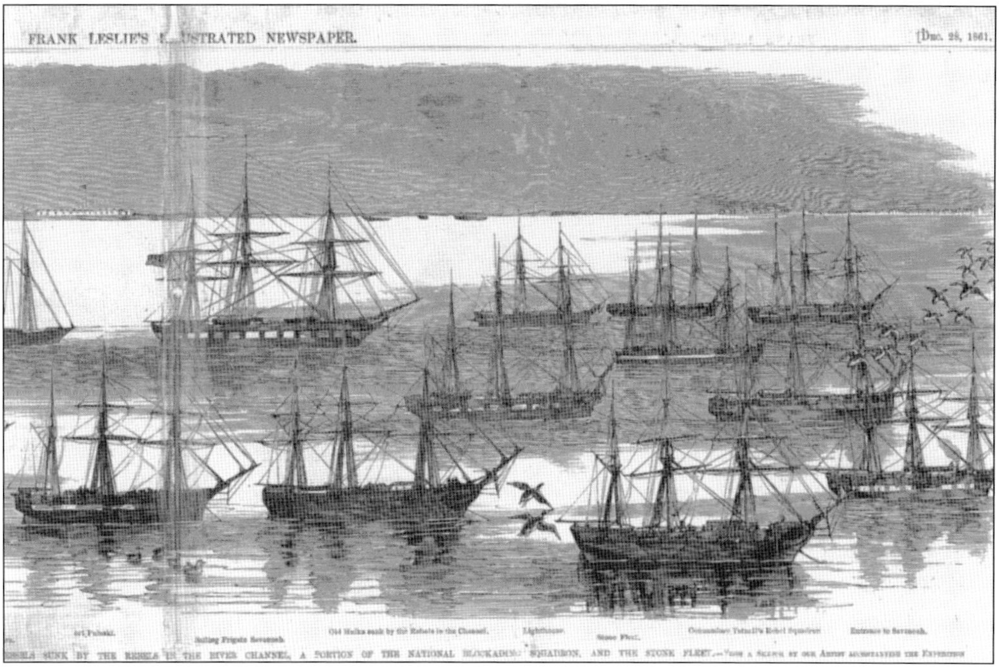

Another artist sketch from the December 28, 1861 issue of Frank Leslie's *Illustrated Newspaper* depicts the Union Navy blockading squadron and the "Stone Fleet" that was put in place to prevent Confederate supply ships from entering or leaving the Port of Savannah. The barricading fleet lay just off the coast of Tybee.

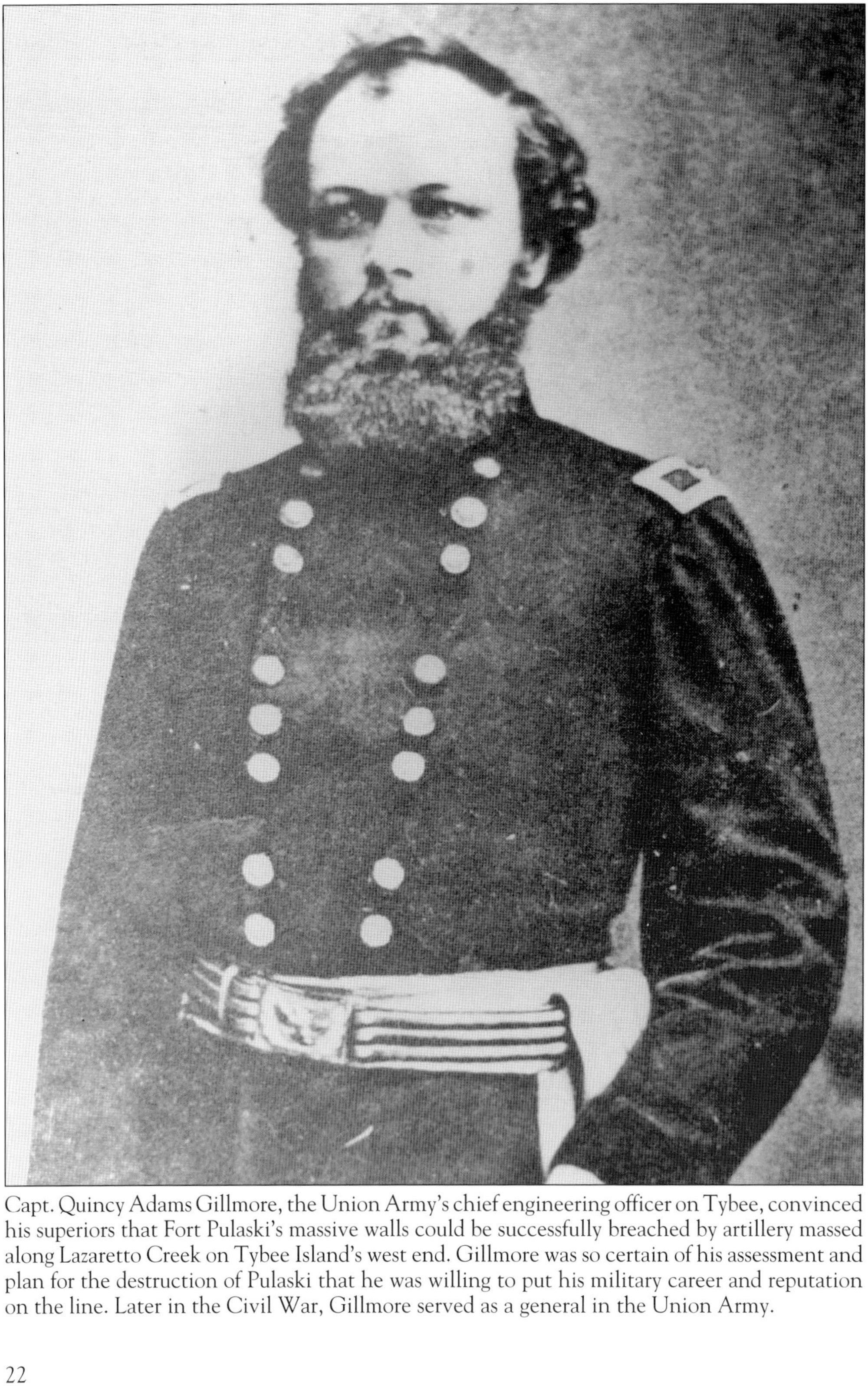

Capt. Quincy Adams Gillmore, the Union Army's chief engineering officer on Tybee, convinced his superiors that Fort Pulaski's massive walls could be successfully breached by artillery massed along Lazaretto Creek on Tybee Island's west end. Gillmore was so certain of his assessment and plan for the destruction of Pulaski that he was willing to put his military career and reputation on the line. Later in the Civil War, Gillmore served as a general in the Union Army.

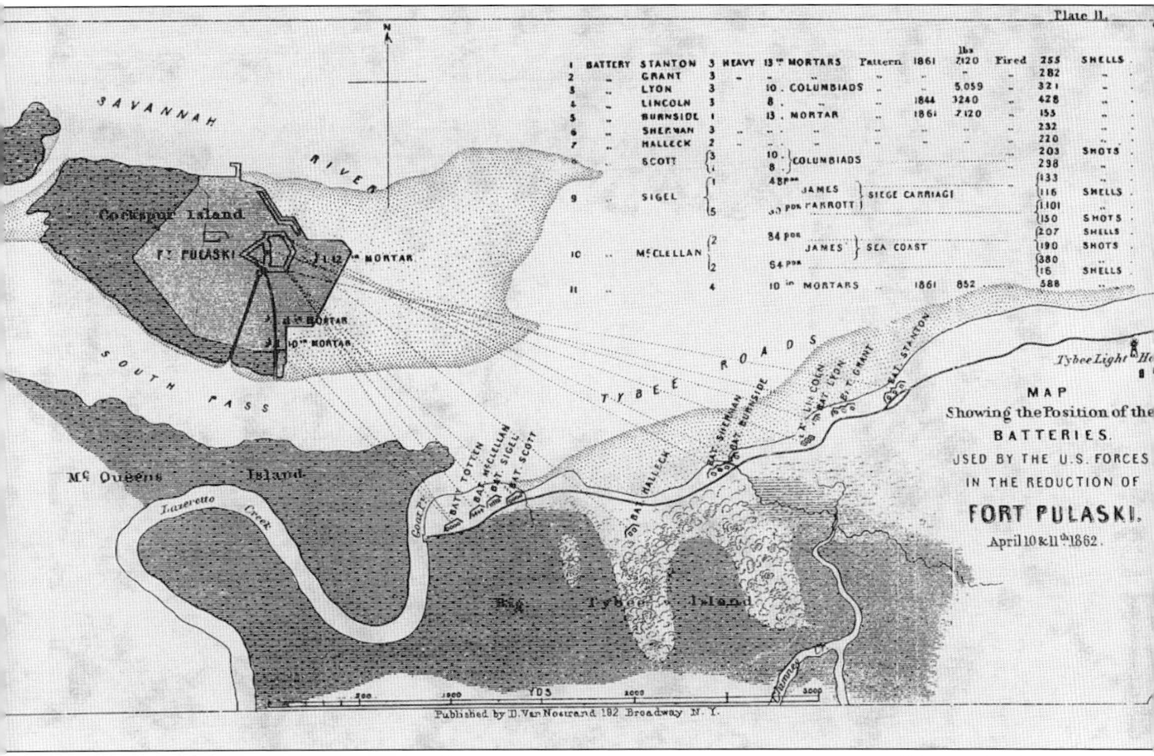

This map shows the positioning of Gillmore's Union batteries for the reduction of Fort Pulaski. Eleven earthen batteries were constructed and each was named for an important Union military officer or government official. Included among the 36 Union guns were 10 new rifled cannon. Rifling for artillery was developed in 1858, but had not yet really been put to such a test as the firing on the massive Confederate fortification. Fort Pulaski was considered to be "state of the art" military fort architecture, and it was said that firing on it would be like bombarding the Rocky Mountains.

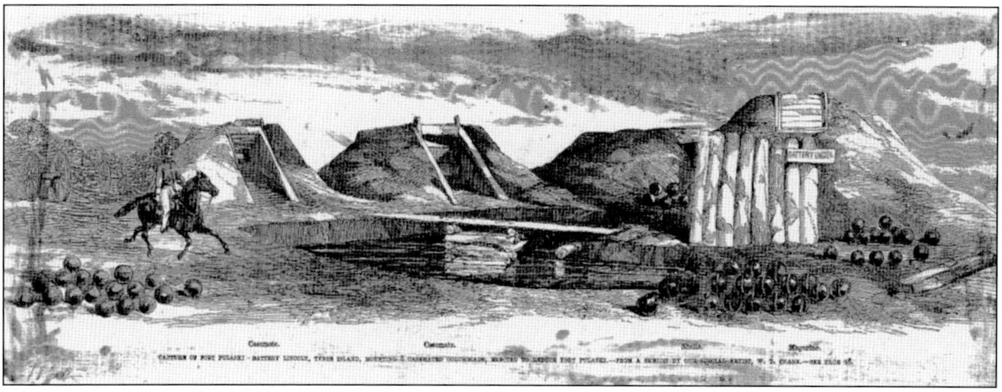

These are artists' sketches of 2 of the 11 Union batteries on Tybee that fired on Fort Pulaski. Battery Lincoln, above, mounted 8-inch casemated Columbiads. The entrance to the powder magazine is protected from possible incoming shells. Battery Stanton, below, was a mortar battery capable of high-angle fire. Union soldiers worked on constructing the batteries during time of darkness, covering their work with tarps to camouflage them during the day. Much manpower was required to tow the big guns from the area of the Tybee Lighthouse to their Lazaretto Creek positions.

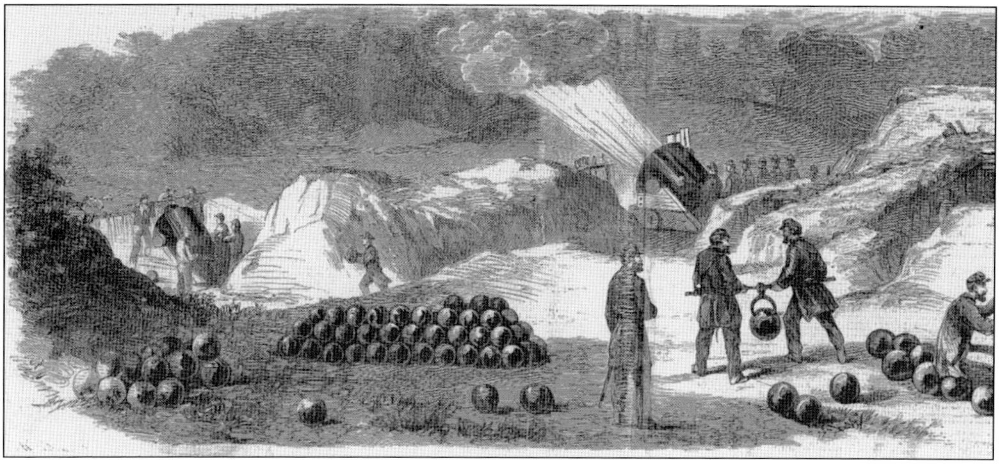

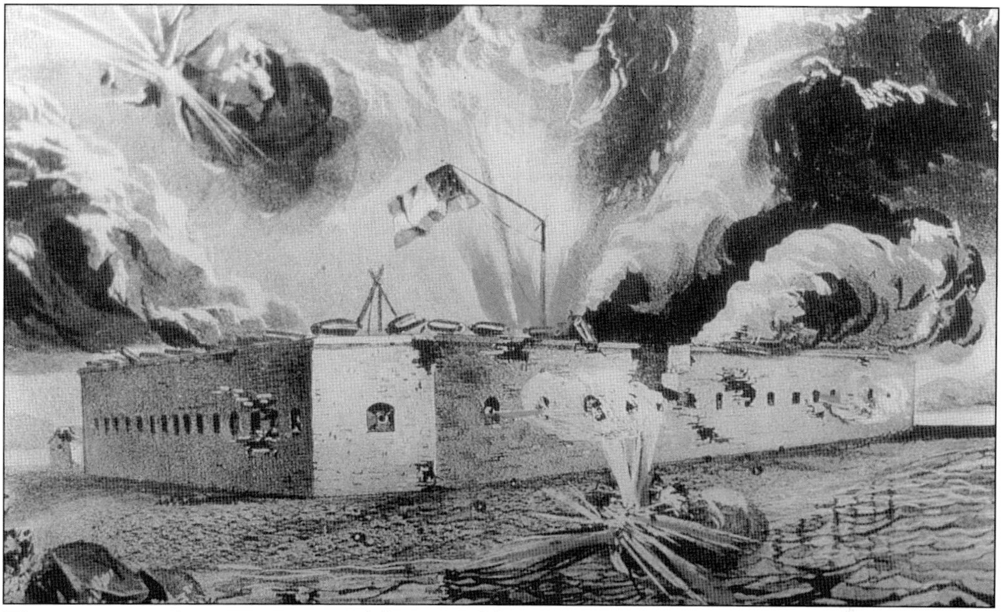

This is one artist's interpretation of the rain of destructive fire from Union guns that fell on Fort Pulaski. Notice that the flag staff has been broken by a Union cannon ball. The bombardment began shortly after 8:00 AM on April 10, 1862, and continued until nightfall. Firing resumed at dawn the next morning. By noon of the second day, the section of wall on the southeast angle of the fort began to crumble and the breach grew wider as the shelling continued.

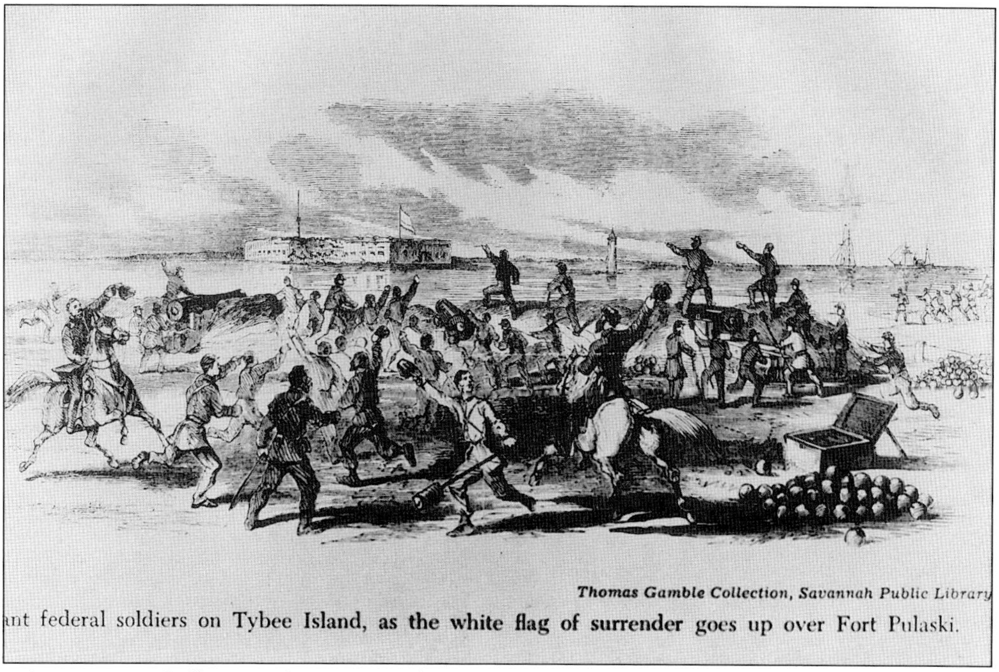

Thomas Gamble Collection, Savannah Public Library

ınt federal soldiers on Tybee **Island, as the white flag of surrender** goes up over Fort Pulaski.

When Union shells started to impact dangerously close to the powder magazine in the fort's northwest corner, Fort Pulaski's Confederate Commander, Col. Charles Olmstead, ordered the white flag of surrender to be raised. This brought cheers and celebration among the Union gunners on Tybee Island. (Thomas Gamble Collection.)

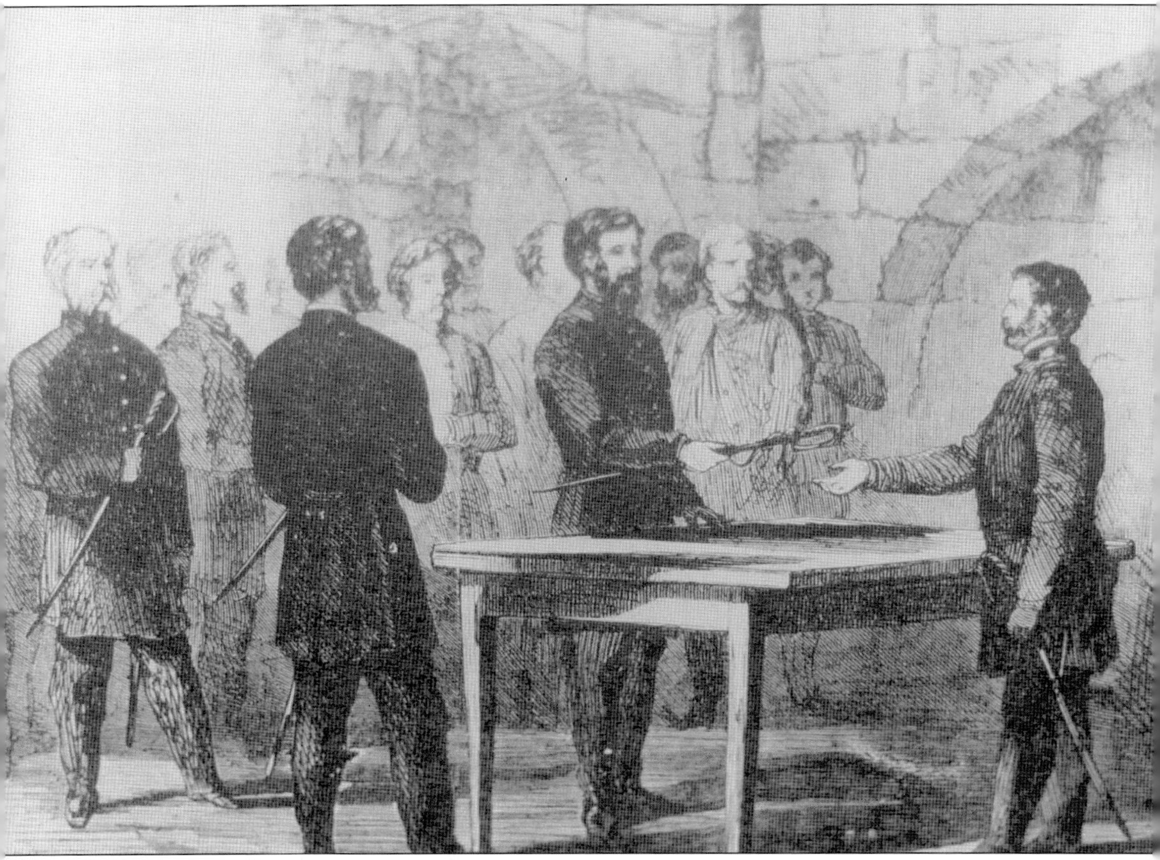

The above scene depicts the formal surrender ceremony after the fall of Fort Pulaski. As was customary, the Confederate officers are offering their sabers to the victorious Union commander. The fort's Confederate commander, Colonel Olmstead, surrendered his sword, saying, "I yield my sword, but I trust I have not disgraced it." His decision to surrender Fort Pulaski weighed heavily on Colonel Olmstead's mind for the remainder of his life.

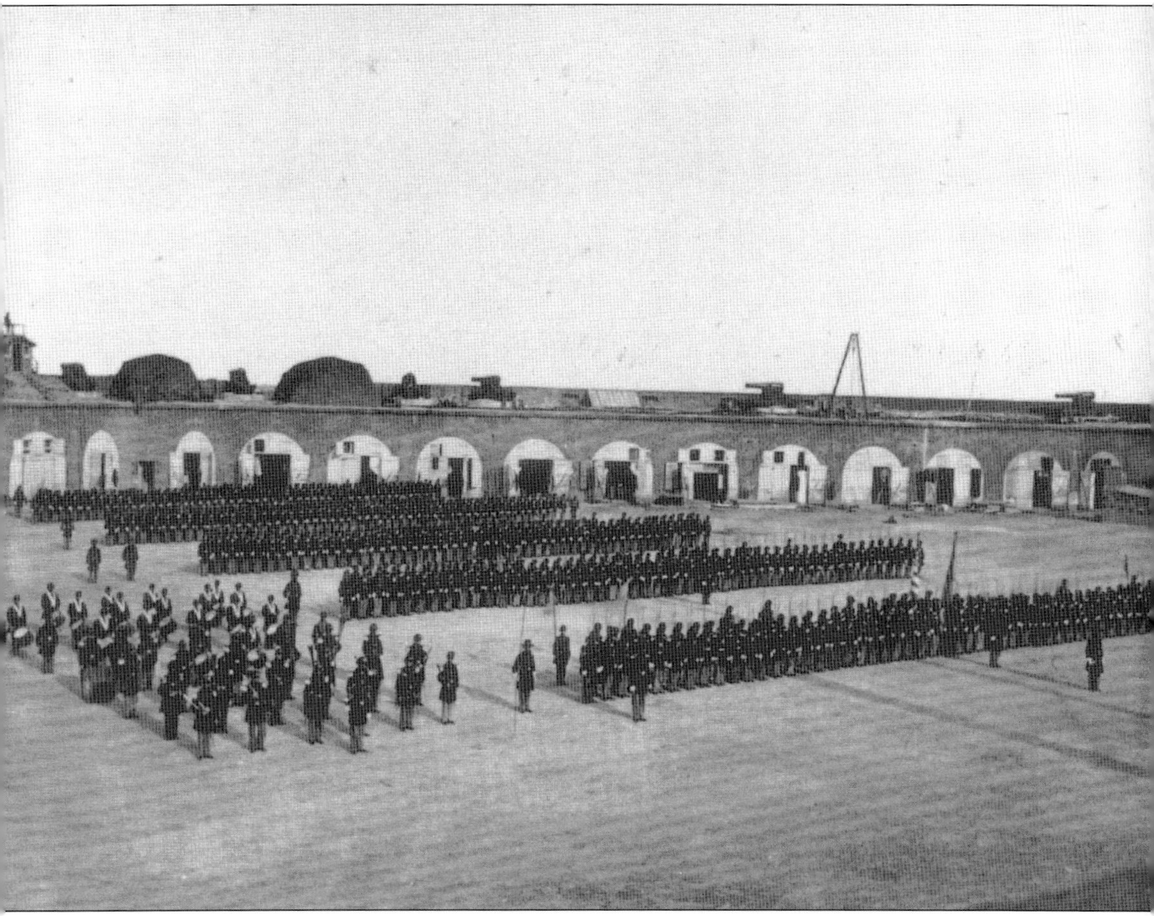

This photograph from 1863 shows troops of the 48th New York State Volunteer Infantry on dress parade inside the walls of Fort Pulaski. Organized in Brooklyn, NY, the 48th made up the largest part of the first garrison of United States soldiers to occupy the fort during the Civil War. Fort Pulaski is now a national monument operated by the National Park Service. It is open daily for visitors and hosts several living history events a year. (National Park Service photo.)

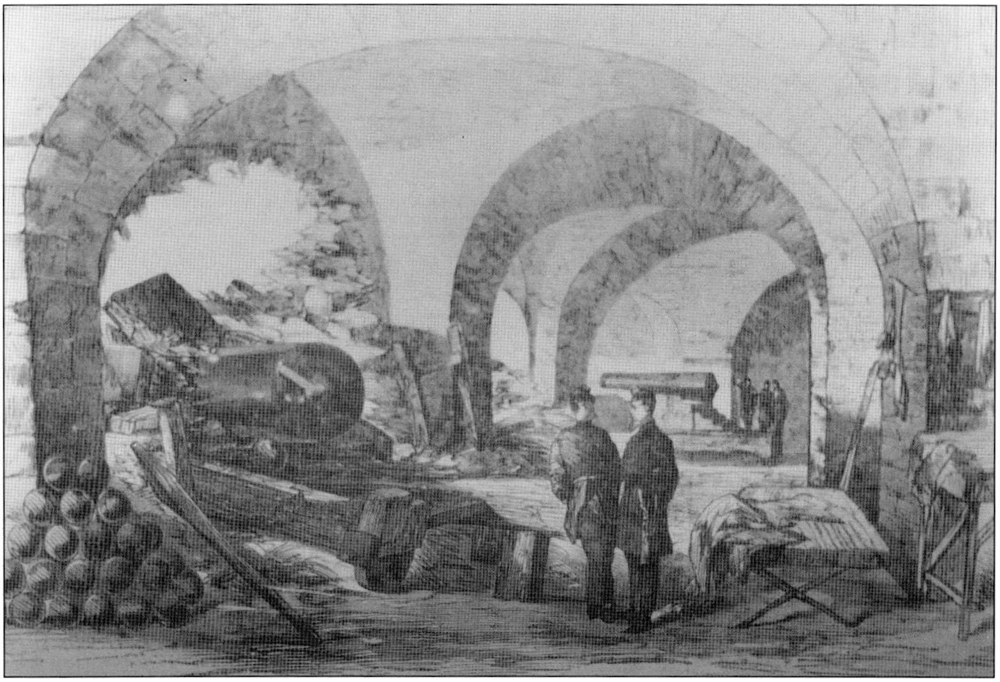

These two photographs show only a small part of the extensive damage inflicted on Fort Pulaski by the Union's rifled cannon. The rifling put a spin on the projectile as it left the barrel, making for better range, accuracy, and force of impact than could be realized from smoothbore guns. This was the only Civil War military engagement on Tybee, but it helped to usher in a new era of weapons technology. Brick walled forts, once thought to be invincible, became obsolete. A new design of coastal fort construction was about to emerge at selected locations along the East Coast, including Tybee Island.

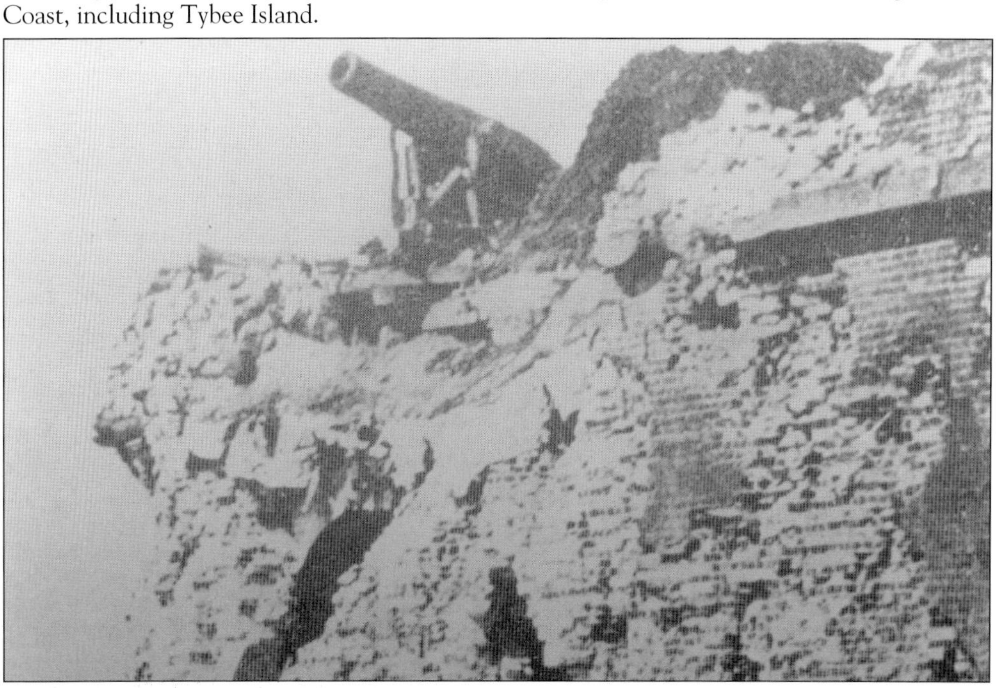

Three

GUNS BEHIND THE DUNES

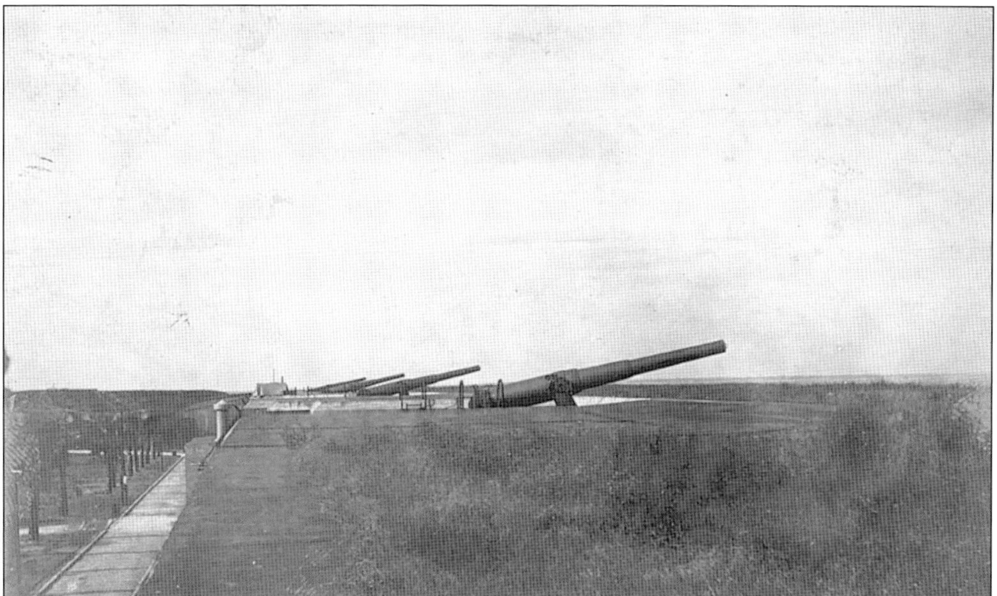

In 1897, the U.S. War Department ordered construction of a series of coast artillery batteries on the north shore of Tybee Island. The batteries represented the Endicott Period of fort construction. The batteries were constructed of reinforced concrete with granite foundations. Sand was banked against the seaward wall to absorb the impact of incoming shells and to make the battery appear to be a sand dune from out to sea.

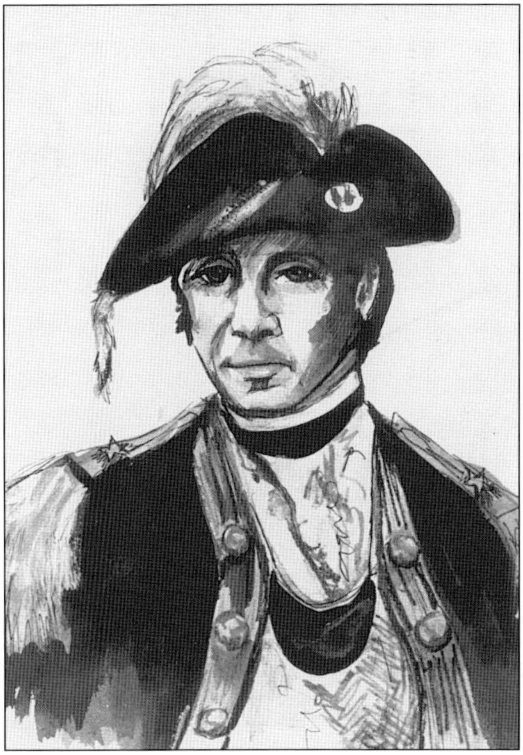

The fortification planned for Tybee Island was first named Fort Tybee and later Fort Graham. When Fort Graham was officially established as a military post in March 1888, the name was changed to Fort Screven, in honor of Brig. Gen. James Screven. General Screven was a hero of the American Revolution, mortally wounded in a 1776 engagement with the British at Spencer's Hill in Liberty County.

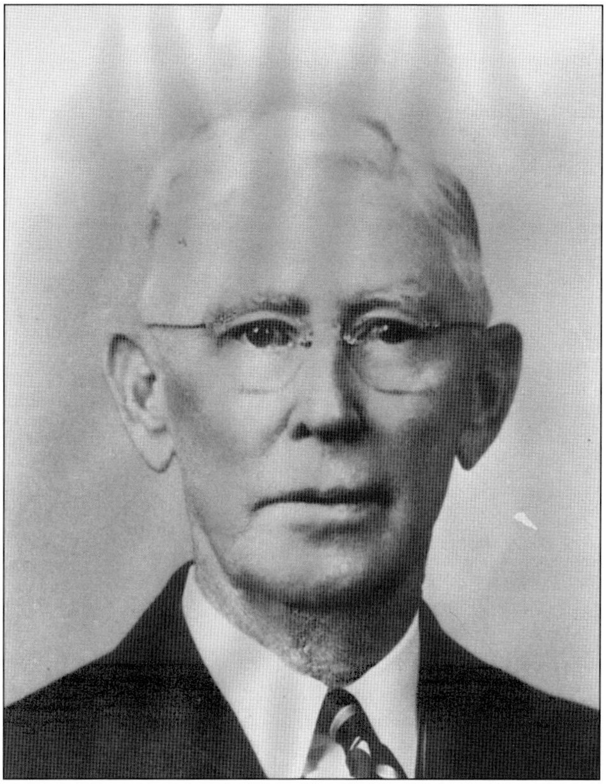

One of the civilian engineers who guided the work on Fort Screven's gun batteries was Thomas Francis Lynch, superintendent of fortifications with the Corps of Engineers. In early 1897, Lynch was transferred from New Jersey to Savannah to supervise restoration work on Fort Pulaski. He was later reassigned to Fort Screven and resided there until his death on July 3, 1958. After retirement, Lynch served for a time as an alderman for the town of Savannah Beach (Tybee).

During a hurricane that struck Tybee Island on August 31, 1898, an Italian vessel was seen floundering off Tybee's shore. Lt. Henry Sims Morgan and five volunteers launched a small boat in an attempt to rescue the ship's imperiled crew. The storm-tossed waves swamped the rescue boat causing it to capsize and dump its occupants into the churning water. Morgan and one companion drowned before they could be rescued. Lieutenant Morgan was a recent graduate of West Point and Fort Screven was one of his earliest duty assignments.

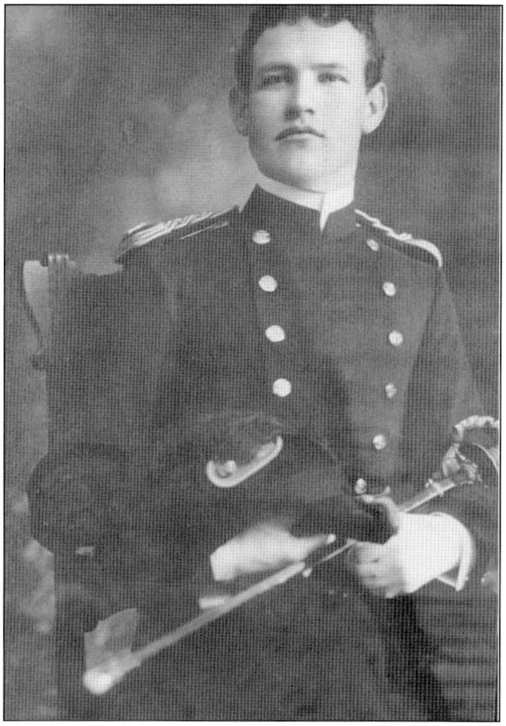

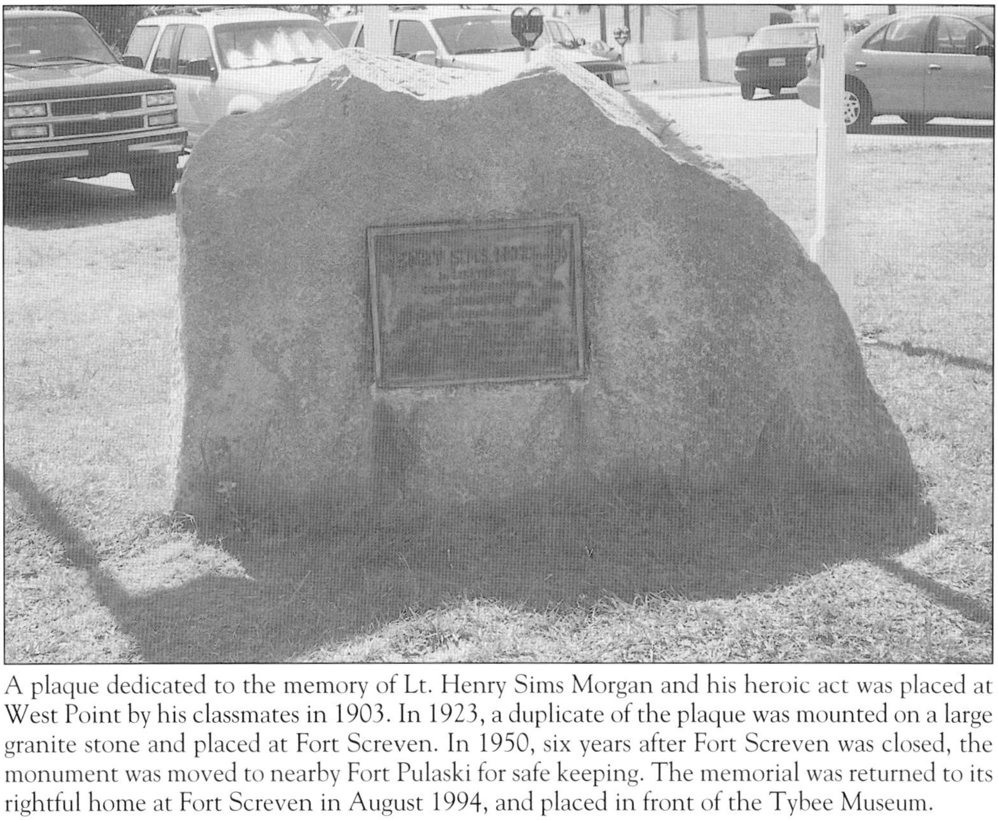

A plaque dedicated to the memory of Lt. Henry Sims Morgan and his heroic act was placed at West Point by his classmates in 1903. In 1923, a duplicate of the plaque was mounted on a large granite stone and placed at Fort Screven. In 1950, six years after Fort Screven was closed, the monument was moved to nearby Fort Pulaski for safe keeping. The memorial was returned to its rightful home at Fort Screven in August 1994, and placed in front of the Tybee Museum.

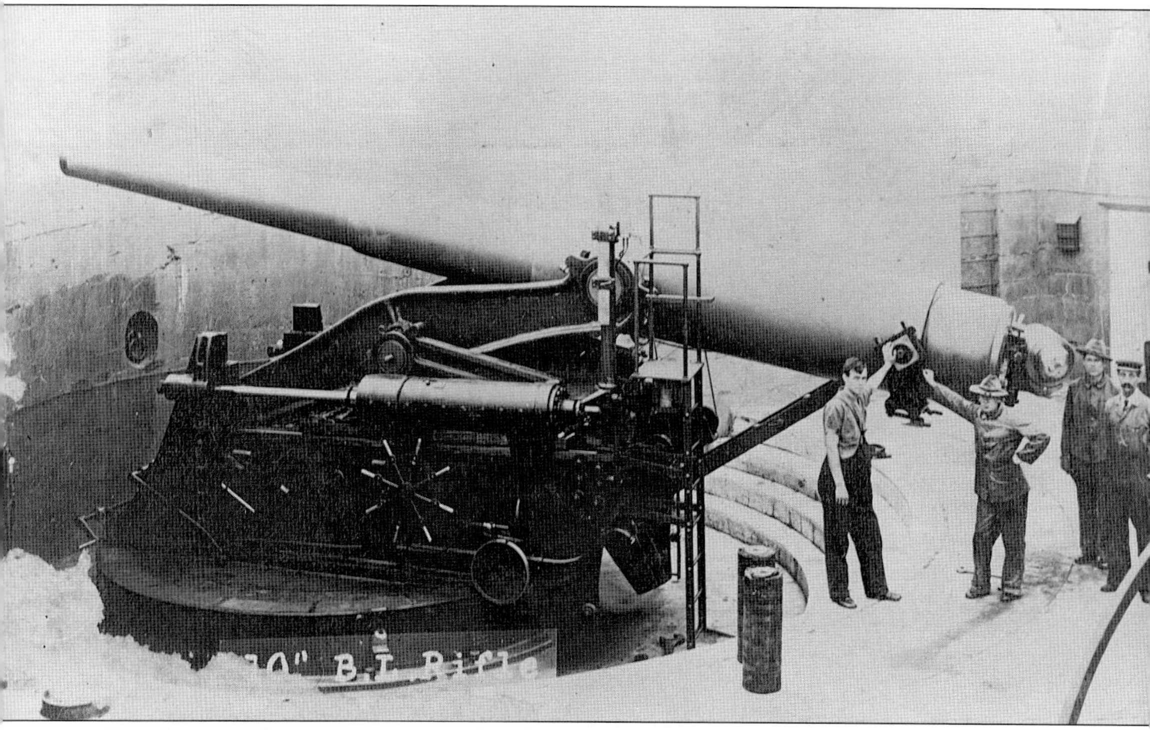

Fort Screven's batteries were armed with some of the most modern weapons available at the time. Government documents, in laying out plans for the fortress, said that it would house "the biggest cannon in the world." This photograph, taken at one of the four gun positions of Battery Brumby sometime around the turn of the 20th century, illustrates the enormous size of the battery's four 8-inch rifles that had a range of 10 miles. Battery Brumby was named for Lt. Thomas M. Brumby who served with the Navy in the Spanish-American War. Battery Brumby was the first of Fort Screven's batteries to be completed and the only one in service during the Spanish-American War.

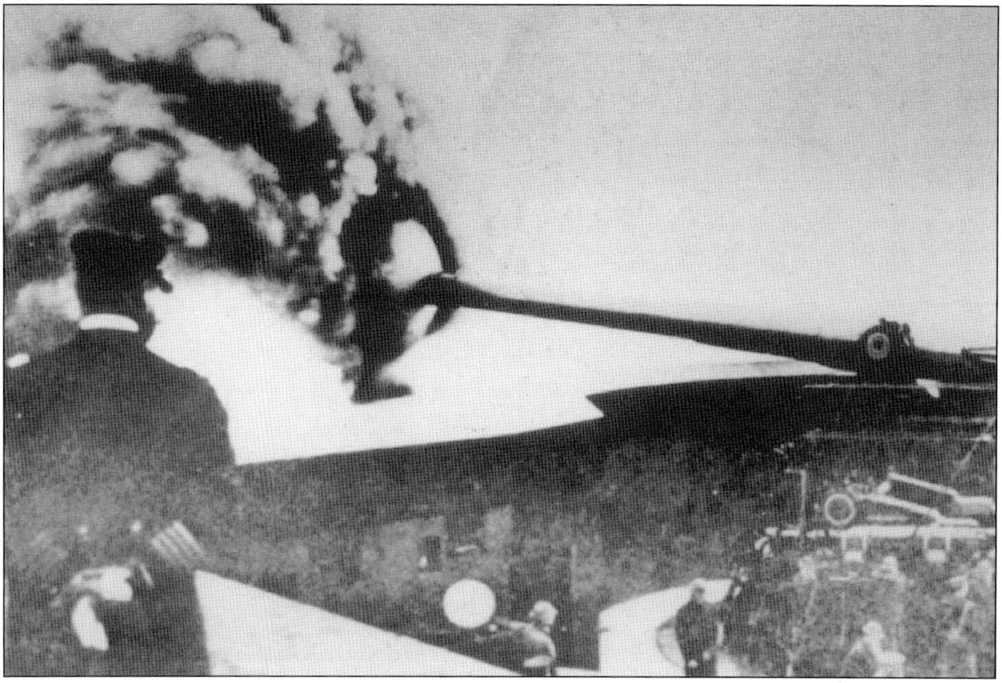

Fort Screven's big guns were never fired at an enemy, but the gun crews kept their skills sharpened by frequent practice firings. These photographs from 1907 (above) and 1916 (below) were taken during full-service drills on Battery Brumby's 8-inch guns. Brumby's 4 guns were manned by 4 officers and 157 enlisted men. The concussion from the big guns often rattled windows and knocked items off shelves in nearby buildings.

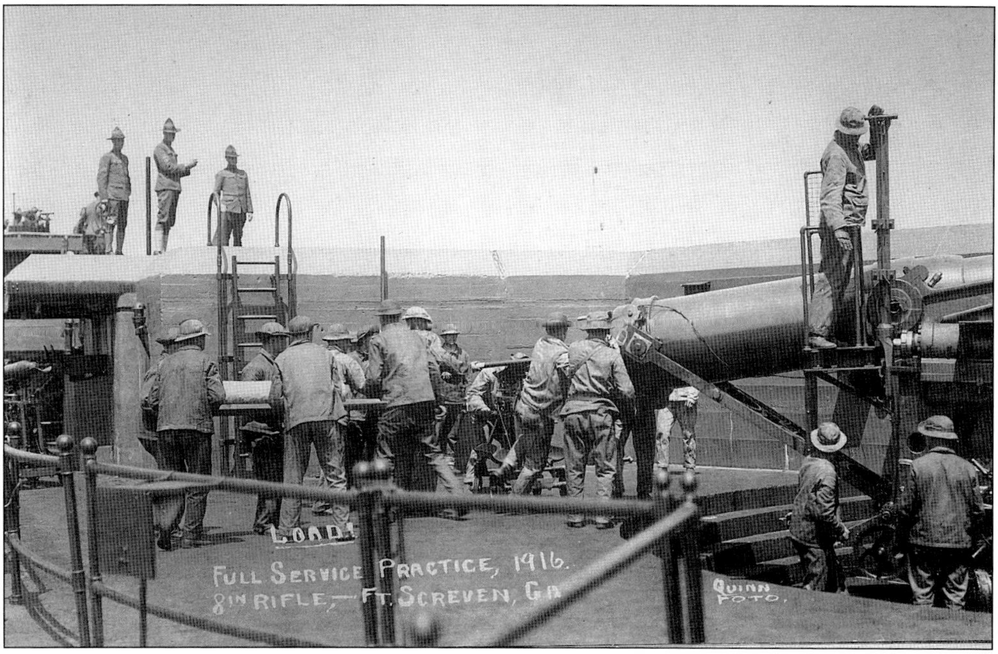

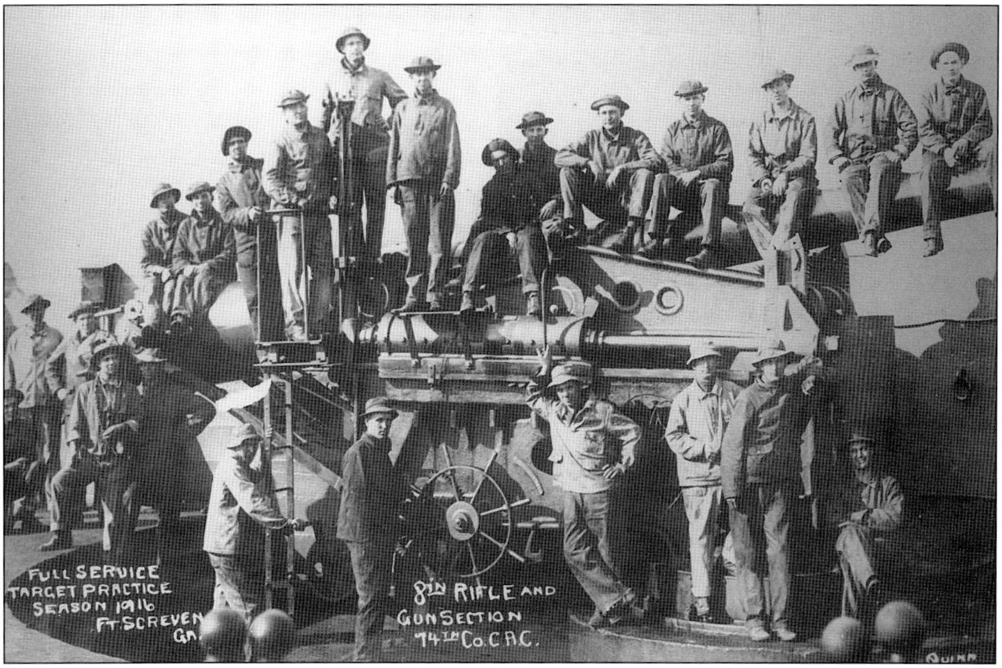

A break could sometimes be taken from loading and firing practice for a photo opportunity, as proven by these photos from 1916. Battery Brumby's 8-inch guns were mounted on disappearing carriages. When the gun was fired, the recoil lowered the barrel below the protective parapet. The crew reloaded the gun while in relative safety and mechanically raised it above the parapet to fire again.

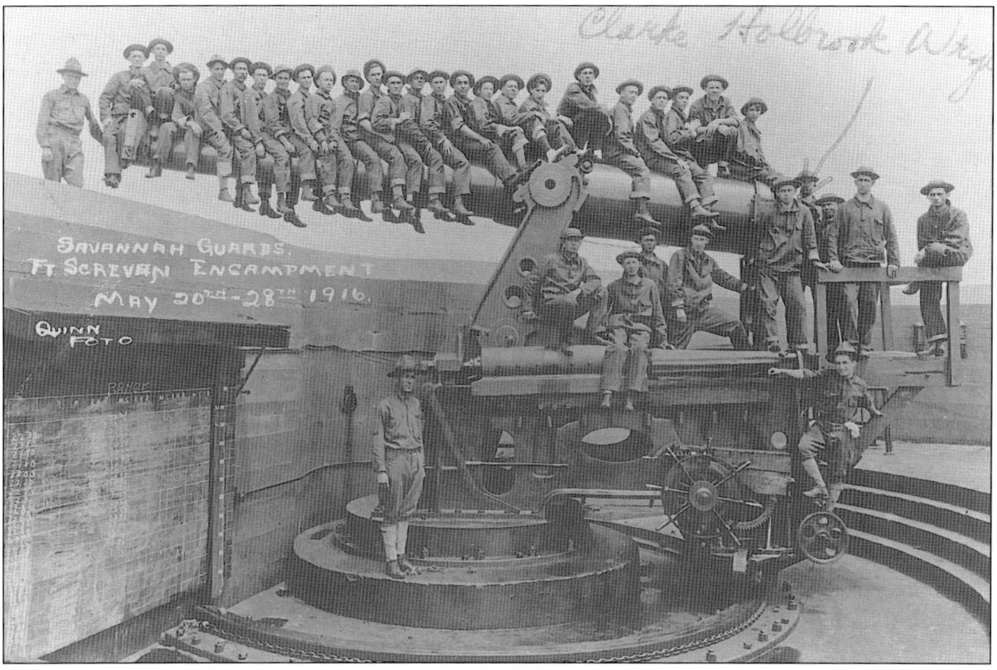

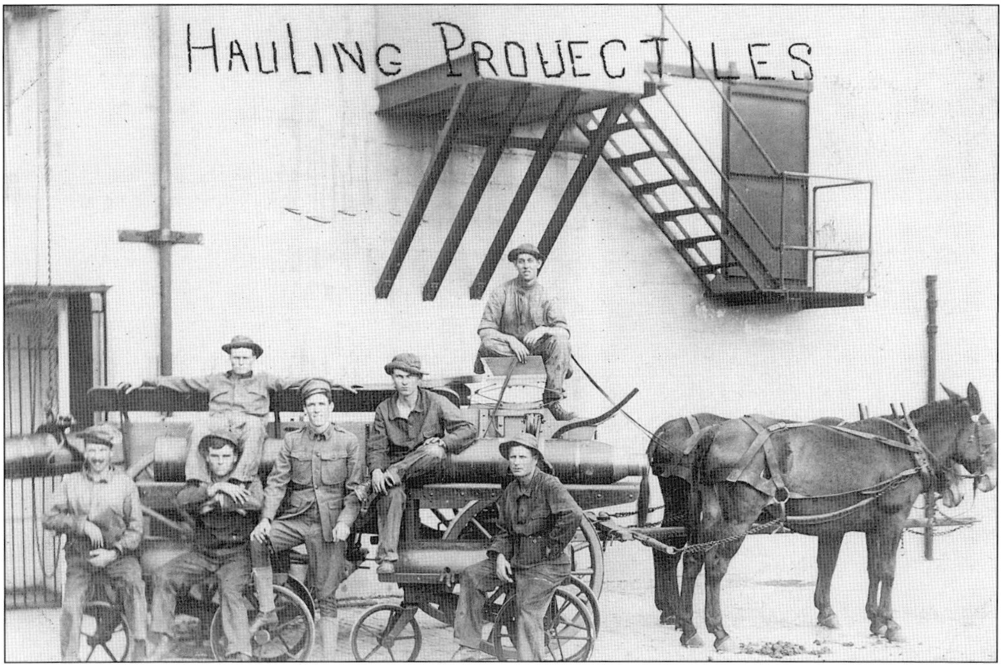

The projectiles fired from Battery Brumby's guns weighed 700 pounds and had to be moved about by mule carts. The projectiles were stored in magazines inside the lower part of the battery and raised to the gun platform by elevator. They were then delivered to the gun by hand carts.

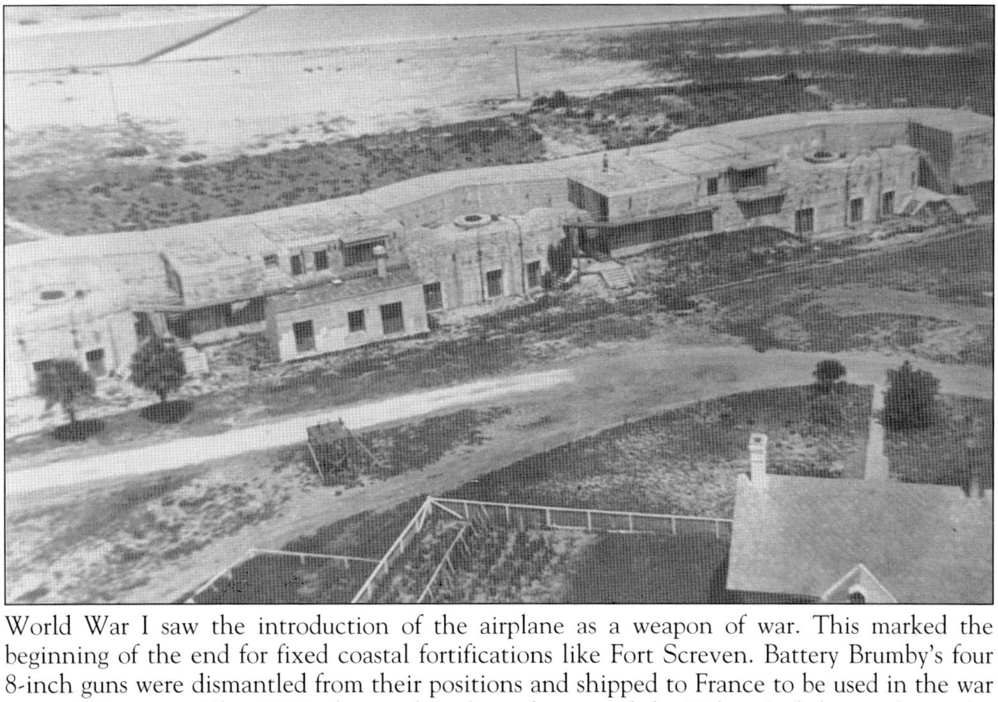

World War I saw the introduction of the airplane as a weapon of war. This marked the beginning of the end for fixed coastal fortifications like Fort Screven. Battery Brumby's four 8-inch guns were dismantled from their positions and shipped to France to be used in the war against Germany. This 1936 photo taken from the top of the Tybee Lighthouse shows the empty gun wells of an abandoned Battery Brumby.

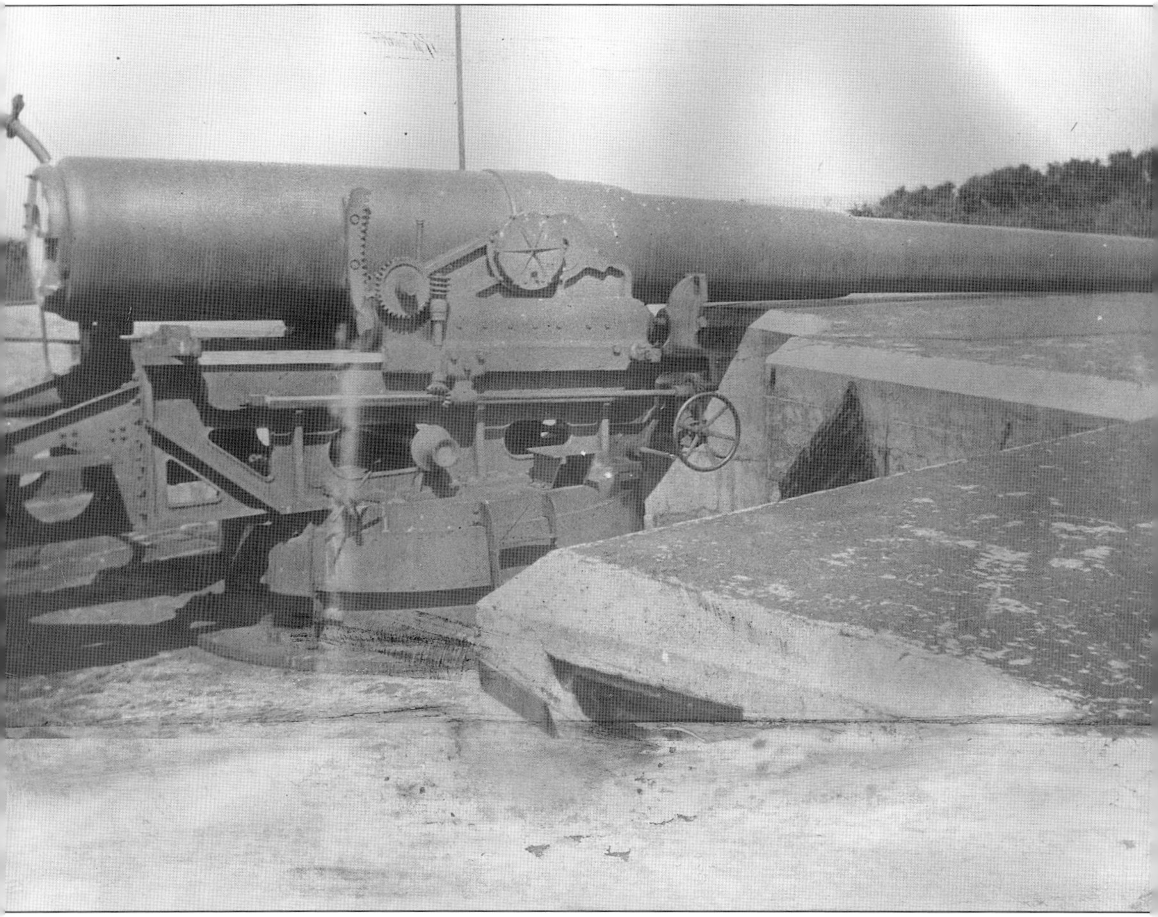

Each of Fort Screven's Coast Artillery batteries was named for a member of the armed forces who had distinguished himself in one of the country's wars. Battery Garland was completed in March 1899 and armed with one 12-inch rifled gun mounted on a non-disappearing carriage. Battery Garland was named for Brevet Brig. Gen. John Garland, a member of the Army in the Florida Seminole Indian War. This battery was serviced by 2 officers and 47 enlisted men; it also became obsolete after World War I and was eventually dismantled and melted down for scrap. Notice in the photo that the gun's breech mechanism has been removed. The restored Battery Garland presently houses the Tybee Museum.

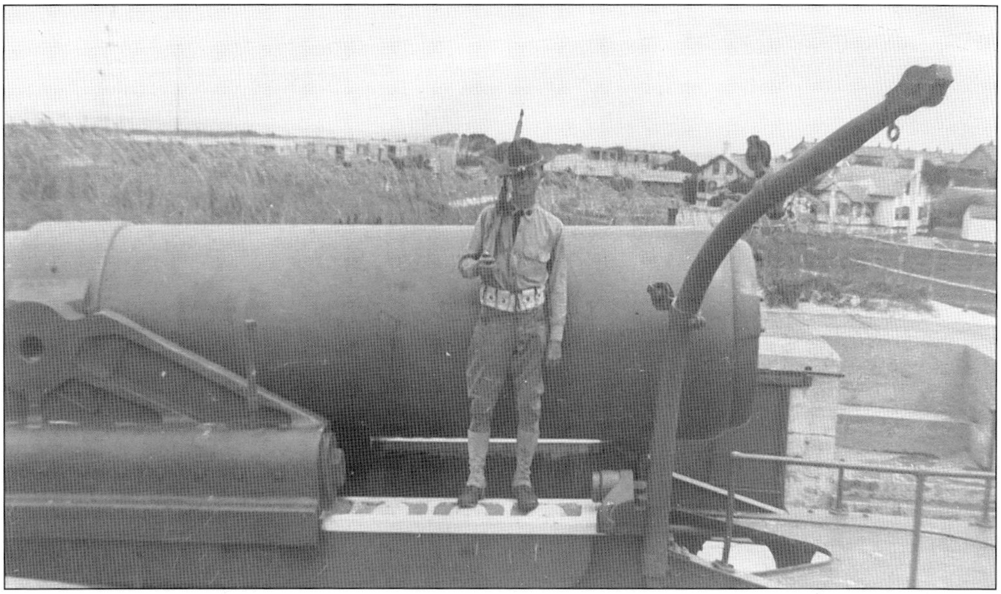

Battery Fenwick was said to be a duplicate of Battery Garland, but supported two 12-inch guns. It was named for Col. John R. Fenwick, an artillery officer who served with distinction during the War of 1812. In the above photograph taken in August 1935, Bill Barnett of the Civilian Military Training Camp (CMTC) stands guard on one of the guns. By this time, the guns were still in place, but no longer active.

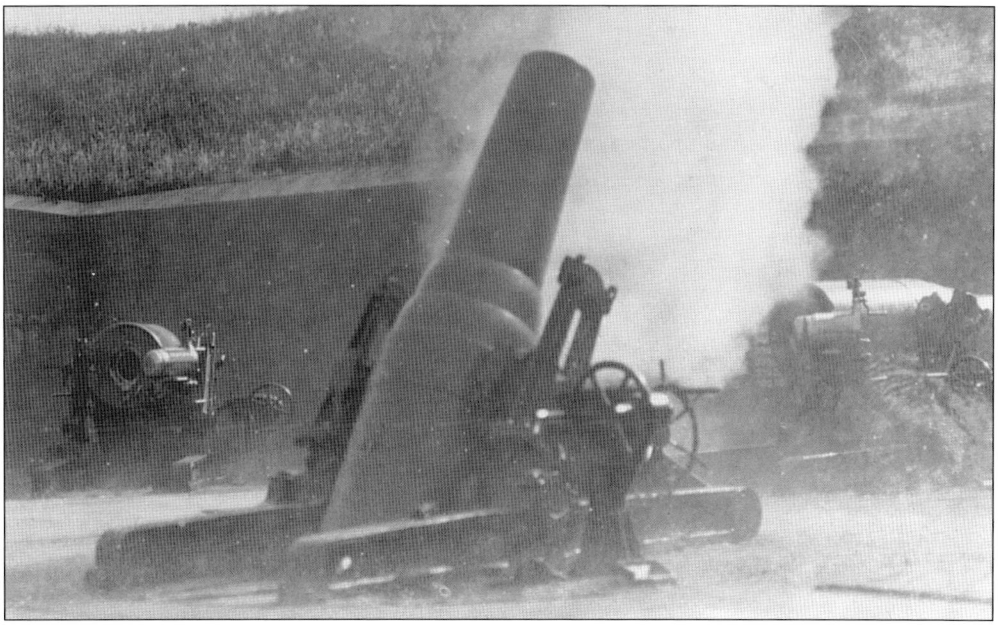

Battery Habersham was named for Maj. Joseph Habersham, who served with the Continental Army during the Revolutionary War. Habersham served as postmaster general of the United States from 1785 to 1801. This battery mounted eight 12-inch steel rifled mortars, arranged in three emplacements. The mortars fired 700 pound shells in a high arc to descend on the decks of ships. Construction of Battery Habersham began in December 1898 and the mortars were in place by June 1900. The battery was served by 7 officers and 219 enlisted men.

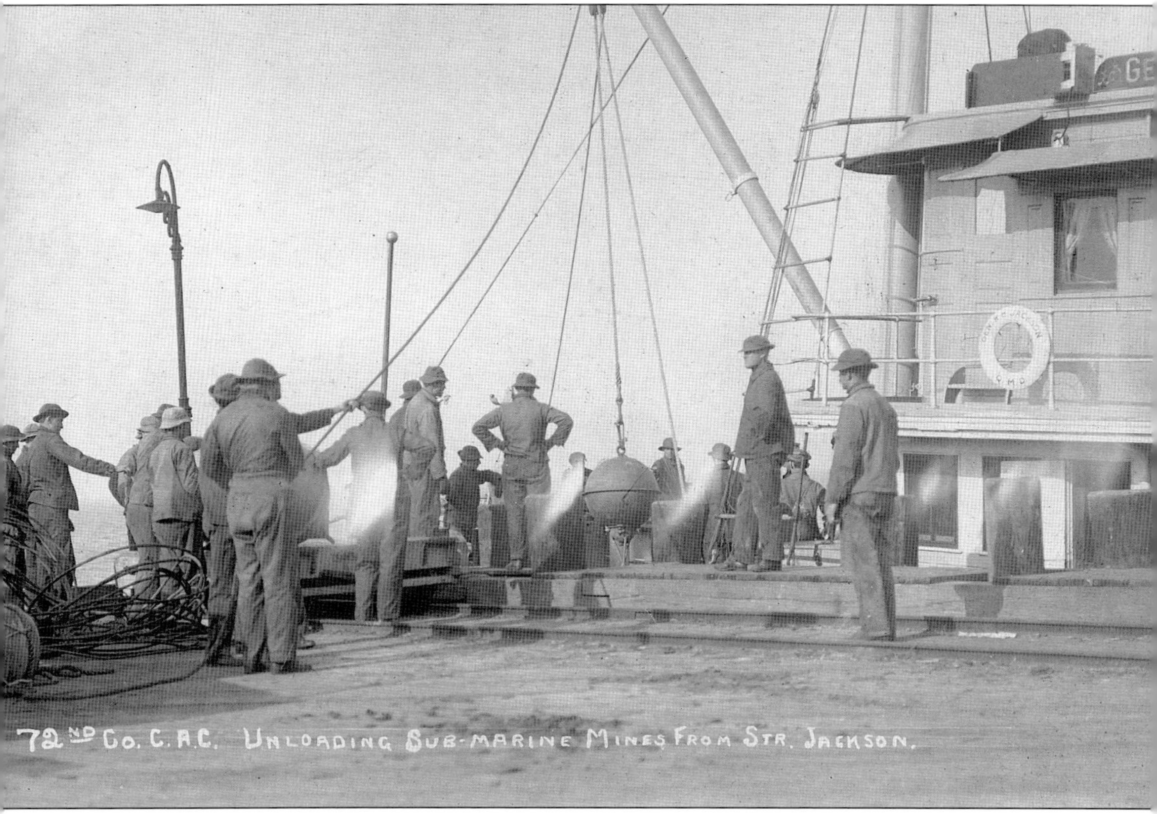

By the early 1900s, submarine warfare became a real concern to those responsible for defending America's coastlines. Of special concern was the submarine fleet being developed at the time by Germany. Capt. J.C. Gilmore Jr. was ordered to Savannah to take charge of establishing an anti-submarine defense at the mouth of the Savannah River. Gilmore established his headquarters at Fort Screven. The defensive plan against enemy submarines included the laying of a mine field to help prevent encroachment of the Savannah River and to protect the harbor of Savannah. The task of laying the mines fell to the men Fort Screven. The above photograph shows men of the 72nd Co. Coast Artillery Corps unloading mines from the steamer *Jackson*.

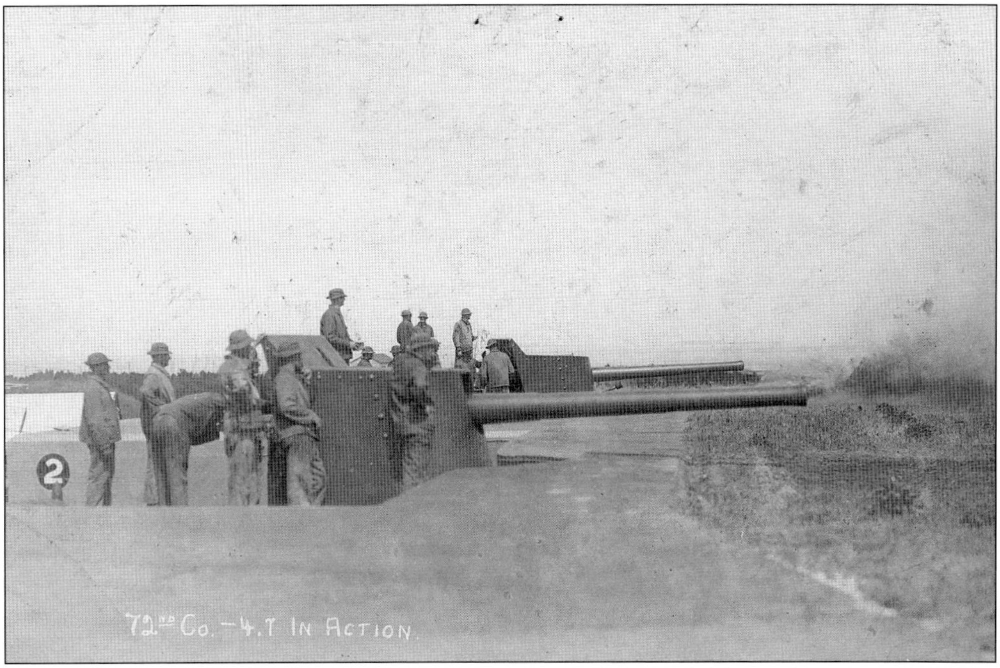

Battery Backus was positioned to guard the submerged mine fields at the entrance to the Savannah River. Construction of Battery Backus began on April 27, 1898, and the first 6-inch rapid fire gun was installed later that year. Two additional gun emplacements were completed in 1900 and all three were armed with 4.7-inch rapid fire guns. The battery was named for Col. Electus Backus, who served with the Army in the War of 1812.

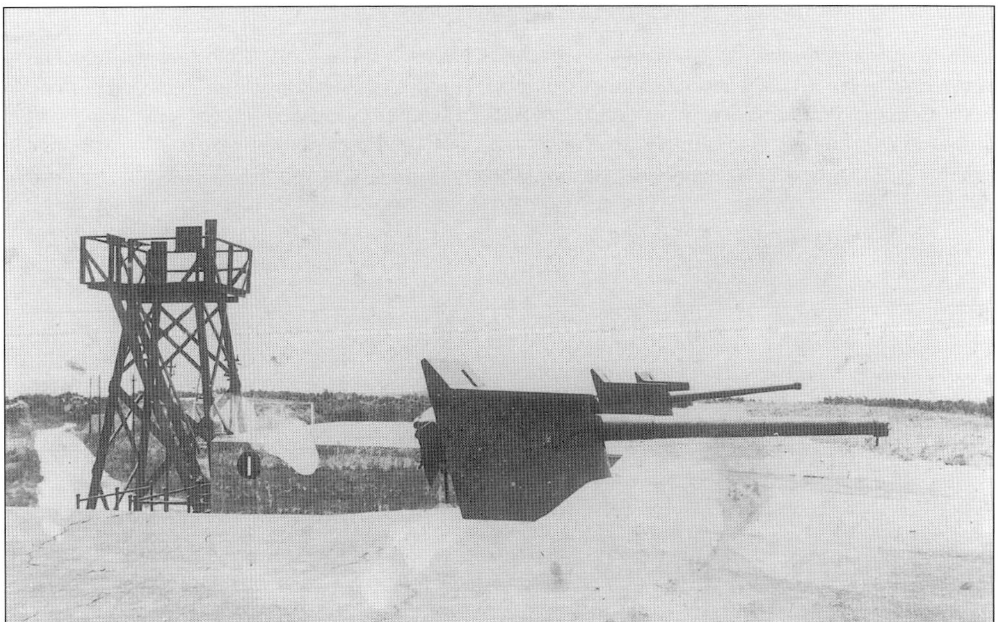

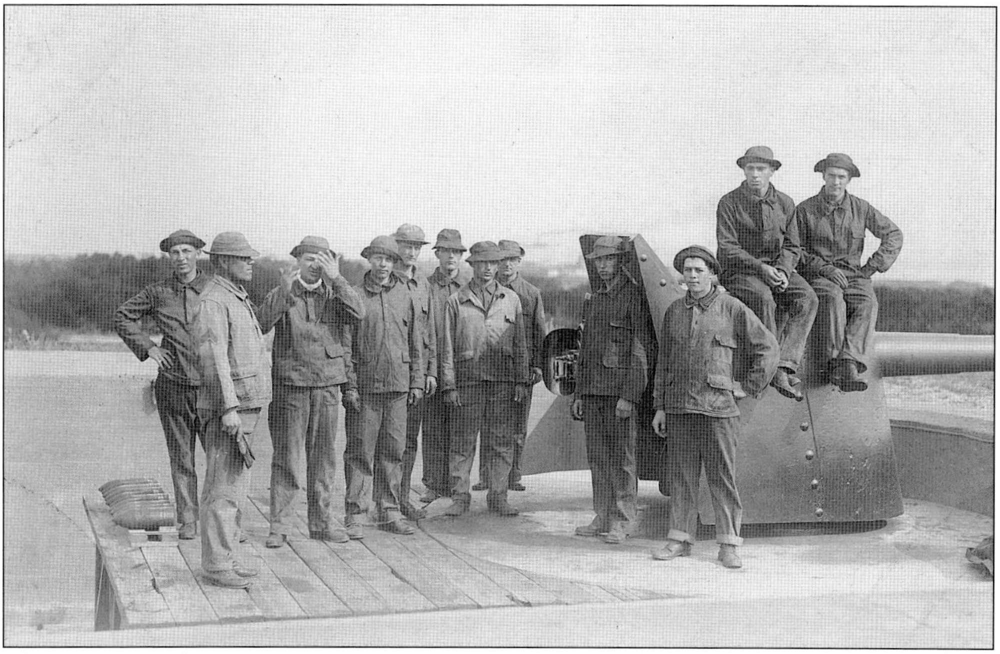

The companion battery to Battery Backus was Battery Gantt, named to honor First Lt. Levi Gantt, who was killed in the Mexican War Battle of Chapultepec in 1847. The battery supported two 3-inch rapid fire guns and joined Battery Backus in covering the mine field.

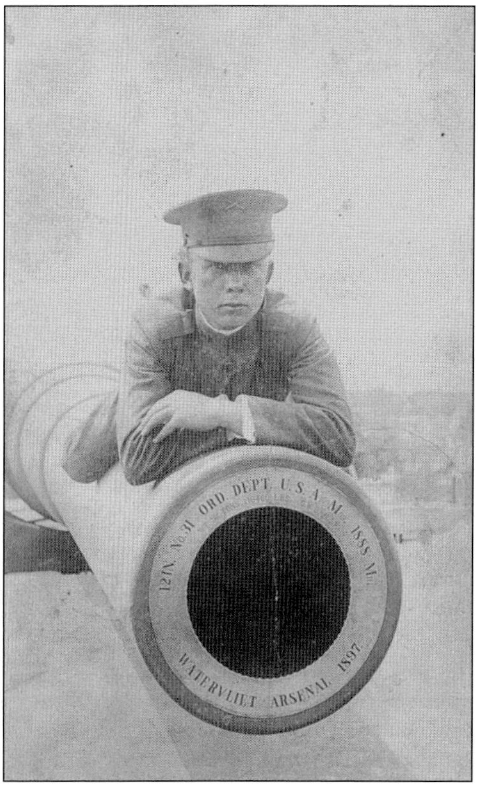

The soldiers who were first stationed at Fort Screven to service the guns that protected the coast were members of the Coast Artillery Corps (CAC) branch of the United States Army. Even though they were never required to repel an enemy invader, these men kept themselves and their guns at the ready. This photo of a young CAC soldier posing near the business end of a 12-inch gun might have been used for recruiting purposes.

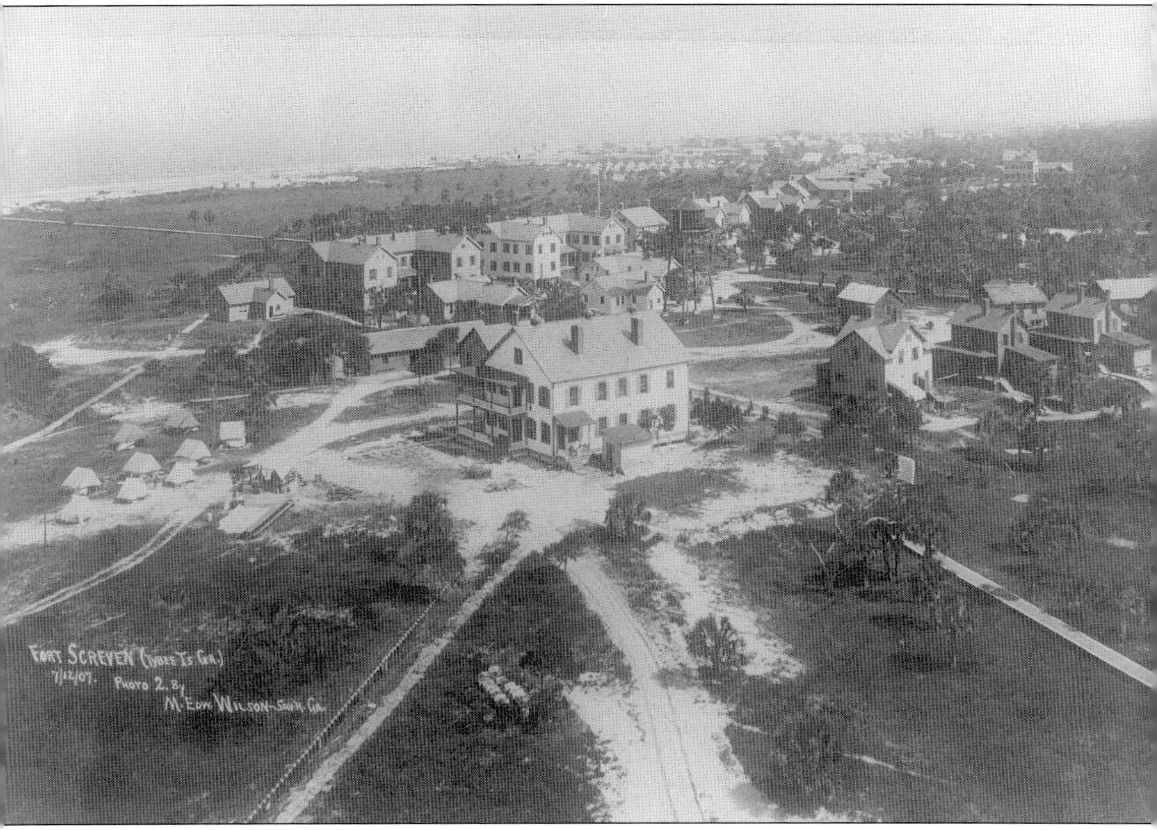

This photograph shows a portion of the Fort Screven military reservation as it looked in 1907, about 10 years after the post was activated. Fort Screven covered most of the north end of Tybee Island. The building program lasted for the next several years. The buildings were numbered in order of their construction.

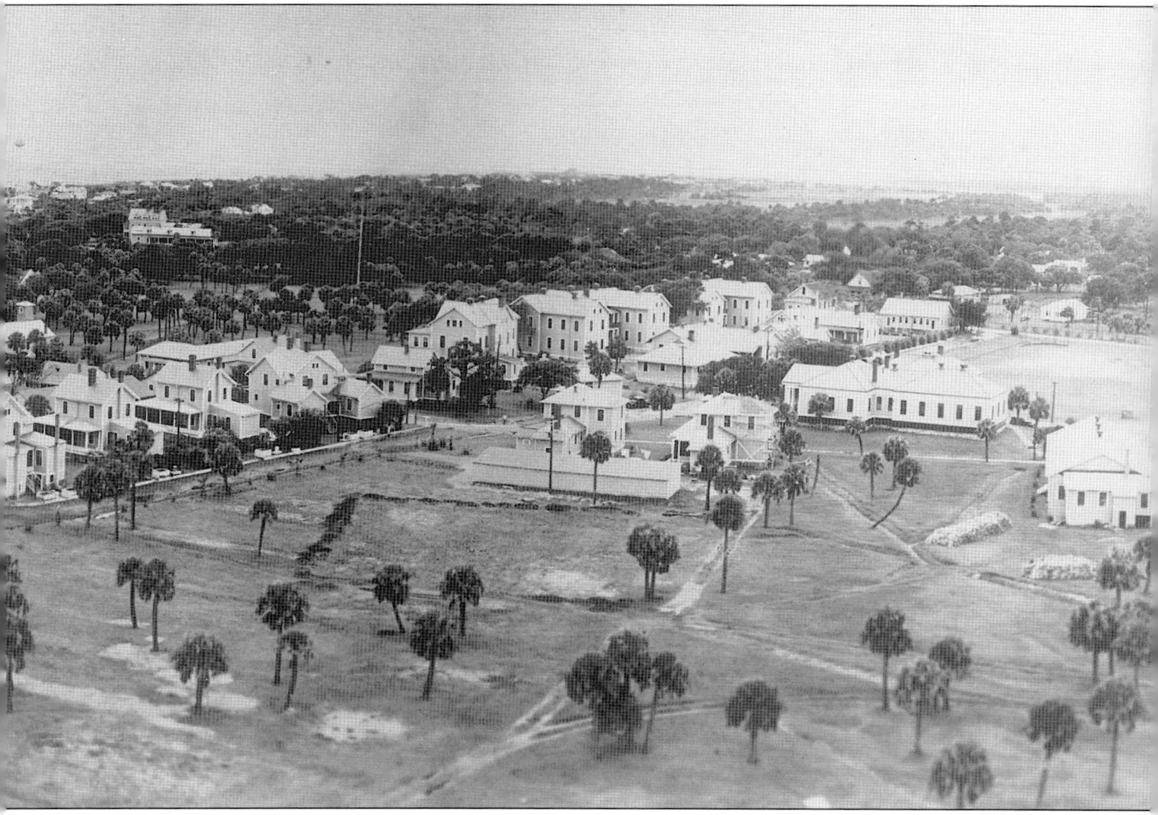

This view of another section of Fort Screven was photographed in 1938. The row of buildings running from the left to the center of the picture are dependent quarters and enlisted men's barracks. The post exchange is to the right center, and adjacent to it is the post baseball field. The building in the upper left of the picture is the officers' mess and club. At the end of World War II, the federal government sold most of Fort Screven's land and buildings to the town of Savannah Beach (Tybee) for a sum of $200,000. Savannah Beach put the property, including 265 buildings and 134.37 acres of land, up for public sale. Even the abandoned gun batteries were sold and are now either private or city property.

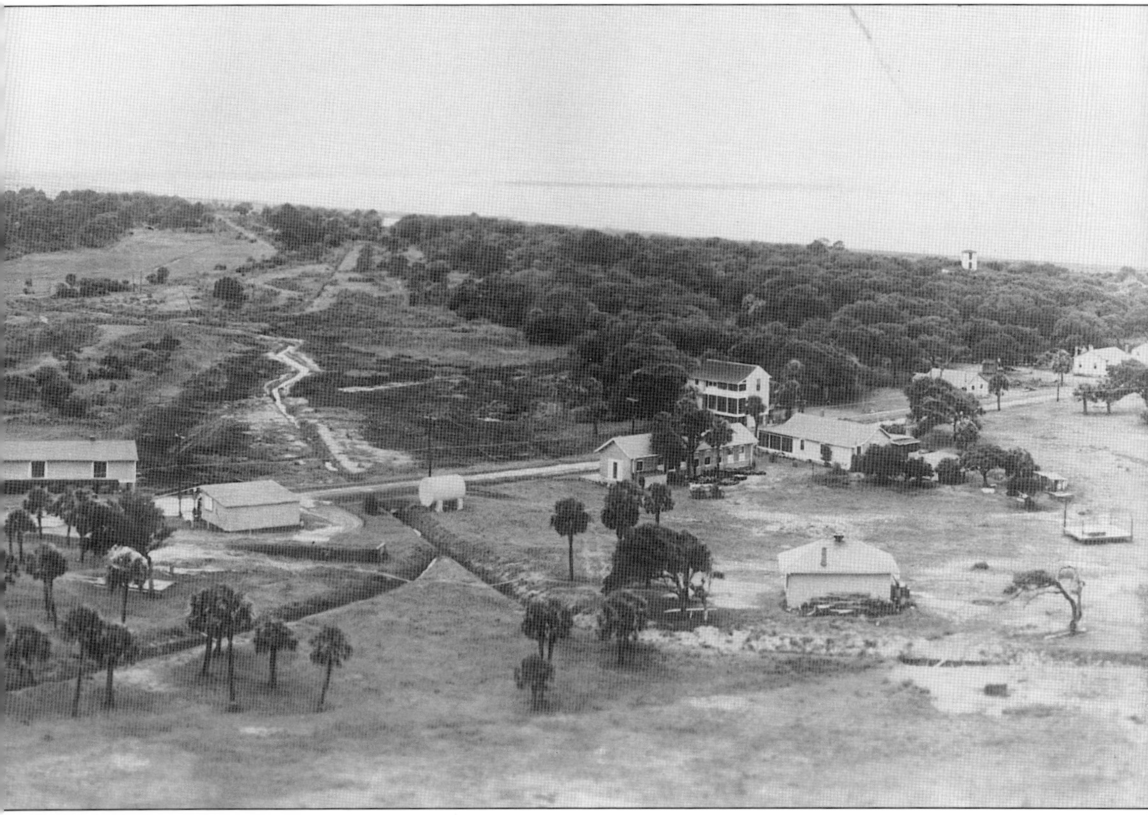

Another 1938 photograph shows a part of Fort Screven's maintenance and ordinance area. The small building in the center is a gasoline station. The post laundry is to the right. The wharf and a training area for members of the Civilian Military Training Corps (CMTC) and reserve officers were to the right, but are not included in this photograph. This area of Fort Screven has been developed and older former military buildings exist in the midst of more modern and expensive private homes.

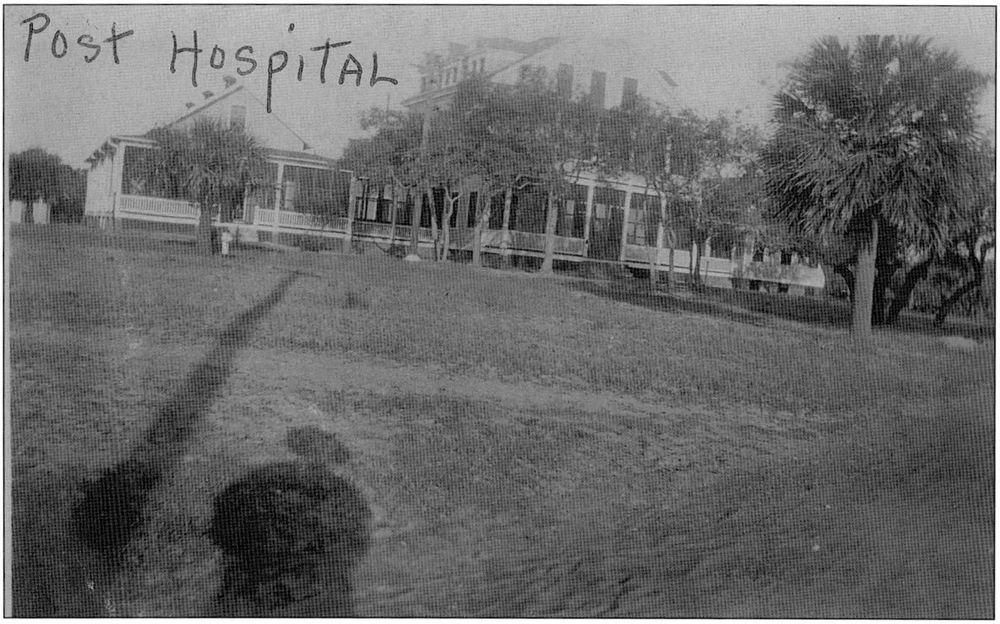

The photograph above, taken in the early 1900s, shows a part of Fort Screven's post hospital complex. The site is now occupied by Tybee Island's nursing and rehabilitation centers. The former hospital day room has been turned into a bed and breakfast inn.

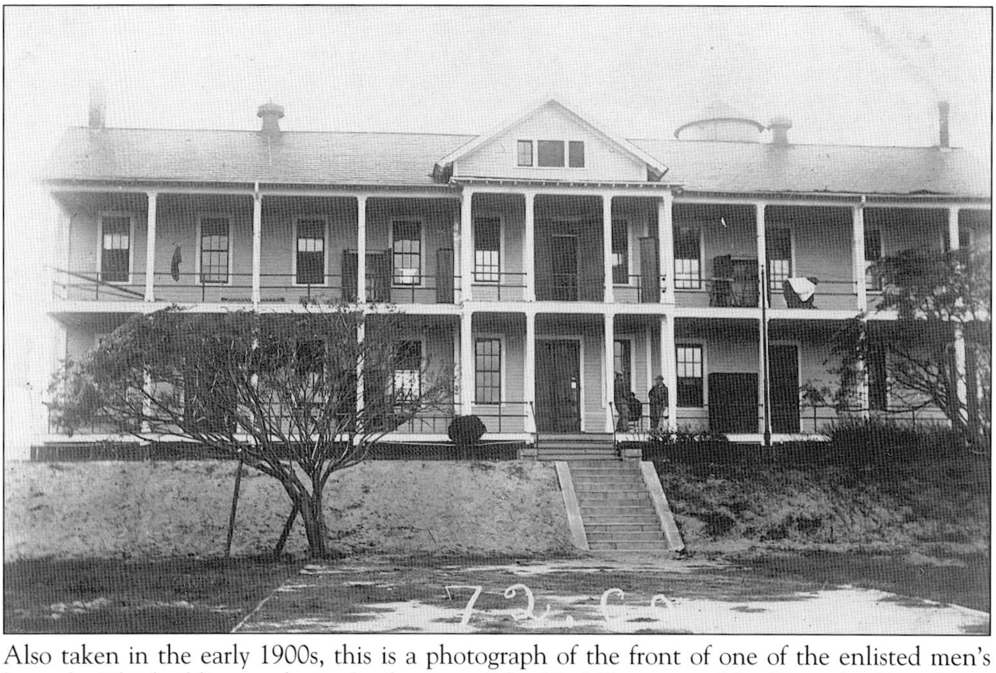

Also taken in the early 1900s, this is a photograph of the front of one of the enlisted men's barracks. This building was home for the men of the 72nd Company of the Coast Artillery Corps (CAC). This barracks faced the post's parade ground, now a public park and playground.

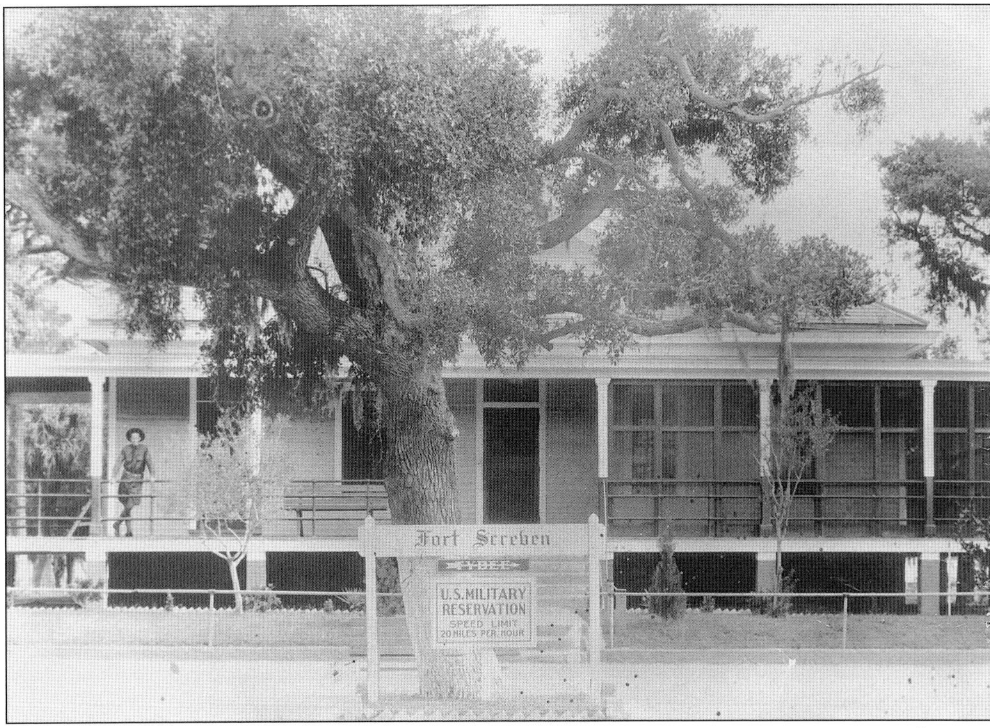

The first building encountered by visitors entering Fort Screven's main gate was the post guard house. The guard detail stayed in this building during their tour of duty. The building also contained holding cells to detain prisoners. The structure is now used as Tybee Island's Community Center.

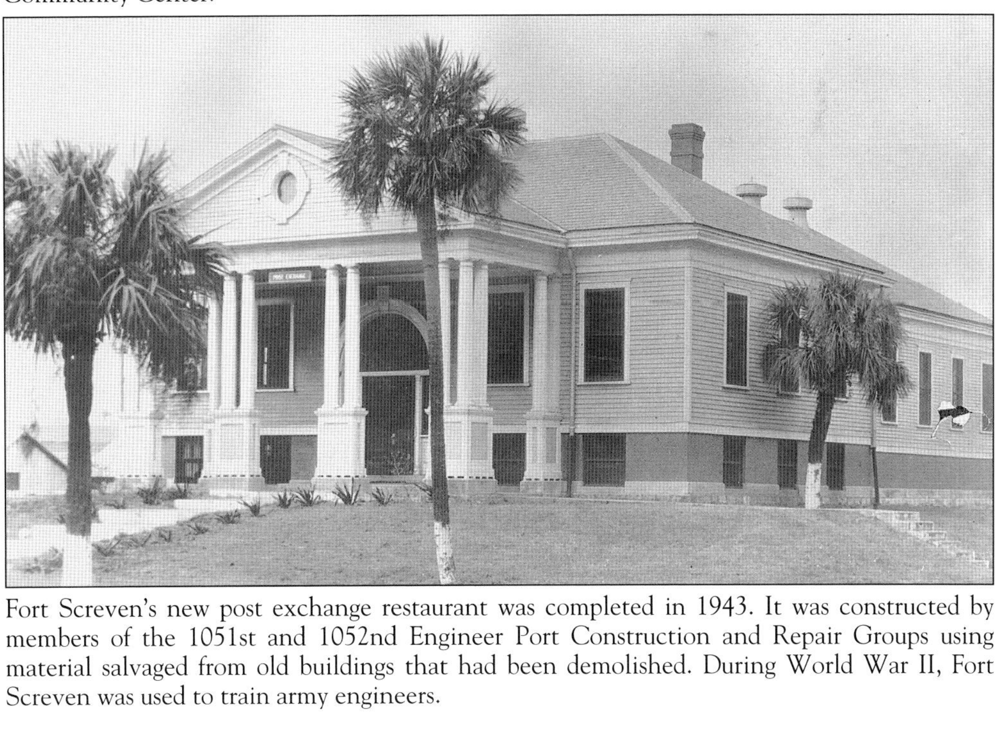

Fort Screven's new post exchange restaurant was completed in 1943. It was constructed by members of the 1051st and 1052nd Engineer Port Construction and Repair Groups using material salvaged from old buildings that had been demolished. During World War II, Fort Screven was used to train army engineers.

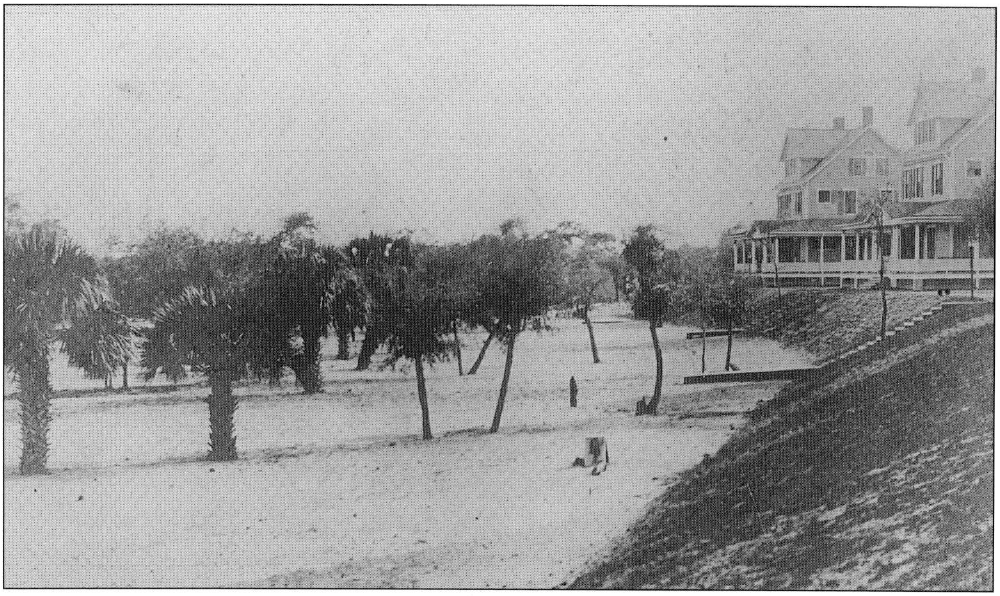

The top photograph from about 1907 shows part of a row of elegant turn-of-the-20th-century frame houses standing atop a ridge, their expansive porches facing the sea. These homes served as quarters for some of Fort Screven's officers and their families, and became known as Officers' Row. The homes were completely furnished and supplied with all the necessities. The open area in front of the row of officer quarters was used at different times as a parade ground, polo field, and rifle range. The Officers' Row houses are now private residences. A later photograph, shown below, is of an Officers' Row building that was once used as post headquarters. It is also now a private residence.

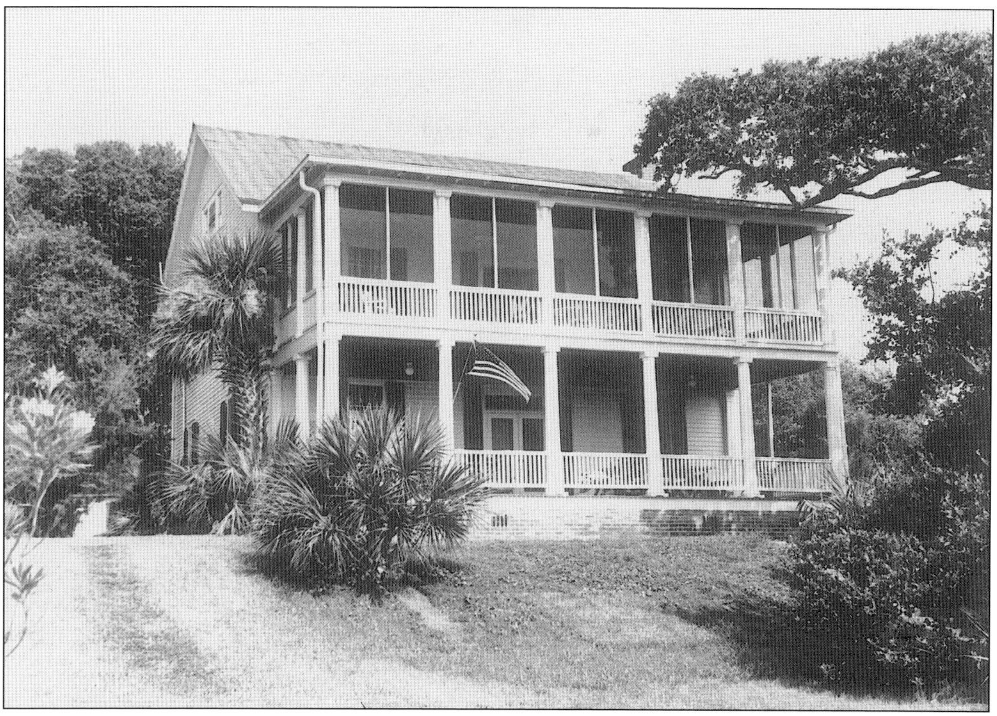

Four

MEN OF FORT SCREVEN

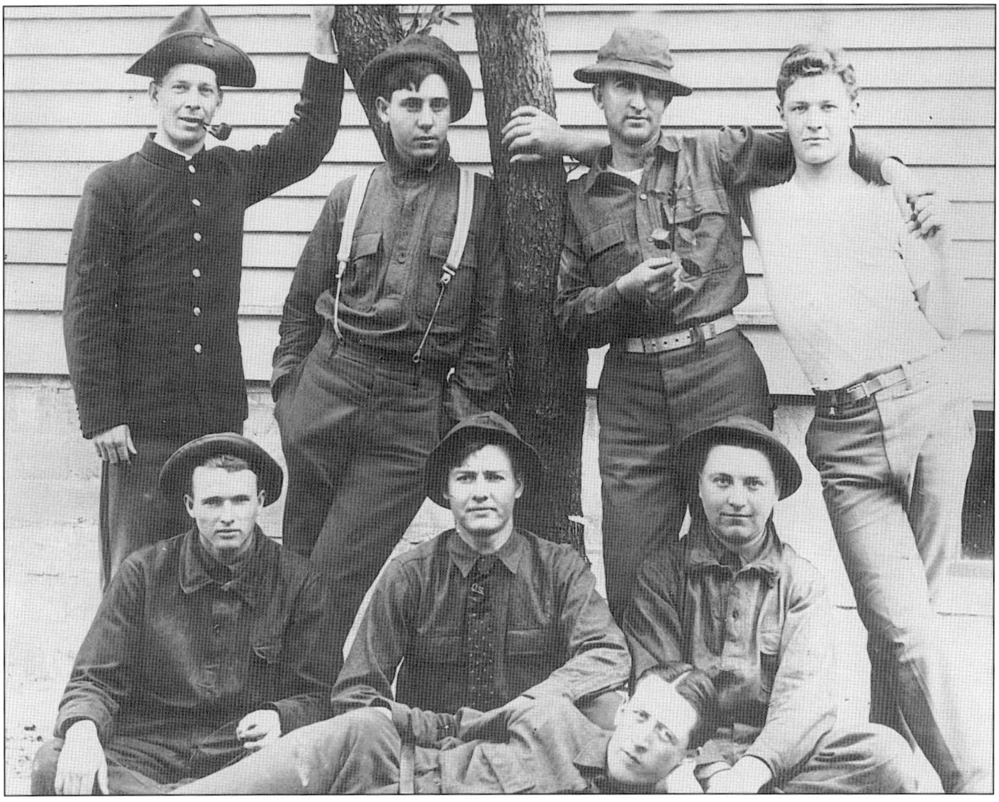

A normal duty day for the Fort Screven soldier included marching and manual-of-arms drills, training classes, bayonet and grenade practice, and the honing of marksmanship skills. And, of course, the day also included maintenance, housekeeping, guard duty, and all of the other duties that make for a smooth-running military post. The soldiers of Fort Screven did get breaks from their daily routines to pursue other activities, such as posing for pictures.

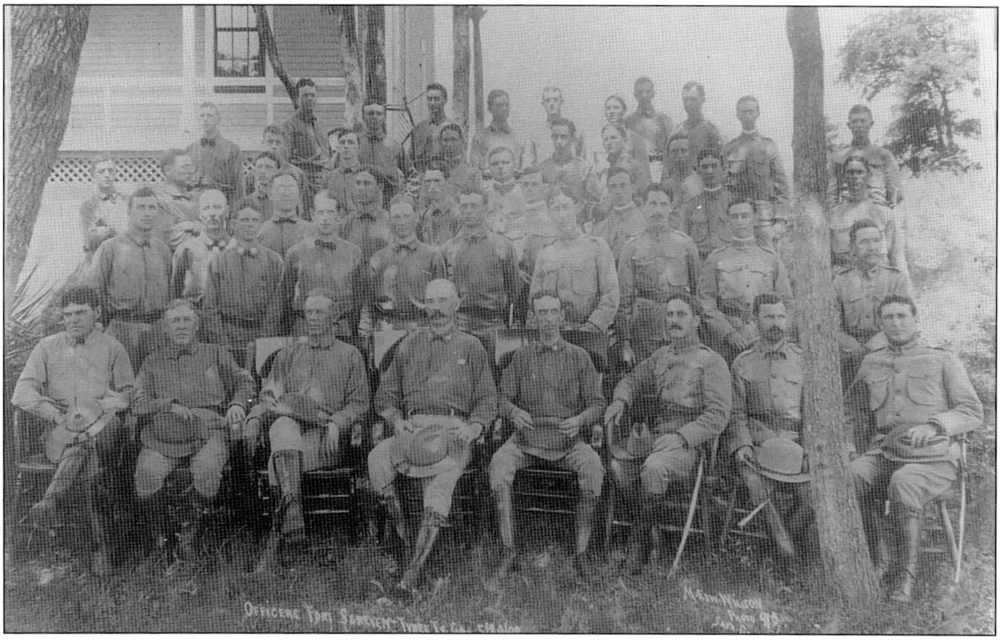

During the early 1900s, Fort Screven and its coastal batteries were commanded by a succession of Coast Artillery Corps officers. Few of them were above the rank of captain. During these early days, officer assignments to Fort Screven were usually of short duration. Above is group photograph of the fort's officer corps in 1908.

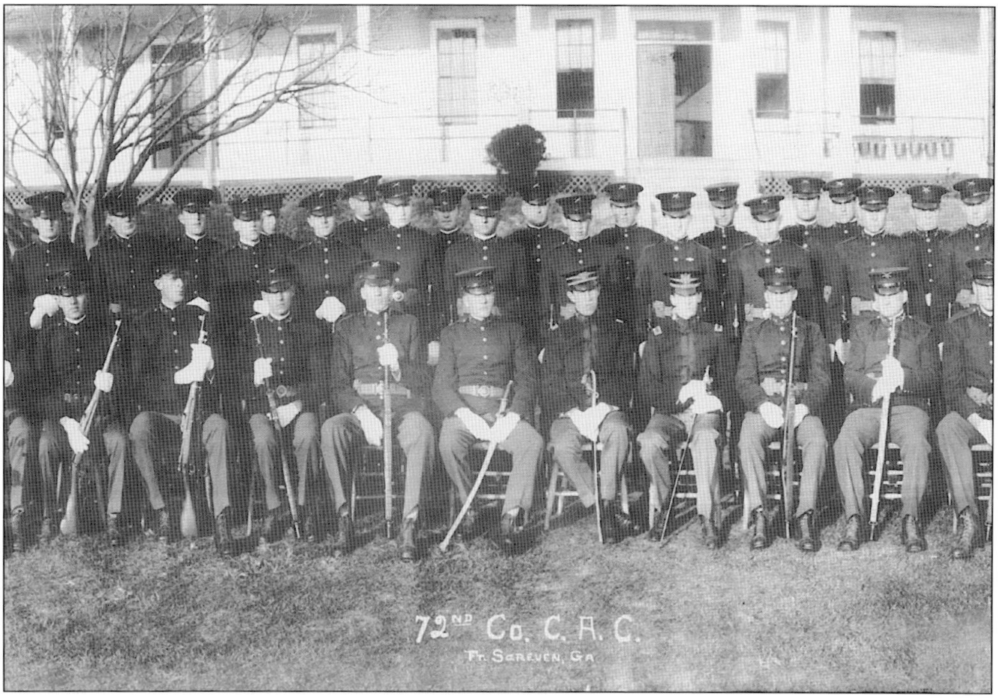

This early 1900s photograph of the officers and men of the 72nd Co. CAC could have been taken following a formal parade or review. The men are wearing their dress, or "class A," uniforms.

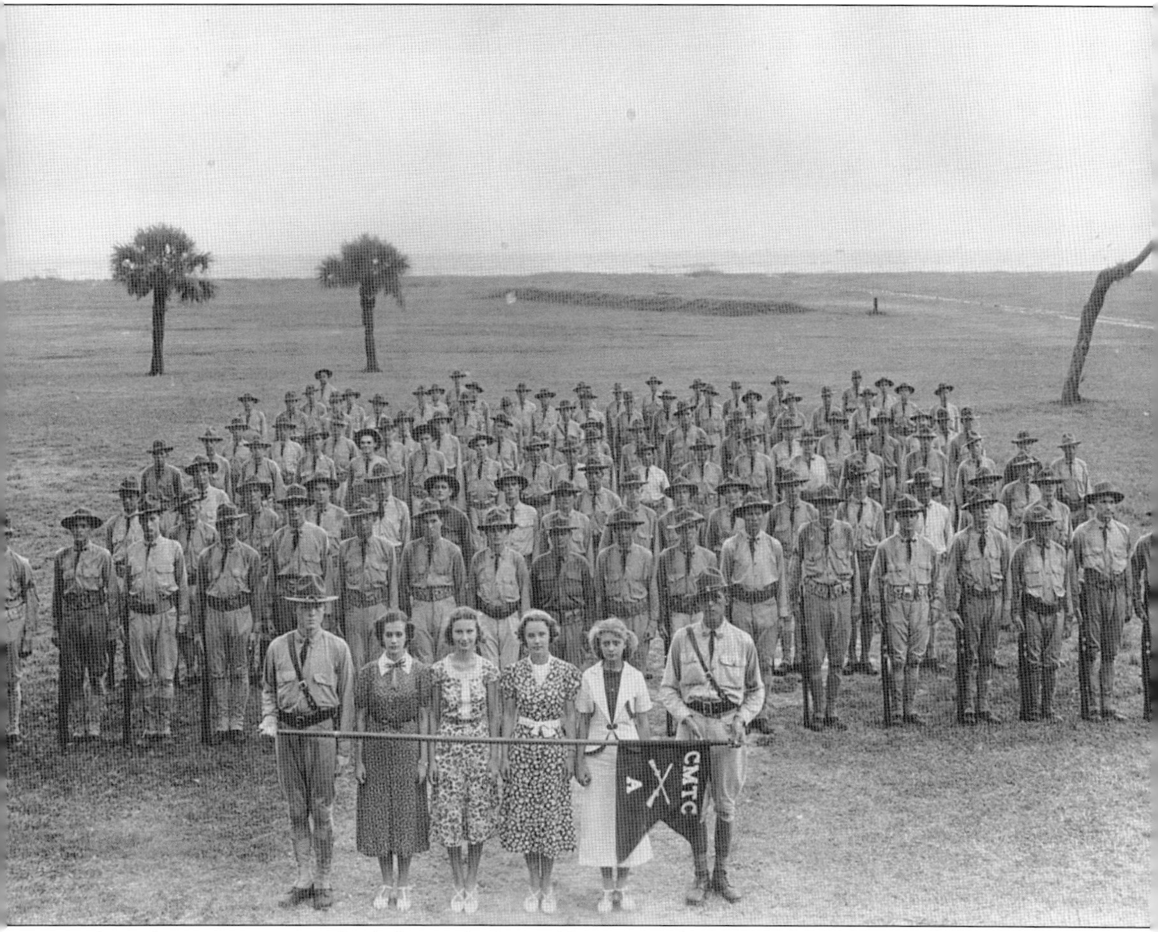

When the Armistice marked the end of World War I, "the war to end all wars," most all of Fort Screven's big guns were dismantled and removed from the fortifications, and the fort was threatened with closure. During the summer of 1921, the post was used as a training site for men of the Citizens Military Training Camp (CMTC) from Georgia, South Carolina, and Florida. Many reserve and national guard troops traveled to Fort Screven for their summer encampments and training. This photograph taken in the early 1920s is of Co. A of the CMTC. The identities of the young civilian ladies are unknown.

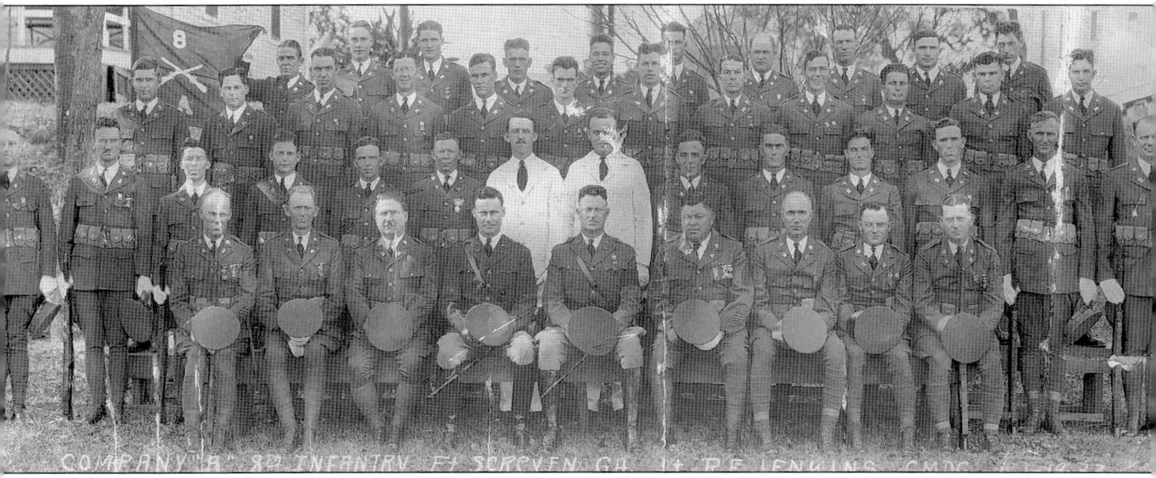

Fort Screven was saved from being closed when the 8th Infantry Regiment arrived at the Port of Savannah aboard the troop transport *St. Mihiel* on February 7, 1923. The regiment had served with the occupation forces in Germany from 1919 to 1923, and were the last American troops to return from Europe after World War I. The citizens of Savannah gave the men of the regiment a gala welcome that included the ringing of the city's bells, parades, speeches, receptions, balls, and a salute fired by the historic "Washington Guns" of the Chatham Artillery. The 1st Battalion was transported by train to Fort Screven, where it spent the next 15 years. The remainder of the regiment was sent to its new station at Fort Moultrie, SC. The 1933 picture above is of Co. A, 8th Infantry Regiment.

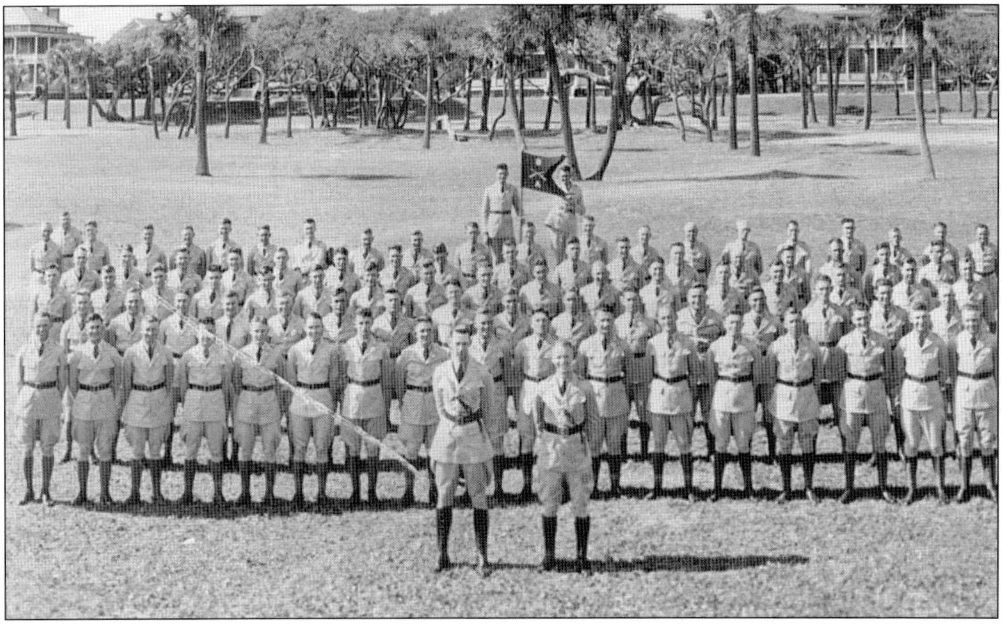

On one sunny day during the middle years of the 1930s, the four companies of Fort Screven's 1st Battalion, 8th Infantry Regiment formed on the parade ground for a photo session. The men are standing at the "parade rest" position. Smiles on some of the faces indicate this was a less formal photo session. In the top photo, the homes of Officers' Row can be seen in the background.

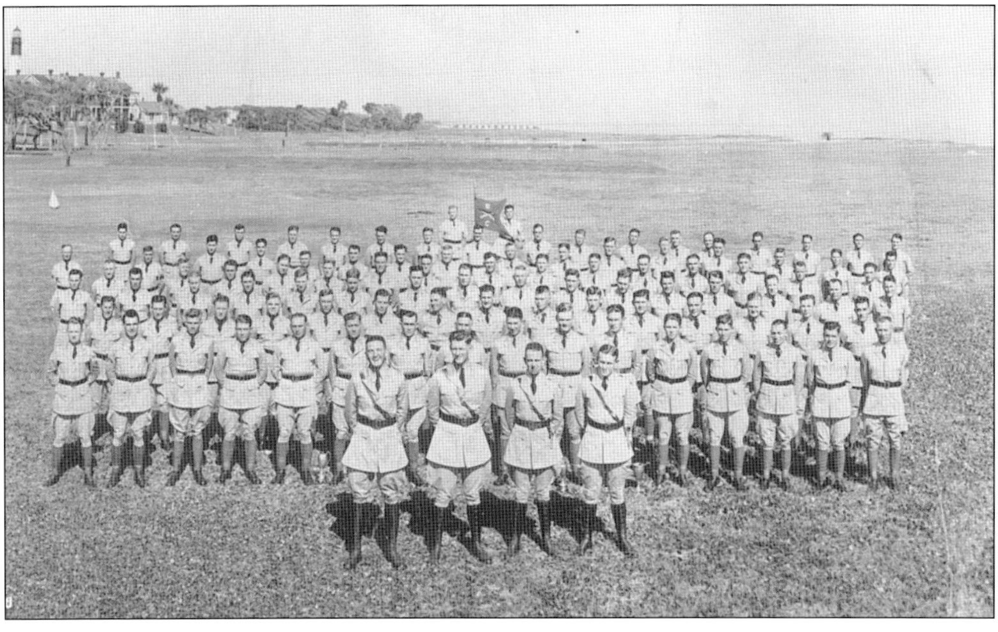

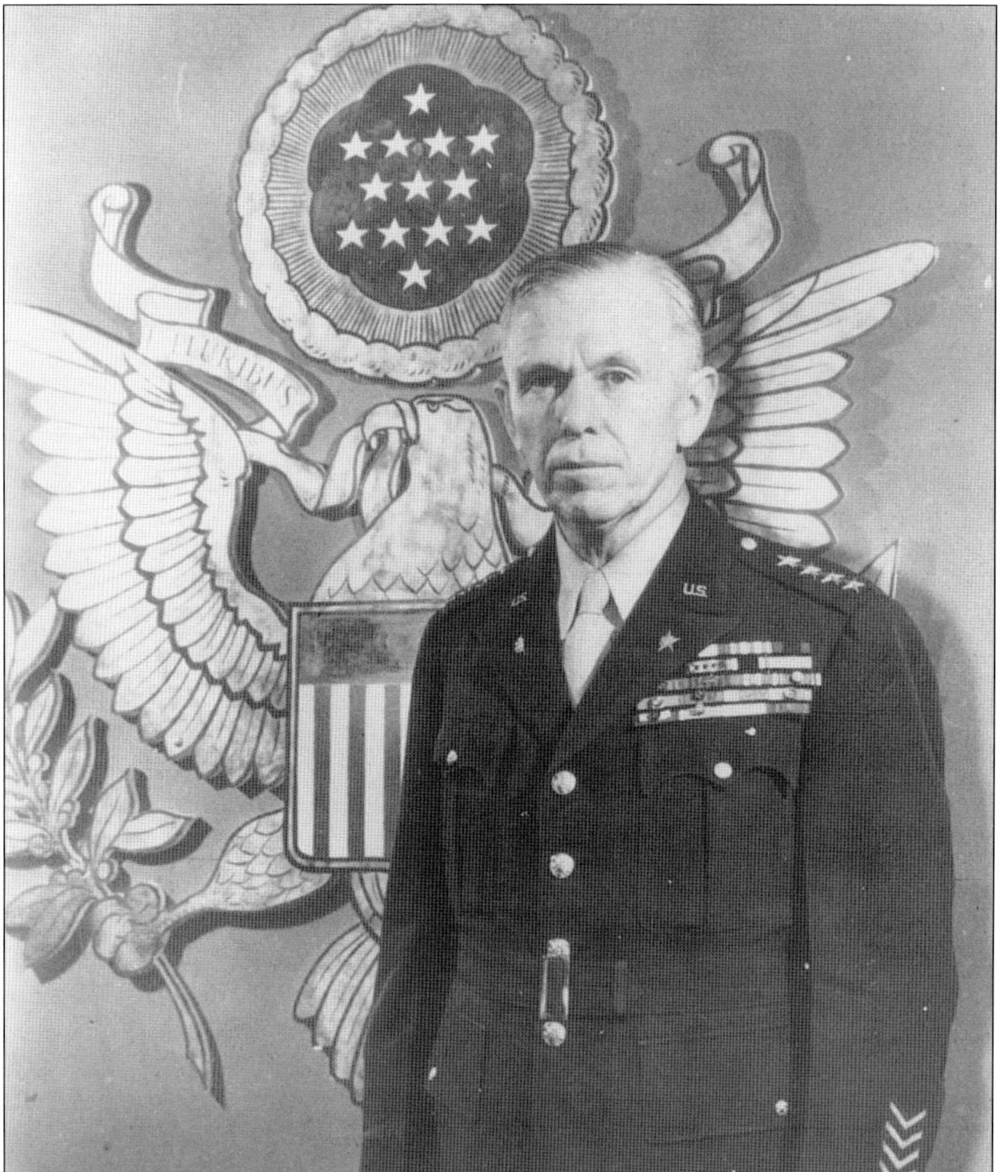

One of Fort Screven's most famous commanders was Lt. Col. George Catlett Marshall. Marshall came to Fort Screven in the Spring of 1932 from duty with the Infantry School at Fort Benning, GA. Determined to improve the relationship between Fort Screven's soldiers and the community, Lt. Col. Marshall and his wife, Katherine, attended church services in Savannah and became acquainted with many of the city's leaders. Another of Marshall's objectives was beautification of the post. Through his efforts, and that of others, Fort Screven gained the reputation of being one of the most beautiful military posts in the country. Marshall's tenure as commander of Fort Screven came at a time when one of the main missions of the post was to organize and train men for the Civilian Conservation Corps (CCC), a national program to ease the unemployment problem resulting from the Great Depression. Fort Screven was the headquarters of District F of the 4th Corps.

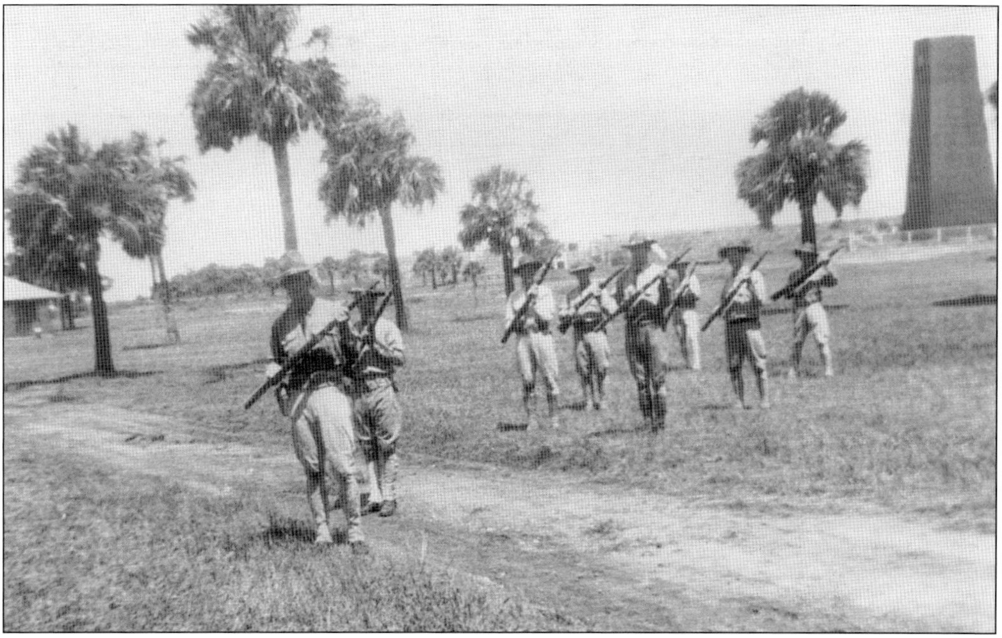

Every soldier soon learns that his rifle is his best friend. Therefore, much of the soldier's training is in the use and care of his weapon. In the above photograph, a squad of 8th Infantry Regiment soldiers practice their manual of arms near the base of the Tybee Lighthouse.

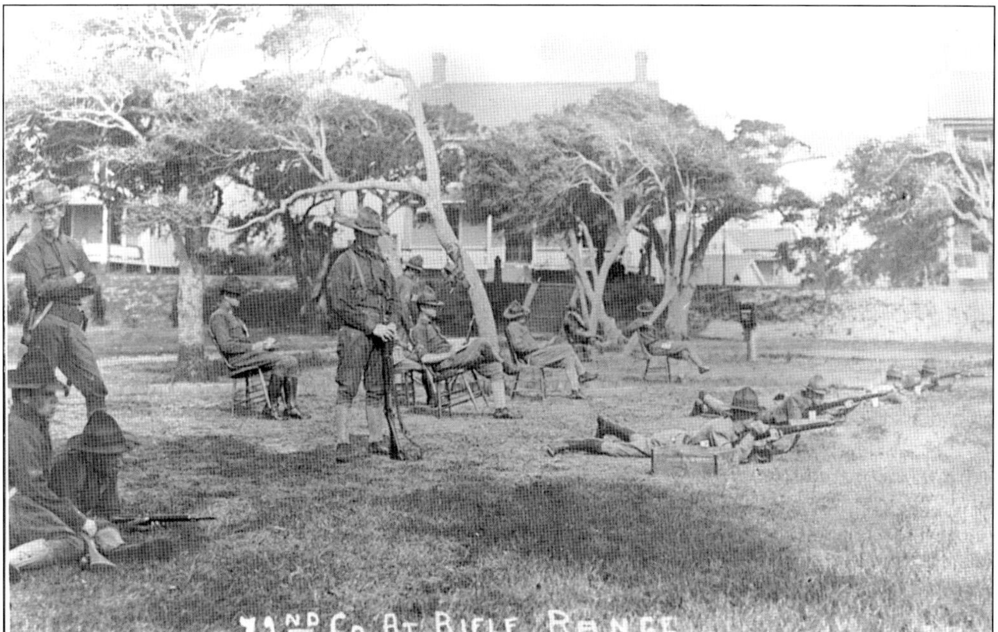

Soldiers were frequently required to "qualify" on their basic personal weapon. Even artillerymen needed marksmanship training with the rifle. In this photograph, members of the 72nd Co. CAC are involved in target practice on the rifle range. Officers' Row is in the background. The "spotters," sitting in the chairs behind the firing line, record the shooters' hits or misses.

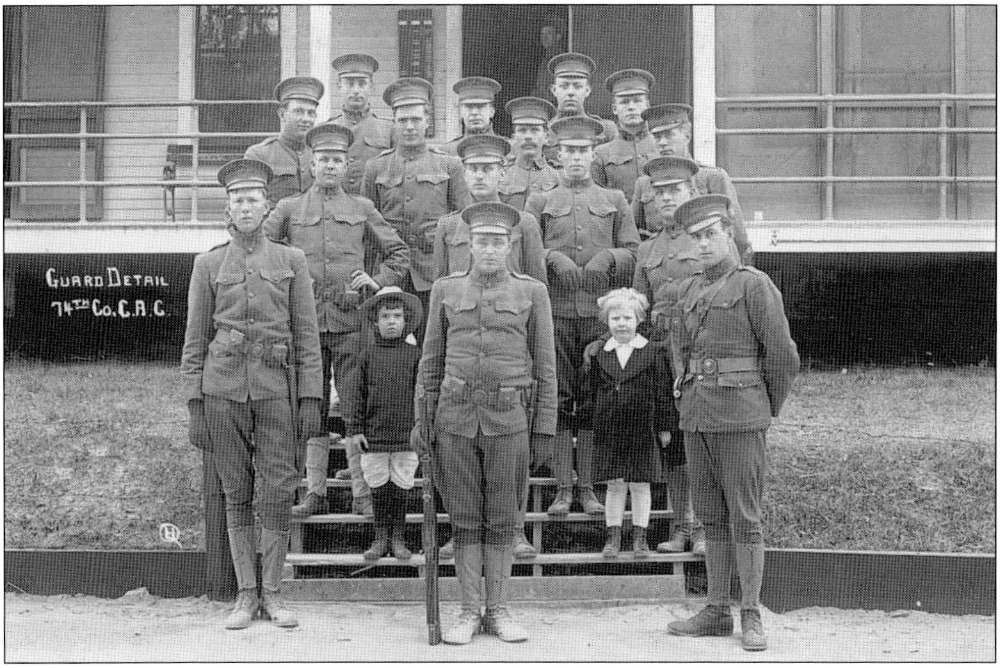

Assignment to the post guard detail was a fact of life for the soldier. The photograph above is from a postcard a soldier wrote to either his wife or mother. The message reads in part, "My heart belongs to you, but my life belongs to Uncle Sam, ha! ha! ha!." The identities of the two children are unknown.

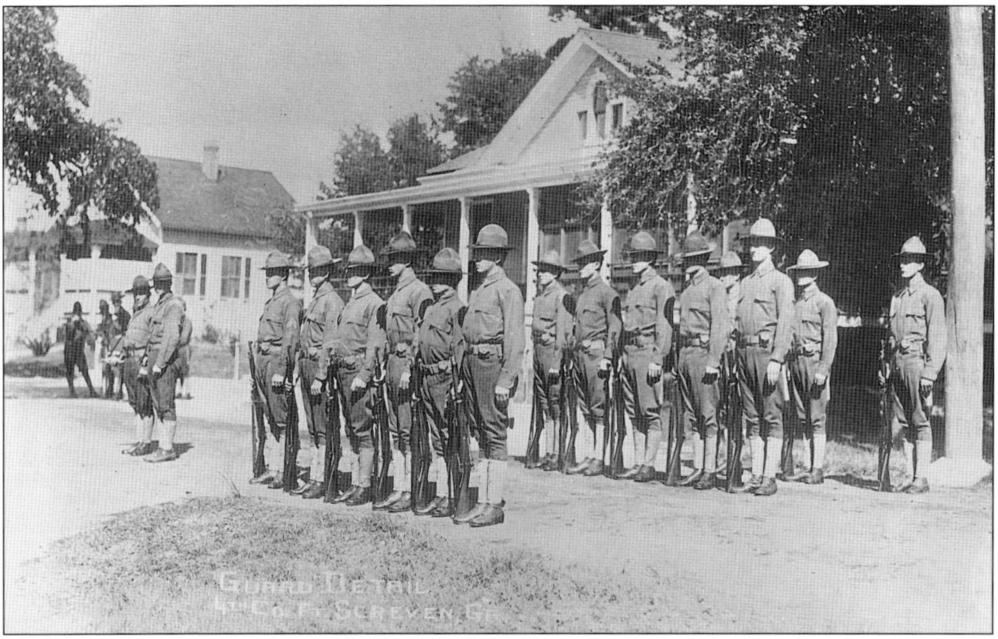

Col. Earl Eubanks, who served as ordinance officer at Fort Screven from 1934 to 1941, described the guard detail in a later interview. "There would be two soldiers on patrol outside the guard house all the time. They would pace back and forth at 120 steps per minute. Of course, no one ever counted to make sure."

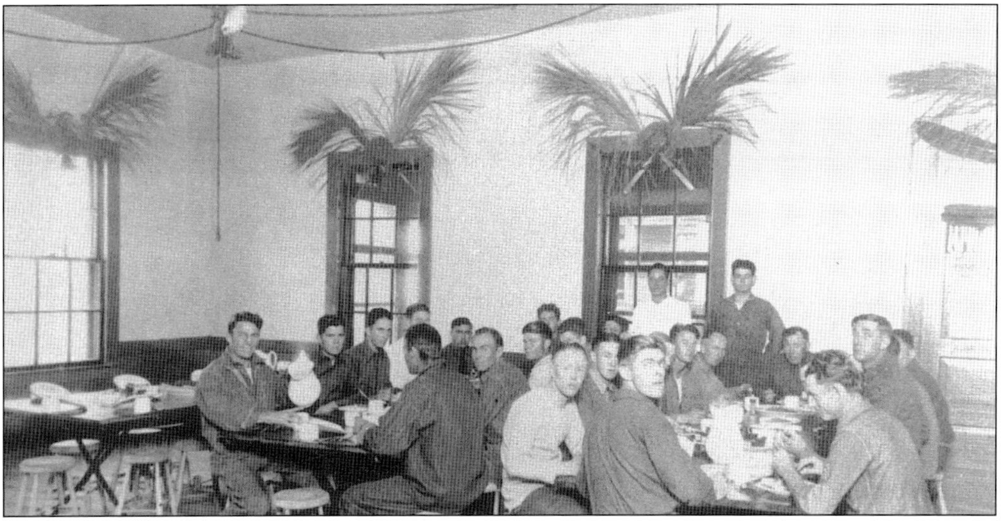

Ask most any soldier and he or she will tell you that one of the most looked forward to times of the duty day is "chow." Among Fort Screven's many military buildings were company mess halls. Meal preparation for hundreds of hungry soldiers did require a lot of work. Many an ex-GI remembers occasionally being assigned to kitchen police detail, better known as KP. The men in the photograph below are shucking oysters, either for the mess hall or for their own consumption.

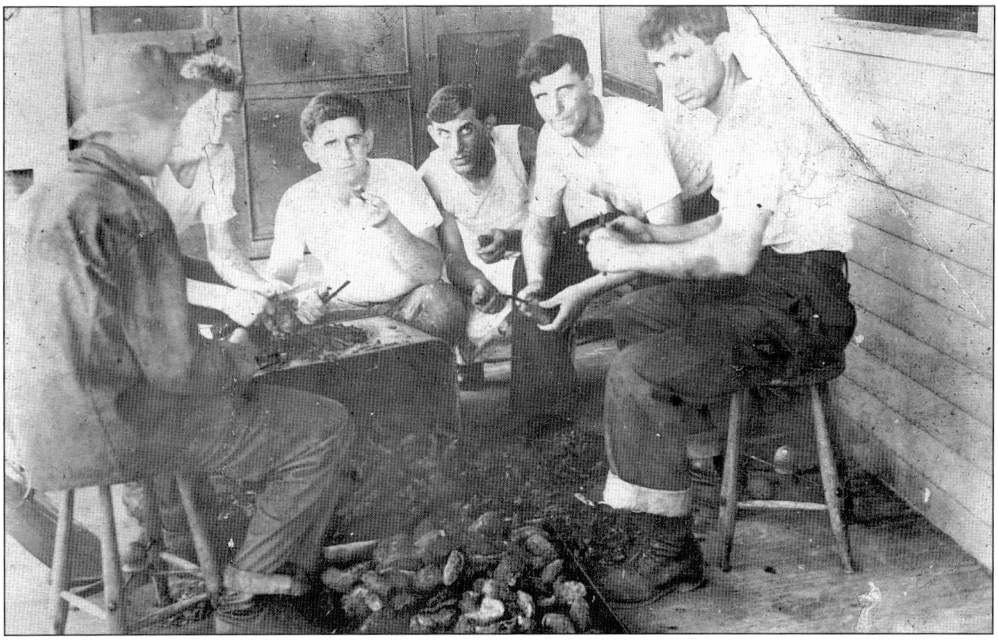

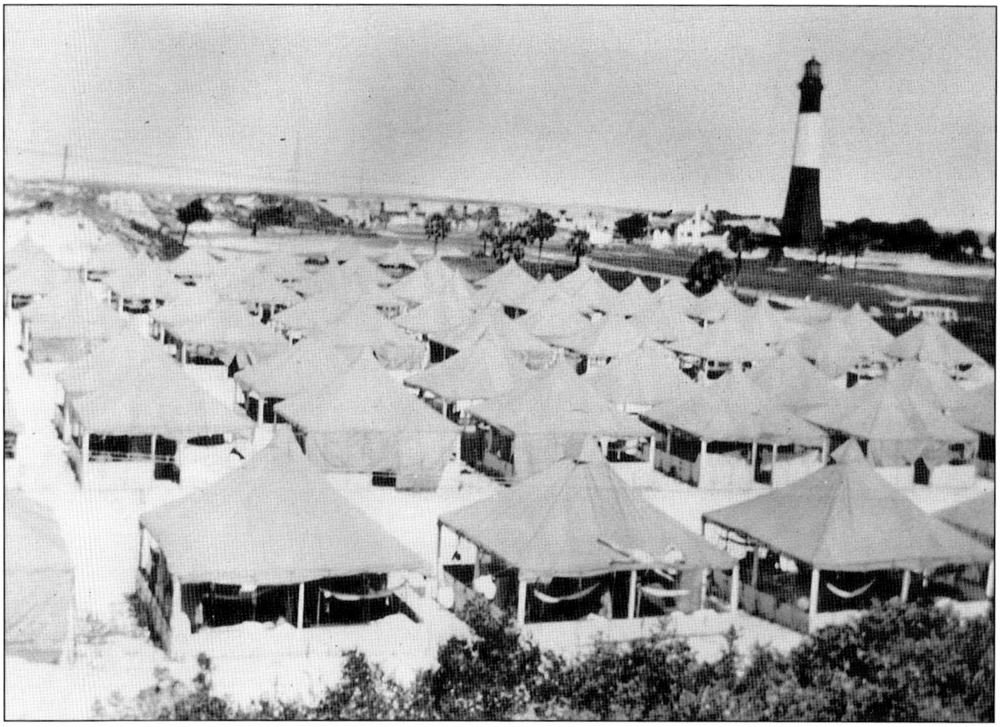

At times, barracks space at Fort Screven could not accommodate all of the soldiers who happened to be present for duty. During these times, citizen soldiers reporting for summer training sessions had to live in temporary wood and canvas shelters called "hutments." This photograph shows the 1936 encampment of the Citizens' Military Training Camp. Notice the lighthouse in the background.

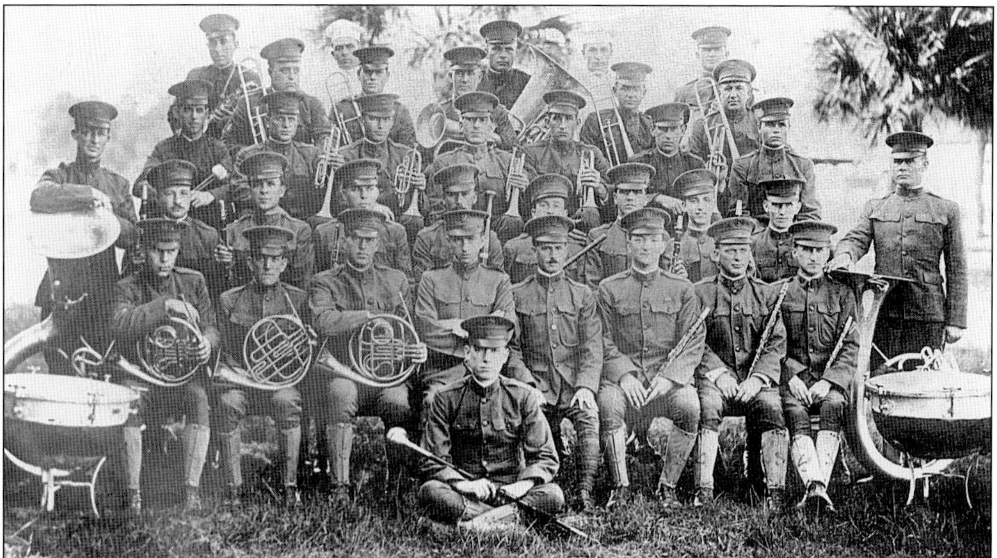

Parades, reviews, and other military ceremonies do not seem to be complete without a band to add to the pageantry. This 1910 photograph of the 14th Coast Artillery Corps Band is taken from a postcard from that time. The band's leader was identified as ? Hernandez.

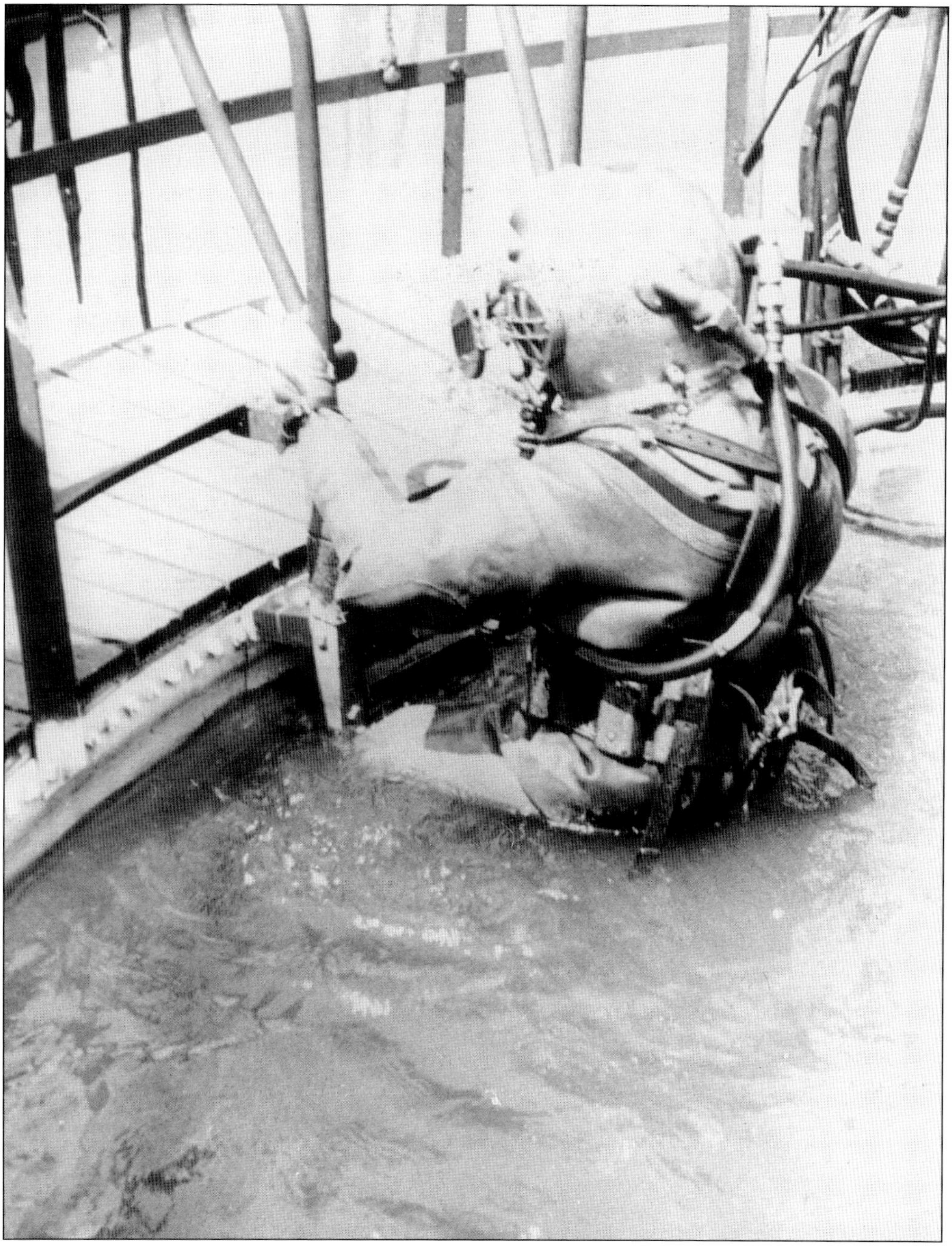

During World War II, Fort Screven became a diving school to train engineer troops for underwater salvage and the repair of bomb-damaged ports. The United States Army Engineer Diving and Salvage School at Fort Screven was the only one of its type in the United States. Members of these engineer units were civilian trained and experienced in various construction trades. Each of the port construction and repair groups went through 12 intensive weeks of training at Fort Screven. An applicant for training to be a diver had to pass exacting physical tests. Even a touch of sinusitis would eliminate the candidate. The diving tank at Fort Screven gave the diver trainee practice in working underwater for extended periods of time.

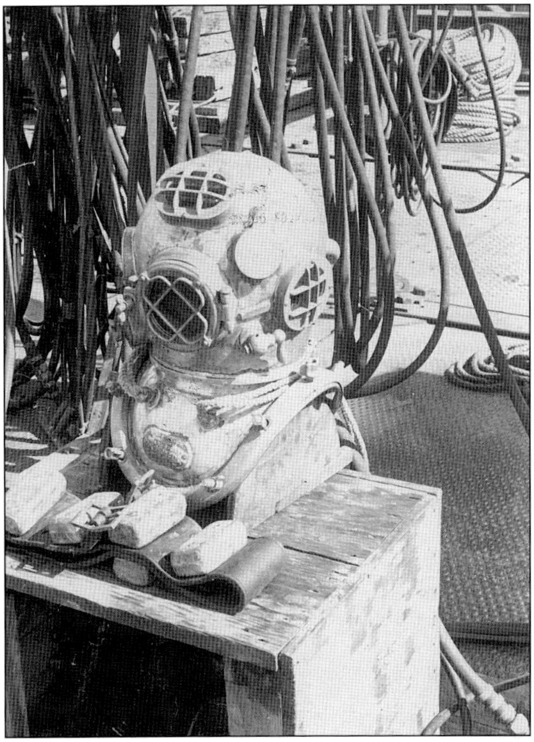

The diving helmet and weighted belt were important parts of a diver's underwater gear. The metal diving helmet weighed 31.5 pounds and had miniature glass portholes with protective brass grill covering. The diving belt added another 83 pounds to the diver's weight and resembled a soldier's cartridge belt.

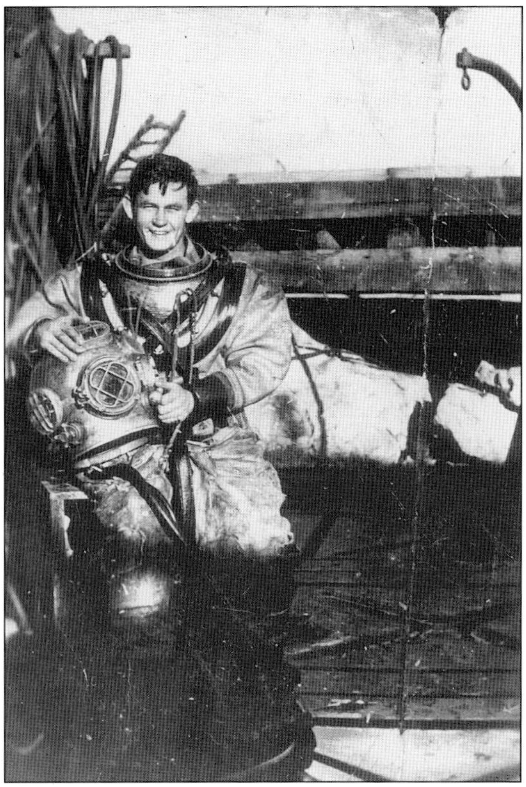

Diver George Lawler of the 1056th Engineers is pictured in full diver's gear, sitting outside the diving tank. The average depth a diver could be expected to descend and work was 90 feet. Beyond that depth, the pressure of the water was too great. It was estimated that the cost to outfit and equip a diver was approximately $7,000.

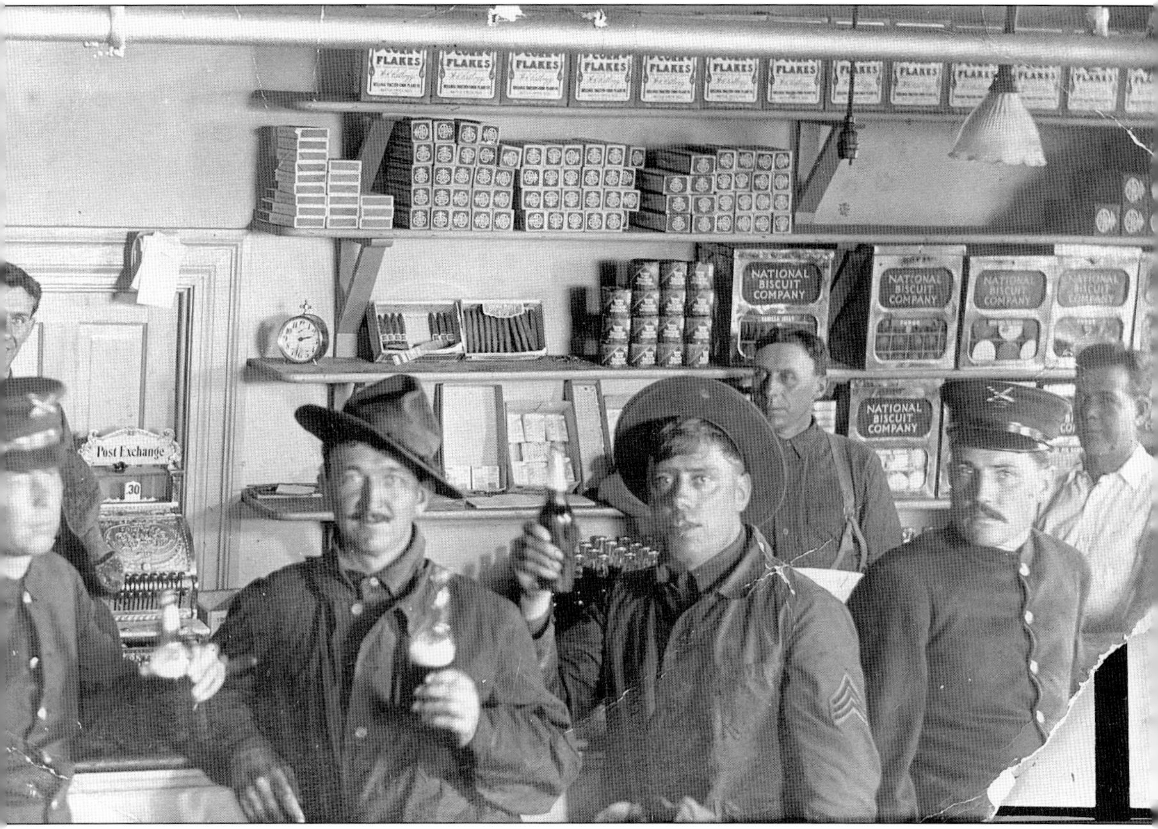

A Fort Screven soldier's life was not all work and no play. During their off-duty hours, unless they had to serve on a special detail, the men often went to Tybee's beach for a swim in the ocean surf. Some walked up the beach to the area of the Tybee Hotel and Tybrisa Pavilion where they might meet young ladies. Others spent their free time in sports, or less strenuous activities such as reading and letter writing. In this photograph, some coast artillery soldiers are enjoying some liquid refreshment at the post exchange.

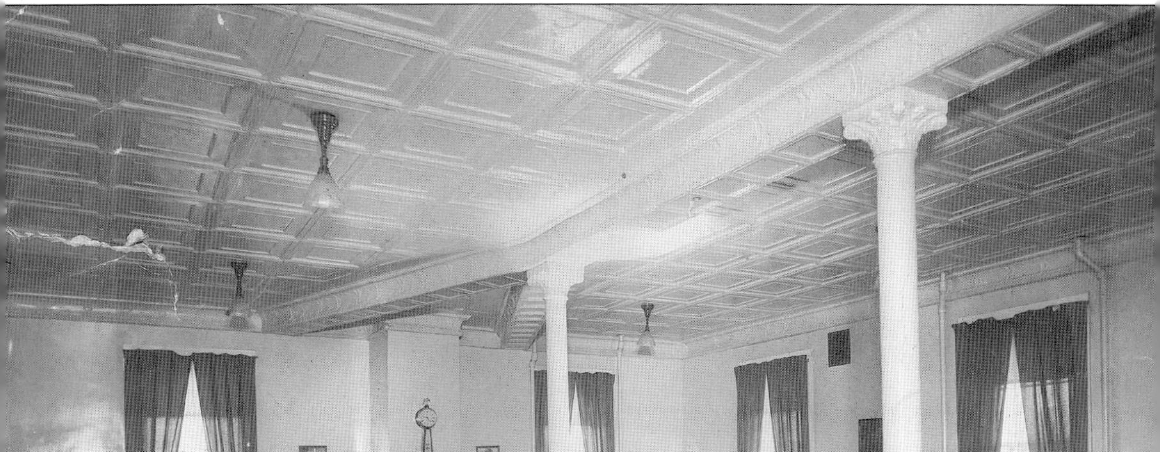

Some chose to spend their leisure hours in some quiet time, catching up on their reading. Fort Screven's commanders and local civilian community groups often worked together for the benefit of the post's enlisted men. In the early 1900s, a branch of the Amy and Navy Young Men's Christian Association volunteered to set up a recreation room for the enlisted men. It was advertised that the room would contain a wide selection of games and reading material furnished by the Helen Gould Circuit Library. Over the succeeding years, recreation facilities were set up in company day rooms and service clubs. In this photograph from 1932, men of the 8th Infantry's Company D enjoy free time in the company's day room.

Cpl. H.C. Raddick and Sgt. C.L. Boles are seen in a relaxed moment on the back porch of their company barracks, *c.* 1940.

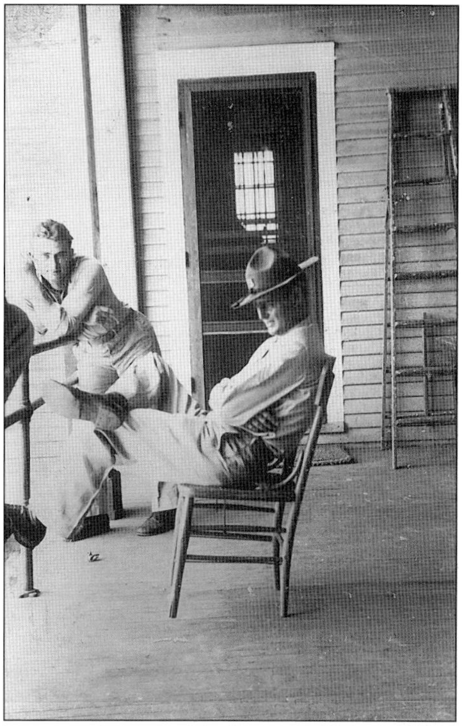

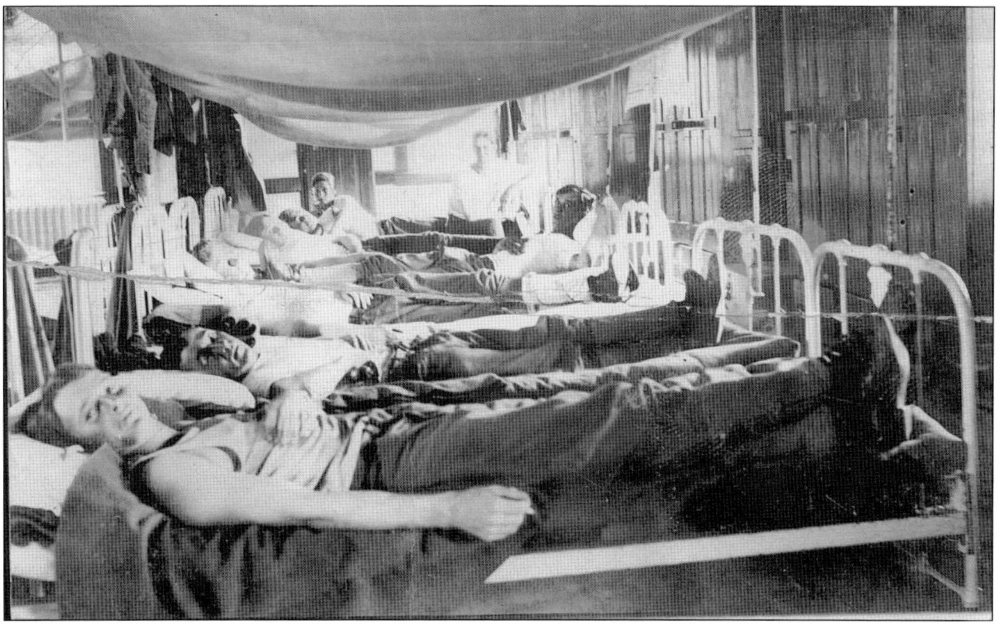

As well illustrated in this photograph, a soldier's sometimes crowded barracks life offered little privacy. Open-bay type barracks, such as the one in the photograph, were for sleeping and for storing uniforms, equipment and personal items. Most off-duty time was spent elsewhere. These soldiers appear to be relaxing on their bunks at the end of a busy day.

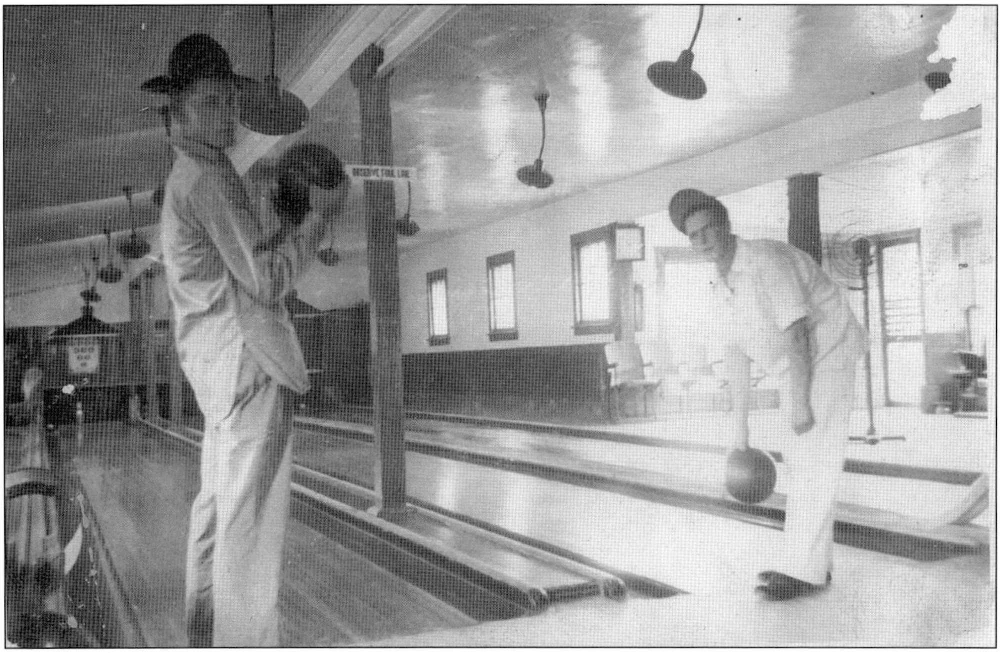

In the top photograph from 1940, A.A. Darwin and C.W. Lyons demonstrate their bowling skills at Fort Screven's bowling alley. In the photograph below, soldiers pass the time with a game of billiards. The photograph was taken in either a company day room or other post recreation facility.

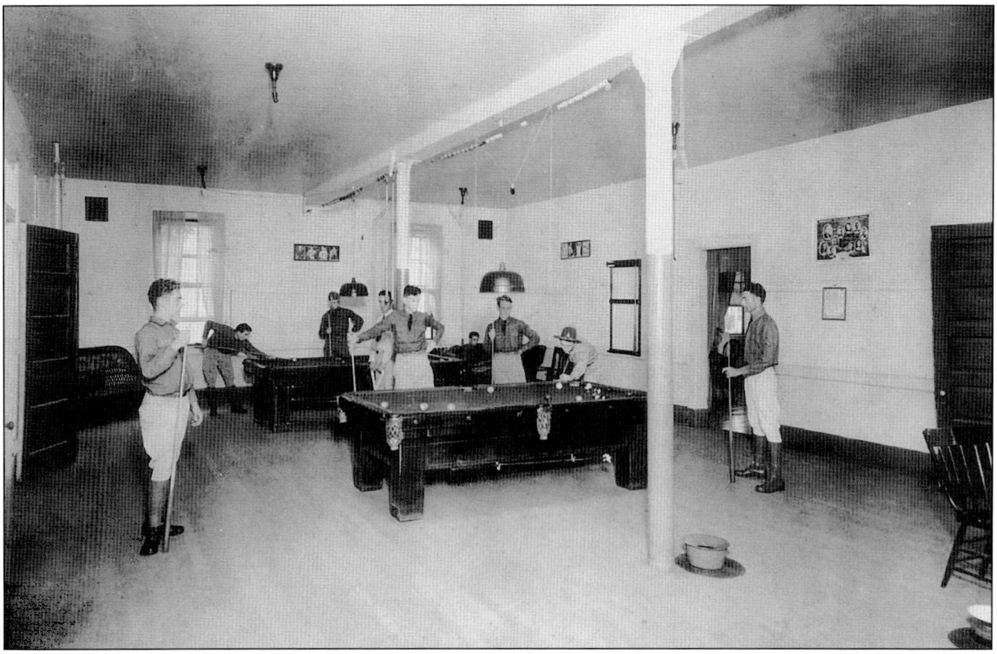

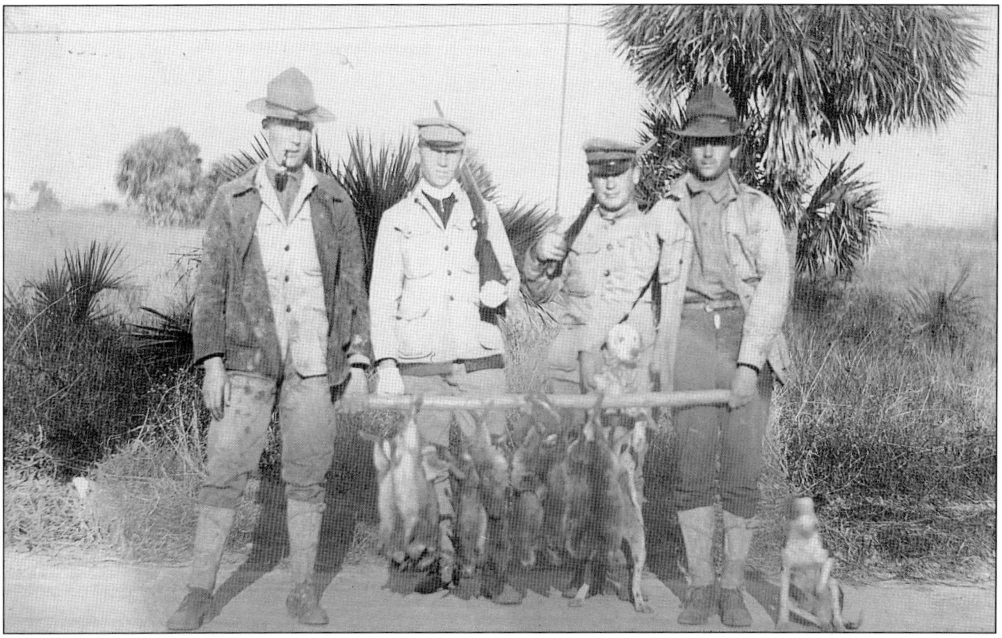

For the more adventurous spirit, off-duty activities on Tybee Island included hunting, and, of course, fishing. In the above photograph from 1909, four proud hunters display their rabbit kill. The photograph below could well be a movie still from an earlier version of the movie *Jaws*. The 14-foot shark was caught in the Savannah River, off Grassy Point, by "Hickory Bill" Barnett, Spike Reider, and Dick Lynott. All three of the men were members of the 14th Coast Artillery Corps Band.

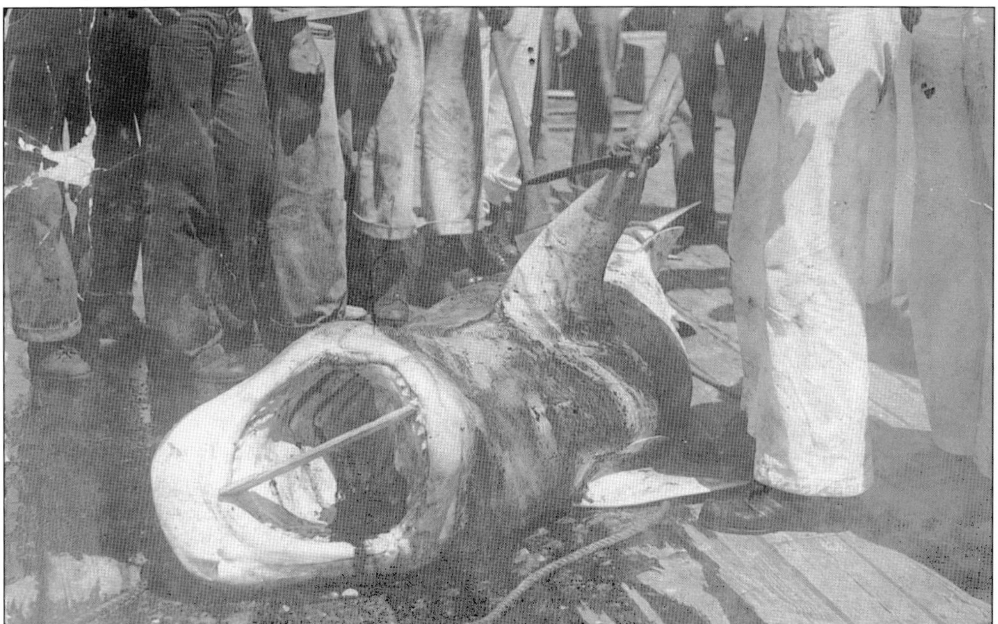

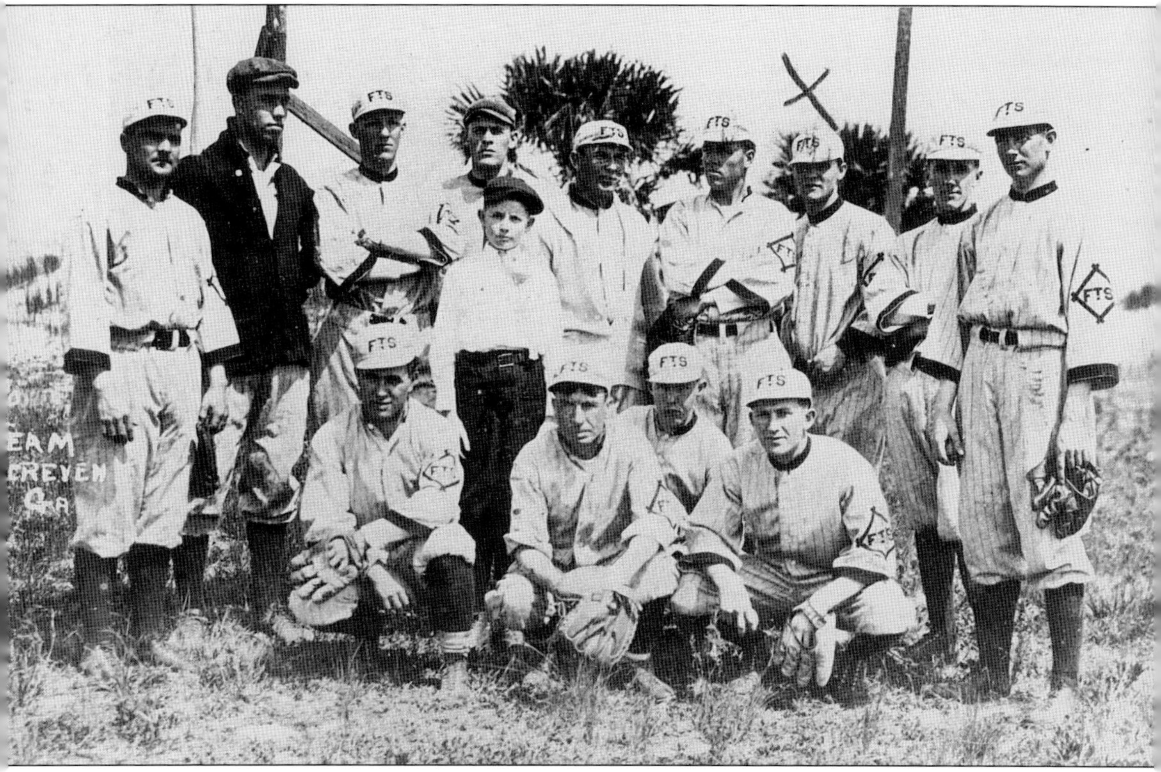

Just as baseball was considered the national pastime, it was also a very popular activity with the men of Fort Screven. Fort Screven teams competed in military, Tybee Island, and Savannah city leagues. The members of Fort Screven's 1916 baseball team posed for this team photograph. They are, from left to right, as follows: (kneeling) Fero, Connelly, Neal, and Repaz; (standing) Dorsey, Schwartz, Burch, Larmore, Cornett, Roberson, Stegall, Bray, and Cecil. The young boy is the team's mascot, Joe Fitz.

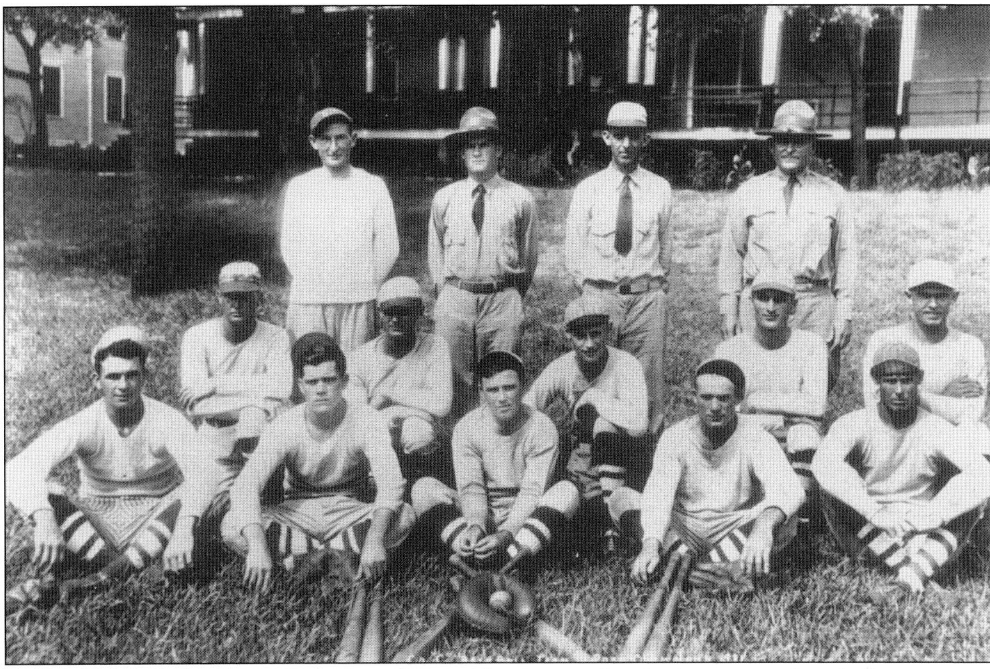

In addition to post teams competing in city leagues, individual company baseball teams vied with each other for the post championship. This photograph from the early 1900s shows a C Company team with their managers and coaches. The names of the men are not available.

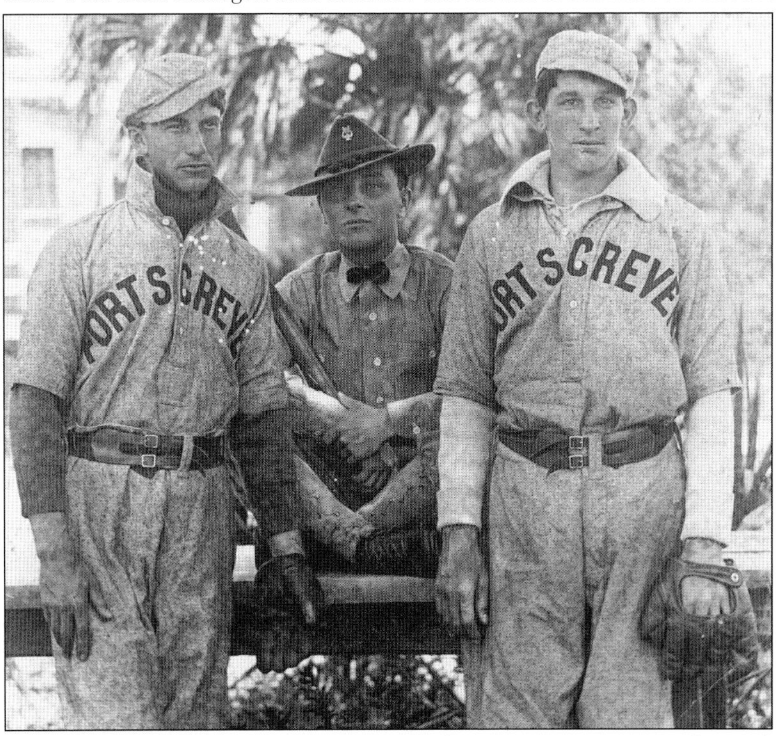

These three soldiers competed in the 1910 Savannah City League as members of the Fort Screven team. They are, from left to right, Bill Barnett, Buzz Walker, and Henry Patenude.

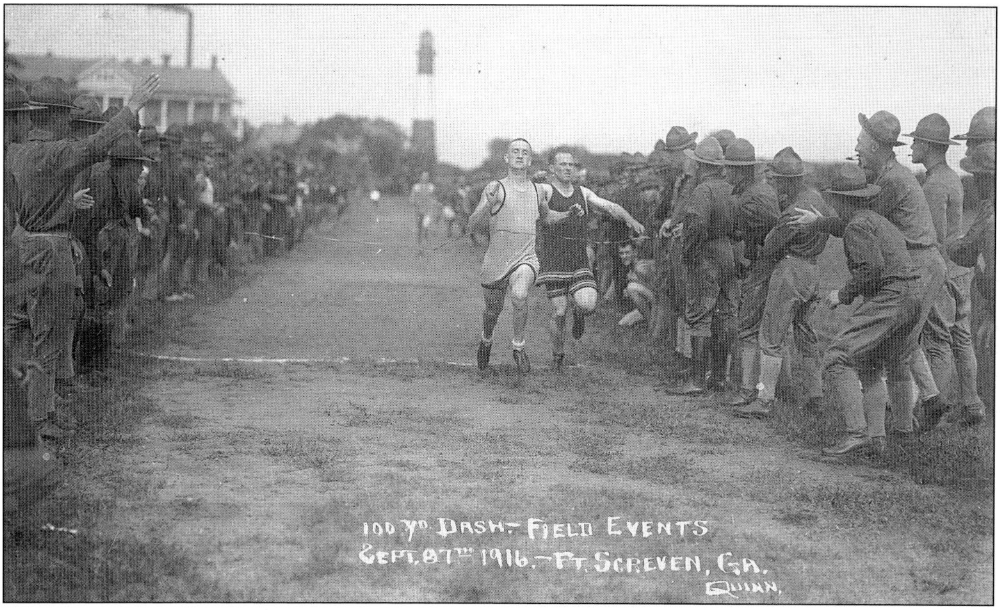

Fort Screven's soldiers competed in other athletic events, such as track and field. This photograph from 1916 shows two runners in the 100-yard dash crossing the finish line to the cheers and encouragement of fellow soldiers. The Tybee Lighthouse is in the background.

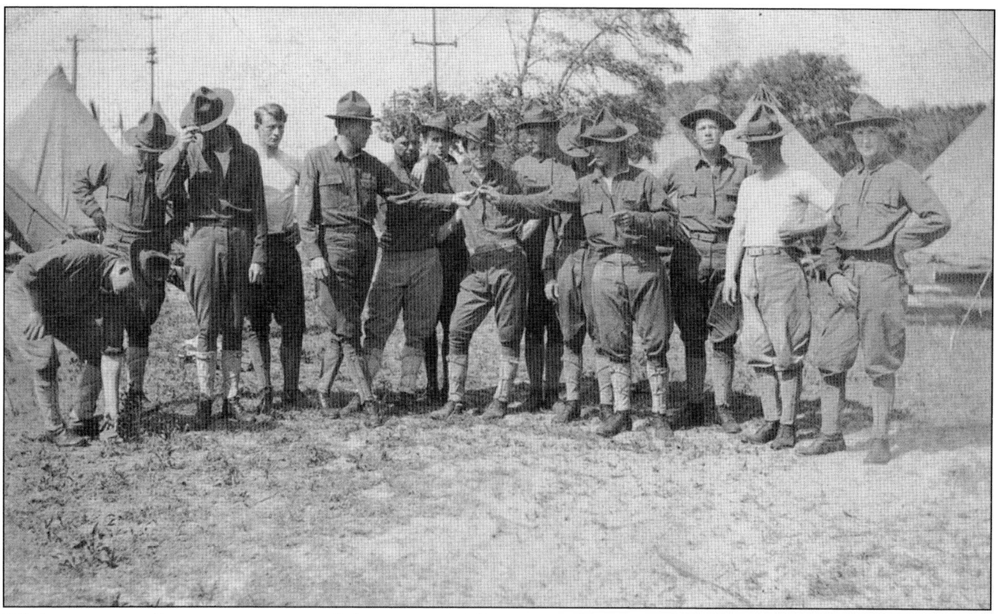

Welcome words to most any soldier are, "Take ten . . . smoke 'em if you've got 'em." These soldiers are enjoying a little break and some time for camaraderie outside their tent quarters.

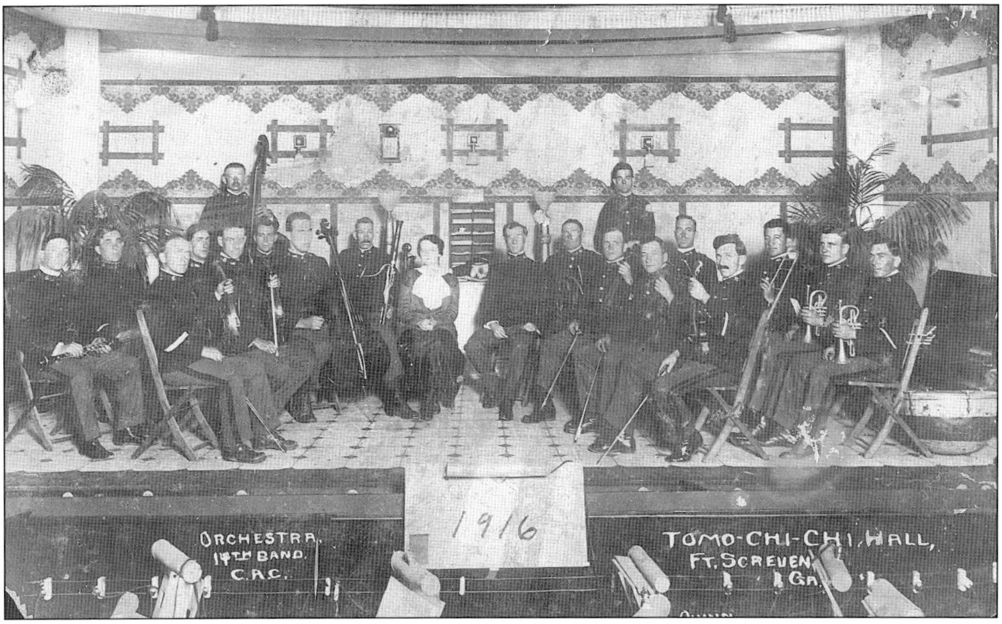

Soldiers and their families, as well as people from the community, attended concerts, plays, and variety shows at Fort Screven's Tomo-Chi-Chi Hall. The theater was named for the Creek Indian chief who befriended the founder of Savannah and the Georgia colony, Gen. James Edward Oglethope, and his settlers when they arrived from England in 1733. This photograph from 1916 shows a concert by the orchestra of the 14th CAC Band.

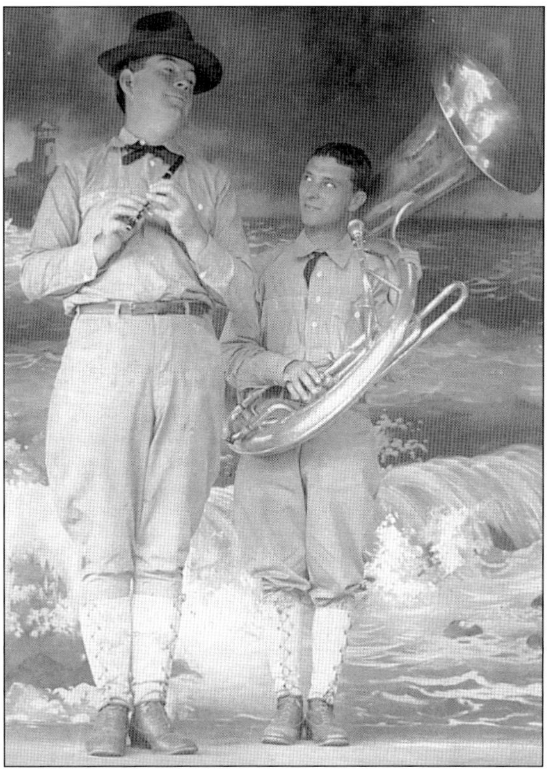

Henry Patenaude (left) and an unidentified partner performed a comedy routine during a 1908 variety show at Fort Screven. At that time, Patenaude had been in the Army for about a year and was a member of the 14th CAC Band. He retired in 1938 with 30 years of military service.

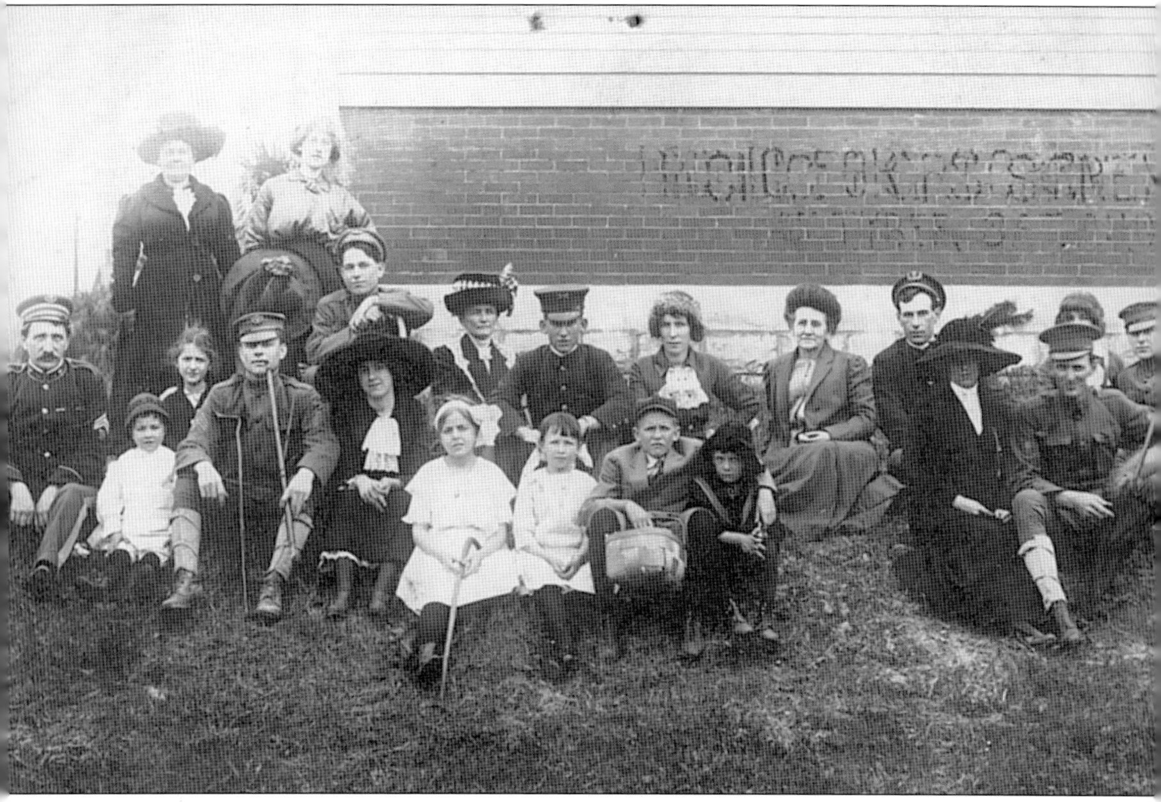

Weekends and holidays were times for visiting and enjoying outings with members of the family. The Army discouraged soldiers of lower ranks from marrying. "If the army had wanted you to have a wife you would have been issued one," the saying went. Some soldiers ignored the advice and married anyway. If they did so, they risked having their "unauthorized" wives denied commissary and other post privileges.

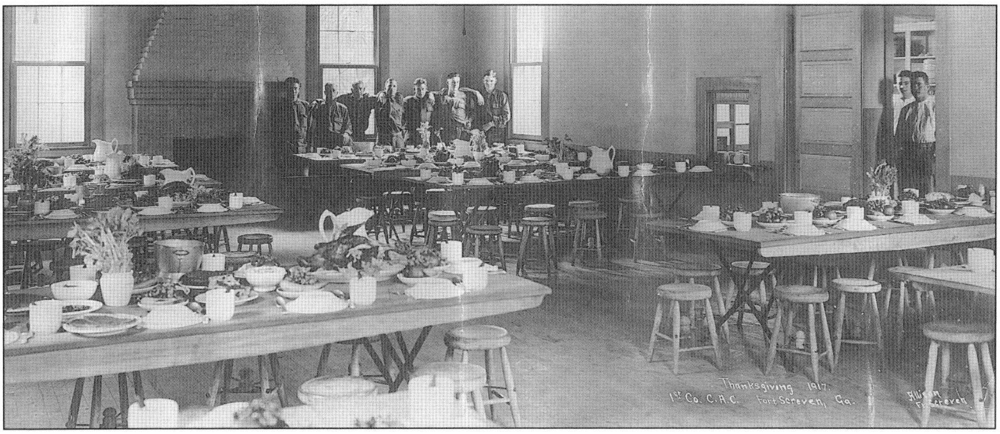

Holidays and other special occasions were times to enjoy good food and fellowship. On those days, the Army cooks broke from the normal daily menus and prepared a special feast to be enjoyed by the soldiers and guests. In the photograph above, the men of the 1st Company CAC were treated to a special 1917 Thanksgiving meal in the company's mess hall. Soldiers and their wives and guests (below) enjoy a special meal in the post gymnasium, now the home of American Legion Post 154.

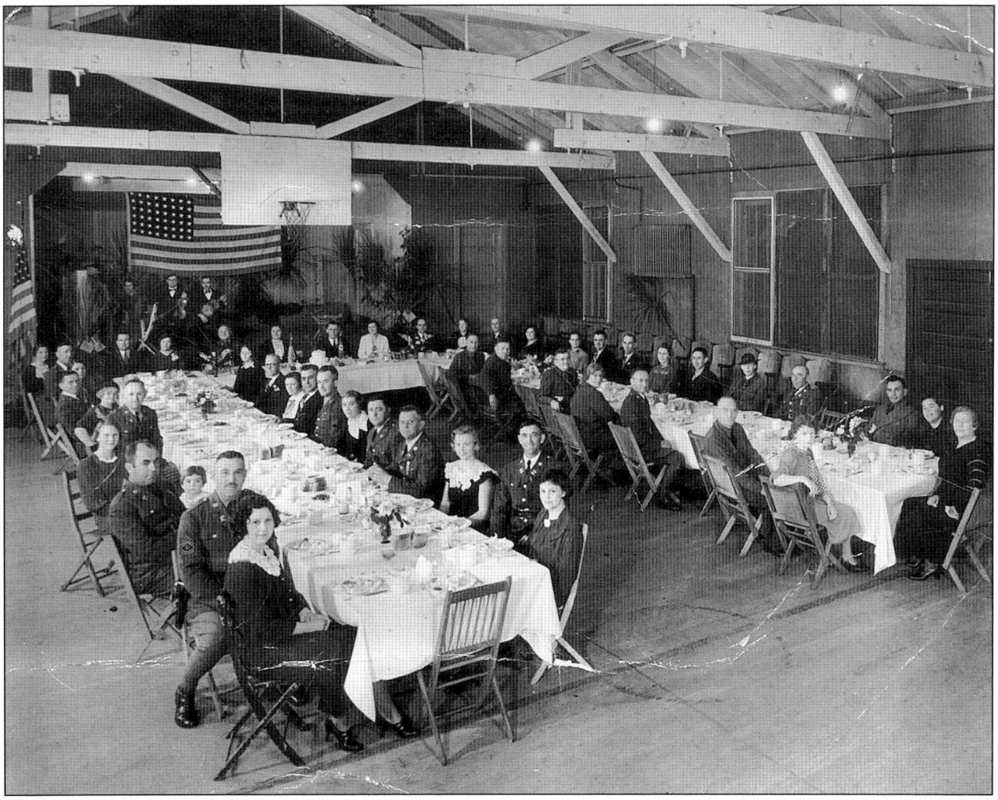

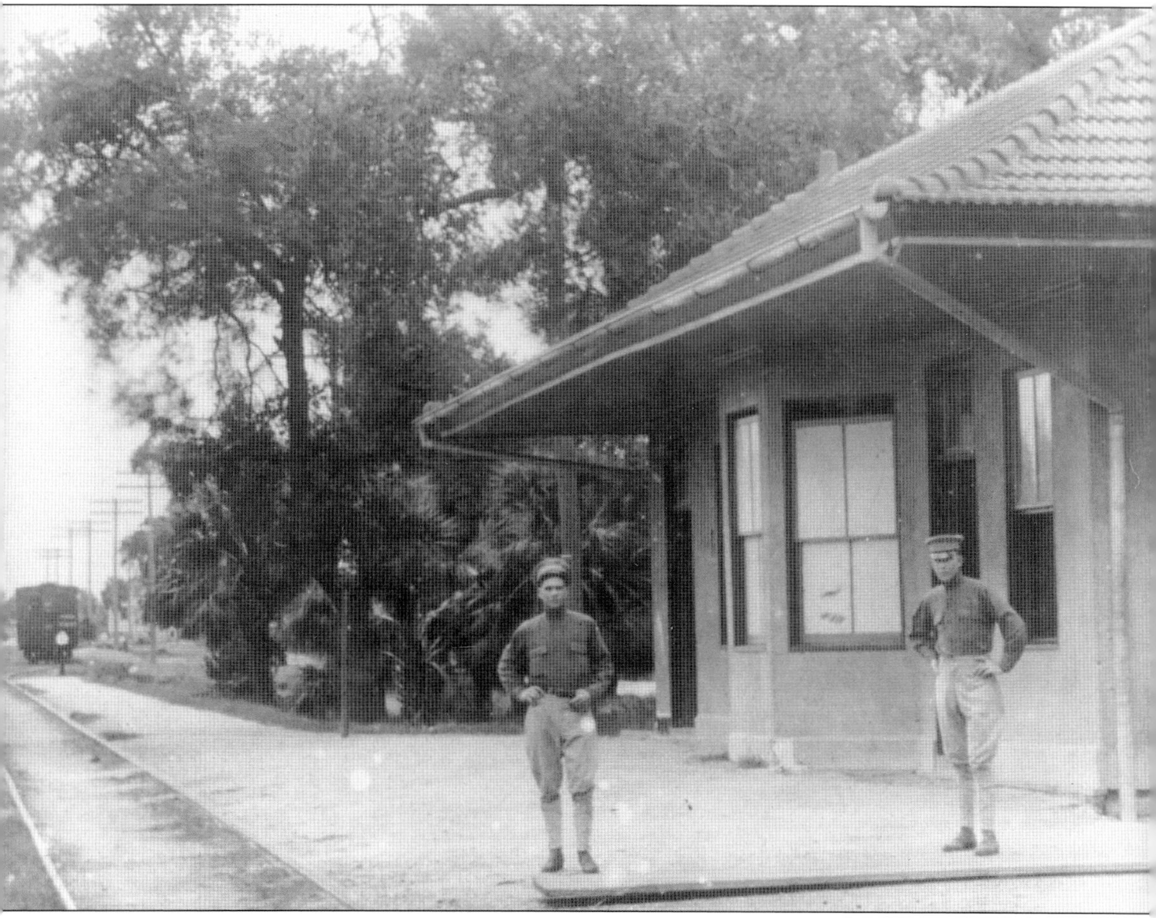

Like all soldiers throughout history, the men of Fort Screven looked forward to getting a pass to go into the city. They traveled between Fort Screven and Savannah by train until rail service was discontinued in 1933. After the train stopped running, the men traveled by car or by bus from Tybee to the terminal located on Wright Square in Savannah for a round trip fare of 35¢. In Savannah, the soldiers could enjoy several good restaurants, movie theaters, and night spots. Because of the low military pay, one or two trips a month into the city was all the average soldier could afford. Then it was back to the post and living on credit, called "jawbone" by the soldiers, until the next payday.

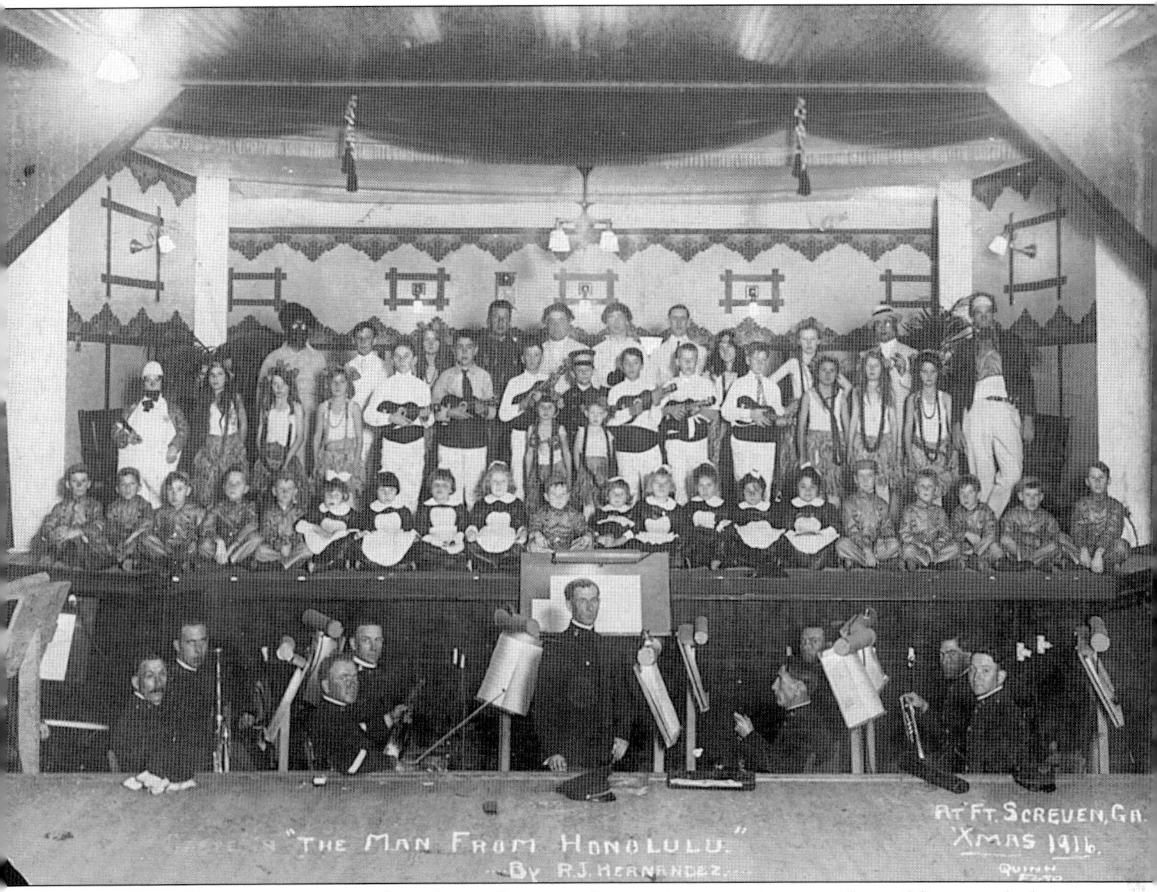

Stage productions continued to be a favorite form of entertainment for soldiers and their families as well as people from the community. In 1916, theater patrons were treated to a musical production of *The Man from Honolulu*. The cast members of the stage productions probably included soldiers, dependents, and people from the civilian community.

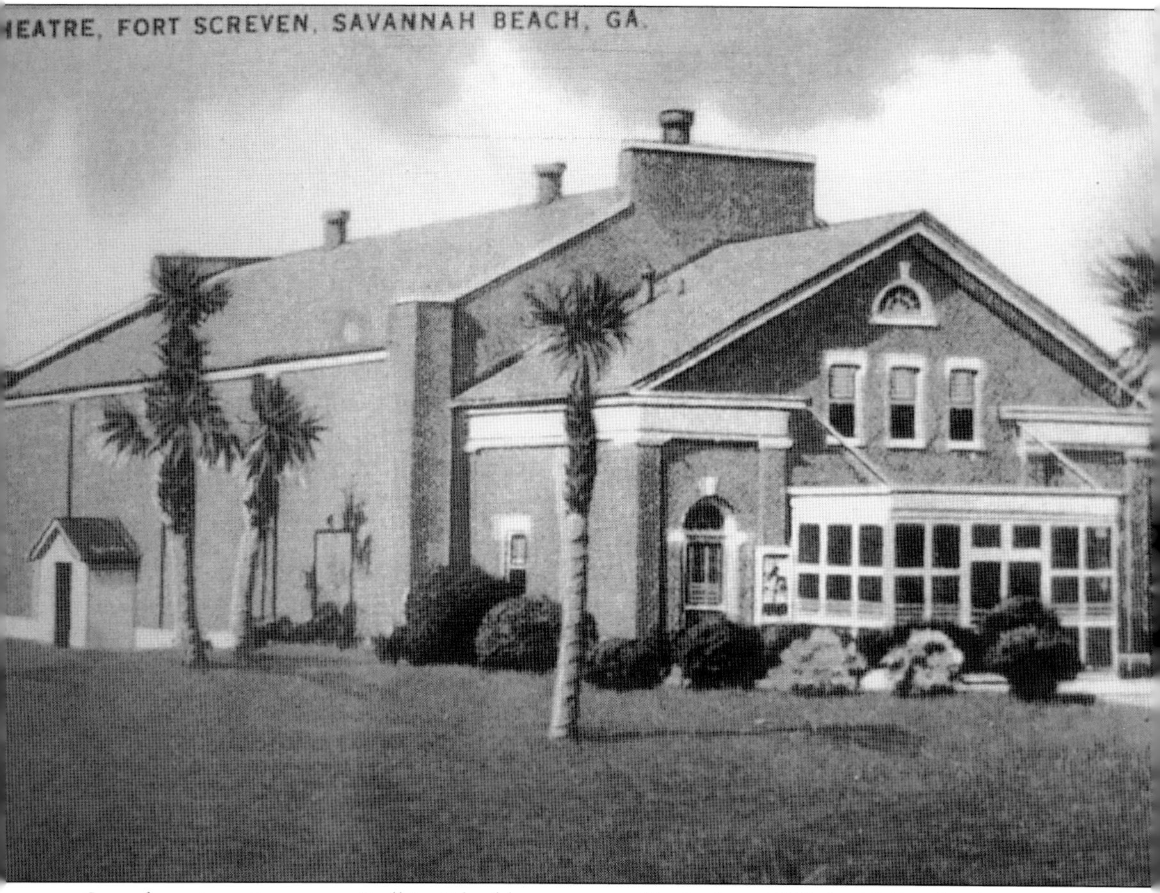

Sound motion pictures, or "talkies," had become a reality by late 1929. In 1930, a brick motion picture theater was constructed at Fort Screven. The post theater was one of the earliest movie houses in the Savannah area to show movies with sound. Many long-time Tybee residents recall attending the post theater with family, friends, or dates.

Five

Georgia's Coastal Playground

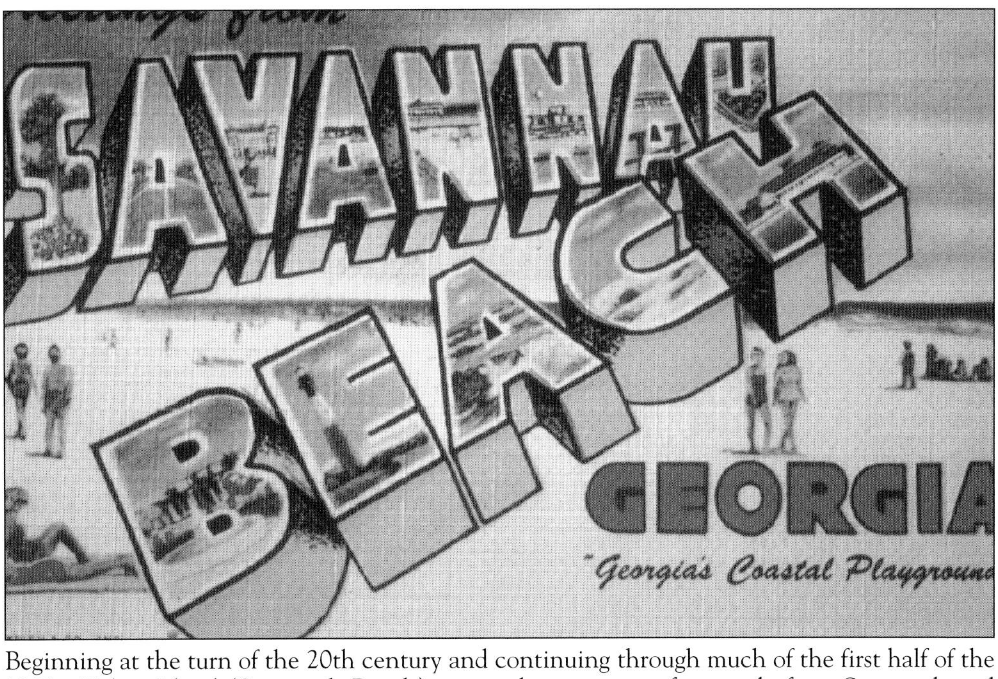

Beginning at the turn of the 20th century and continuing through much of the first half of the 1900s, Tybee Island (Savannah Beach) was a pleasure resort for people from Savannah and nearby communities in Georgia and South Carolina. The number of tourists increased with the automobile and the building of luxury hotels on the island. During its heyday as a beach resort, Tybee was considered one of the premier vacation spots on the East Coast.

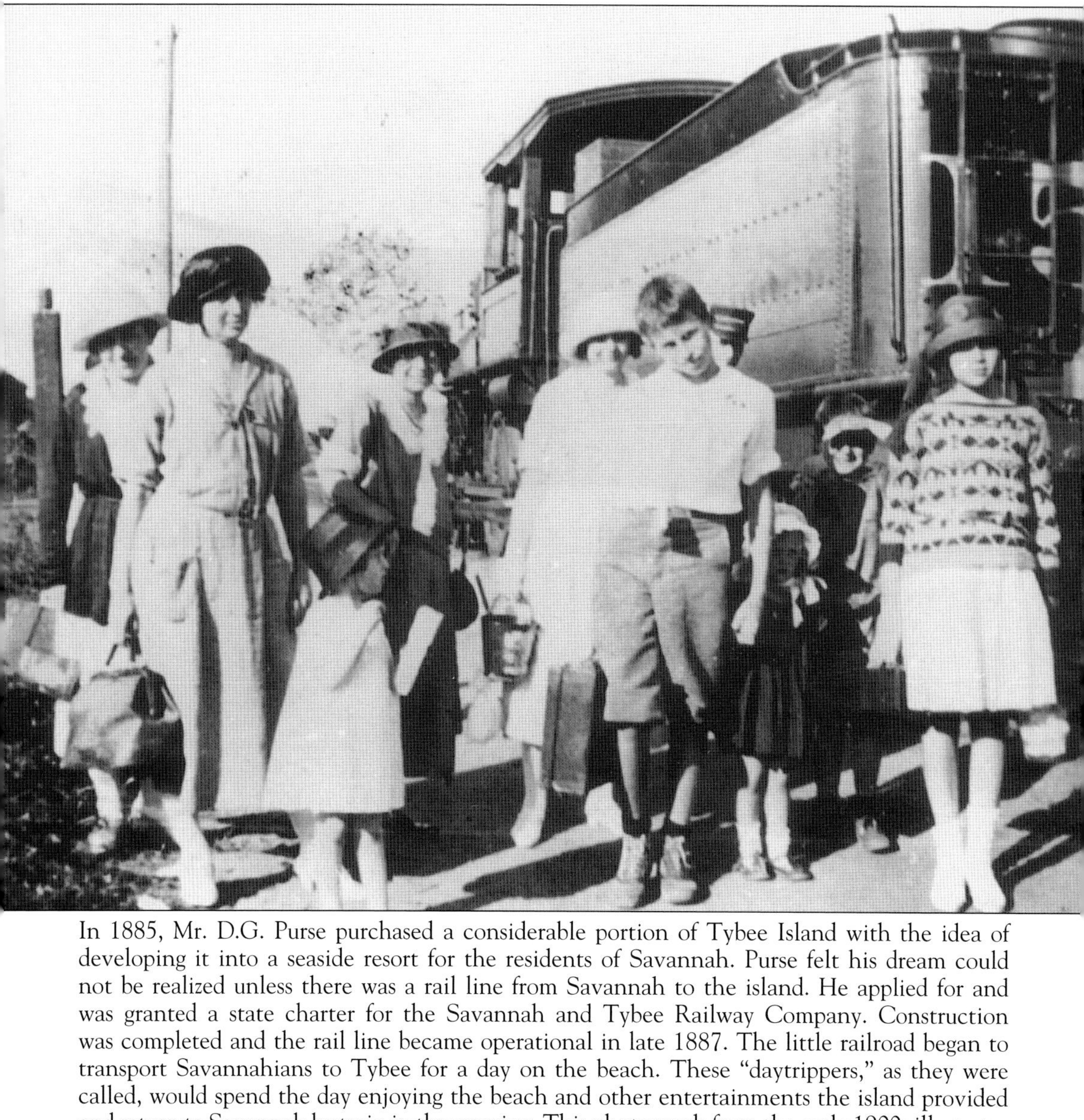

In 1885, Mr. D.G. Purse purchased a considerable portion of Tybee Island with the idea of developing it into a seaside resort for the residents of Savannah. Purse felt his dream could not be realized unless there was a rail line from Savannah to the island. He applied for and was granted a state charter for the Savannah and Tybee Railway Company. Construction was completed and the rail line became operational in late 1887. The little railroad began to transport Savannahians to Tybee for a day on the beach. These "daytrippers," as they were called, would spend the day enjoying the beach and other entertainments the island provided and return to Savannah by train in the evening. This photograph from the early 1900s illustrates that a day at Tybee was often a family outing.

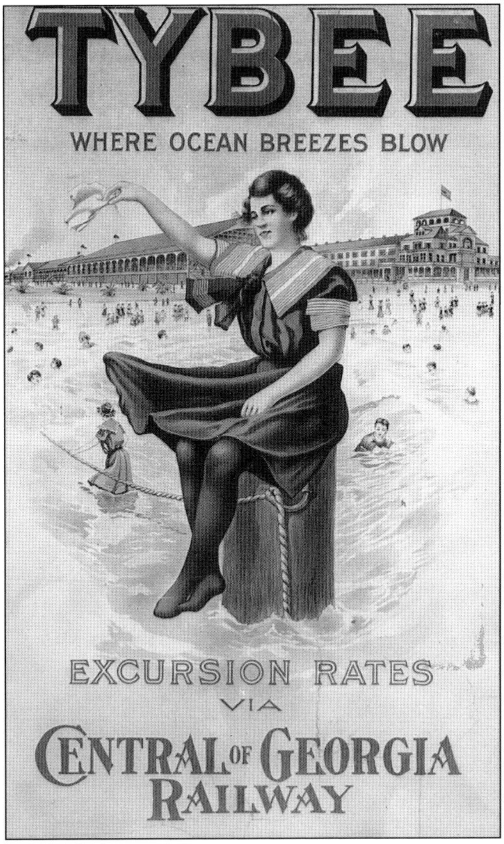

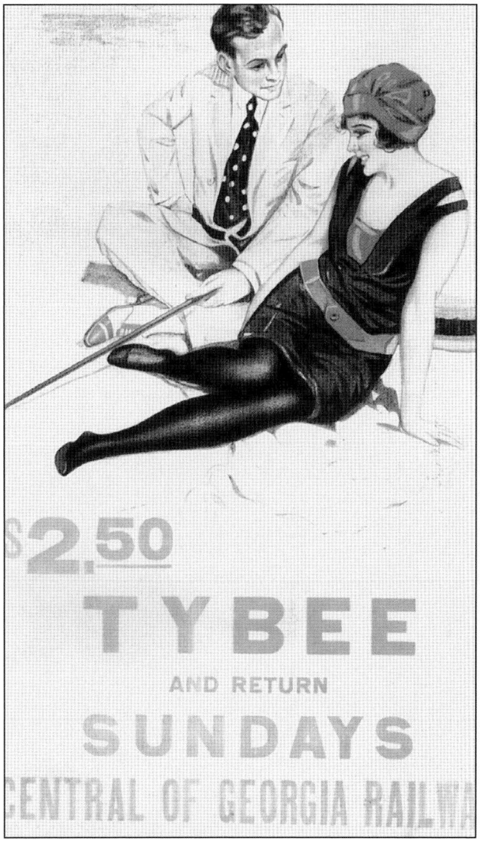

Traveling by sailboat, rowboat, and later by steamboat, people did come to spend the day at Tybee before the Tybee Railroad was constructed. Building of the railroad gave better access to the island and is credited in part for Tybee's later success as a resort area. After years of financial setbacks, the Tybee Railroad was purchased at auction in 1890 by the Central RR and Banking Company, the parent company of Central of Georgia Railway. Central of Georgia launched an advertising campaign to boost tourism to Tybee by offering special excursion rates, as shown by these advertisements.

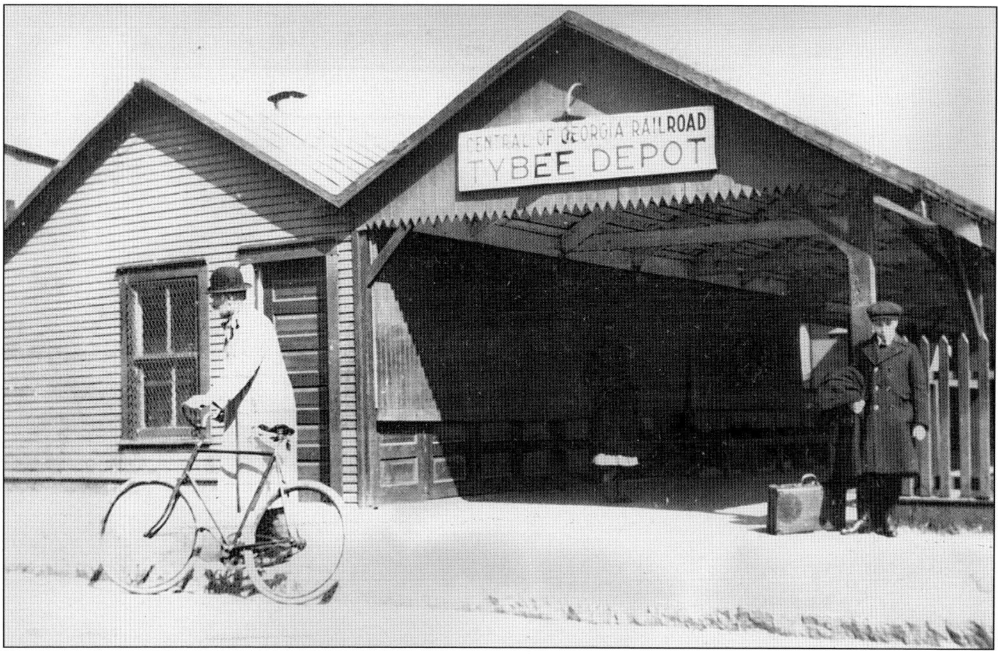

A young boy waits for the train that will take him to Tybee. The main depot, located at 130 Randolph Street in Savannah, was the departure point for trains carrying passengers from Savannah to Tybee. After the railroad's demise, the depot property became the site of the Penn Waller Lumber Company. The bicycle was then, as today, a favorite means of local transportation.

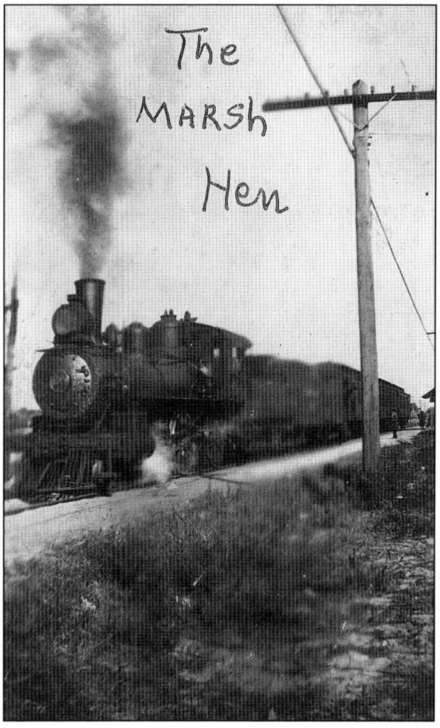

On the trip between Savannah and Tybee, the train passed over several rivers and wound its way through an expanse of salt marshes. One of the steam-powered locomotives that made the trip several times a day was given the appropriate name "The Marsh Hen."

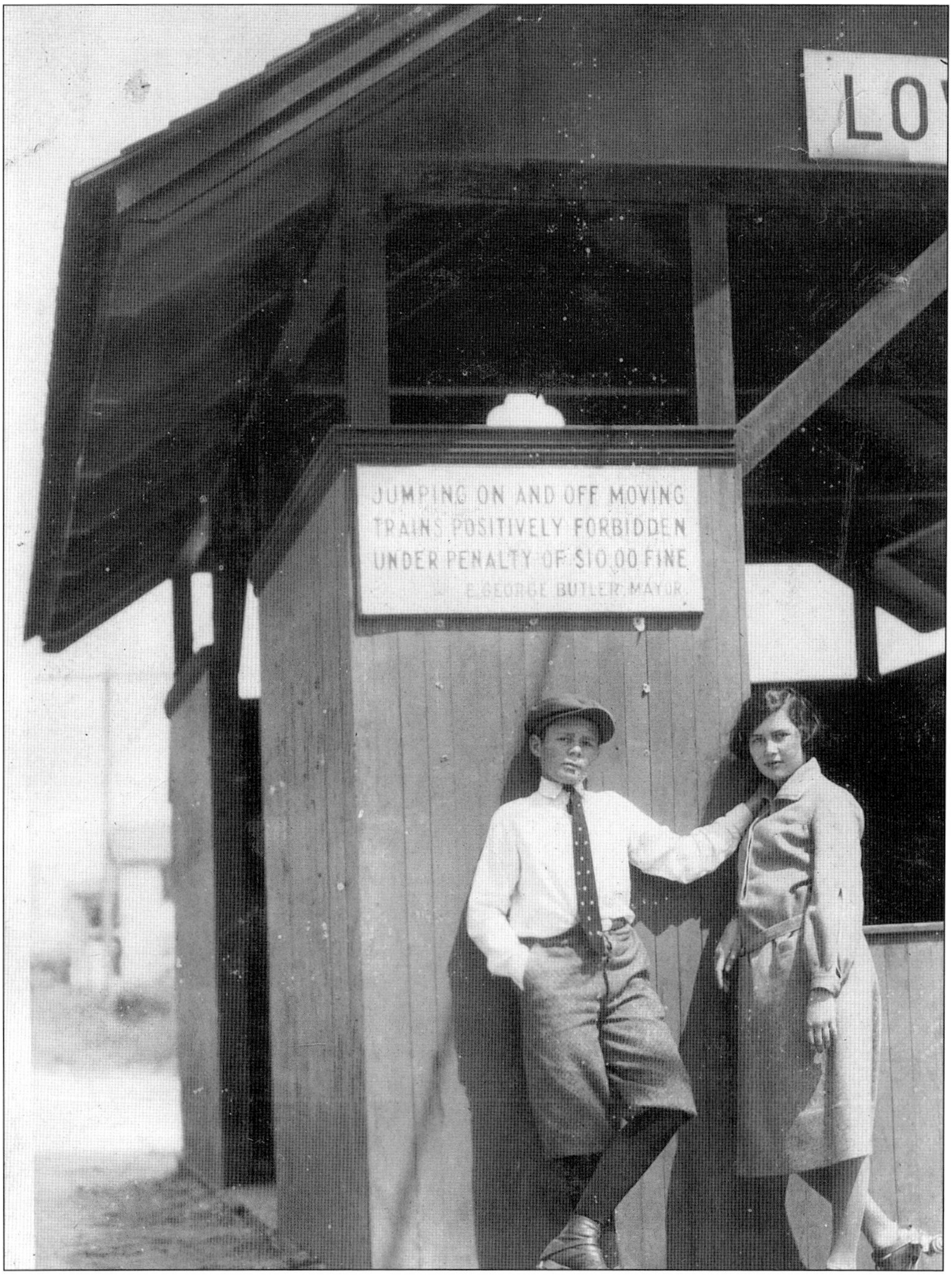

An appropriate caption for this early 1900s photograph could be, "Young love blooms at Lovell Station." Before the Tybee Road was built, island youth rode the train into Savannah to attend school, and returned in the late afternoon. On the 17.7-mile trip, there were picturesque stops at Inlet Station, Tybee Station, Dixon Station, Atlantic Club, Lovell Station, Fort Bartow (Causton's Bluff), and Lazaretto. Note that the young couple in the photograph are wearing roller skates. The sign above their heads cautions, "Jumping on and off moving trains positively forbidden under penalty of $10.00 fine . . . George Butler, Mayor." Good advice.

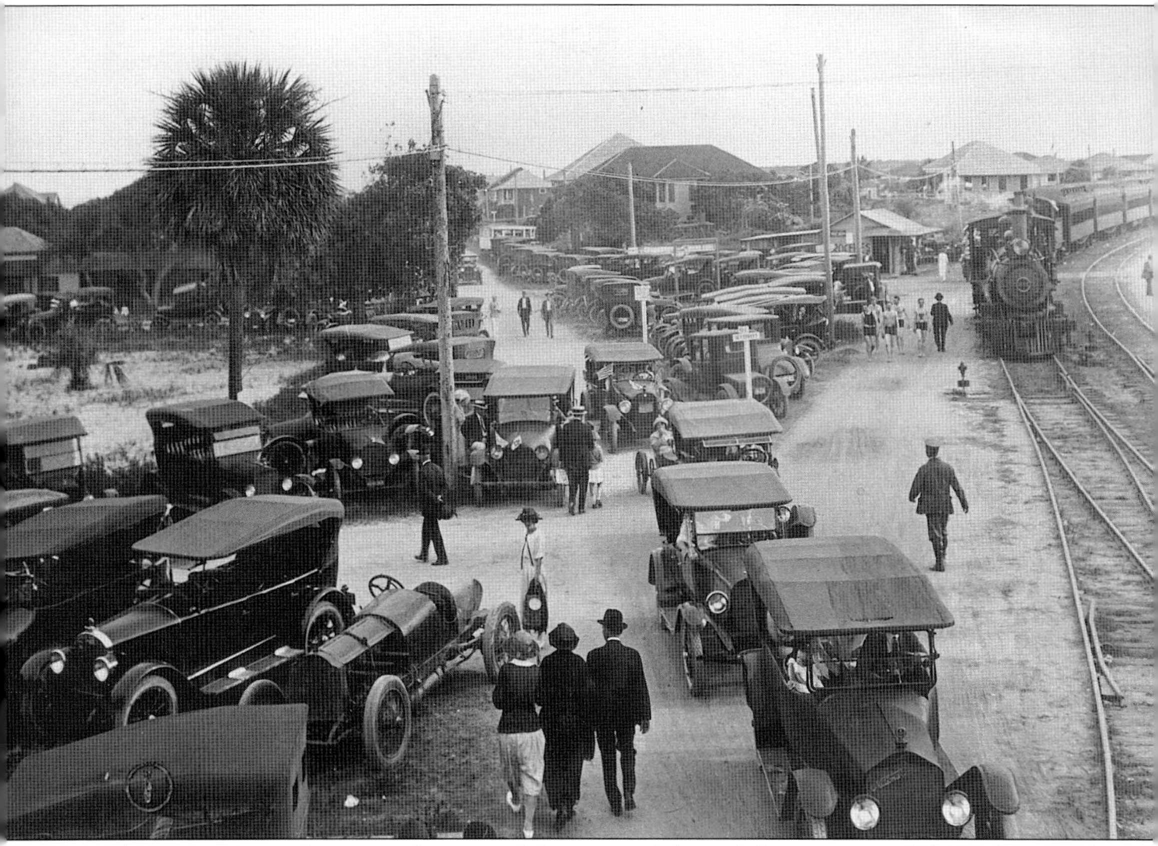

The invention and mass production of the automobile and the opening of the Tybee Road in 1923 gave beachgoers an alternate means of travel to Tybee Island. The number of train passengers decreased with the growing popularity of automobile travel. This scene from a busy summer weekend on Tybee's south end shows both modes of land transportation to Tybee. It seems there were traffic and parking problems even in those days. The train is coming down the middle of Butler Avenue toward its final stop. A turntable was located at the end of the line. A water tank resupplied the locomotives so they could build up steam power for the return trip to Savannah.

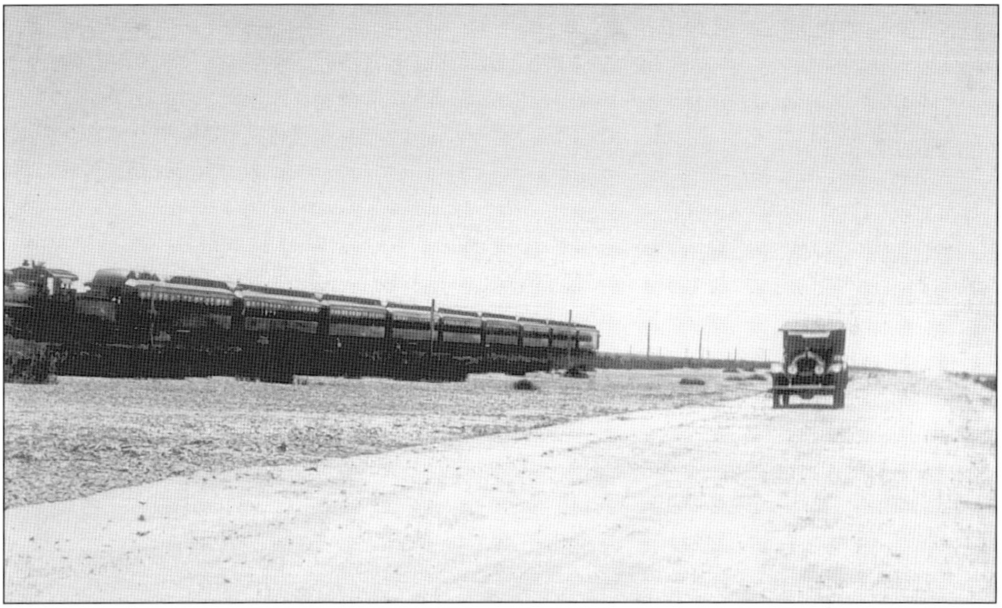

The new Tybee Road and the Tybee Railway operated together for a period of about 10 years. As the automobile became more and more popular as a mode of transportation to Tybee, the number of rail passengers steadily dropped until it was decided there was little justification for continuing the service. The Tybee train made its last run on July 31, 1933, almost 36 years to the day after it began operation.

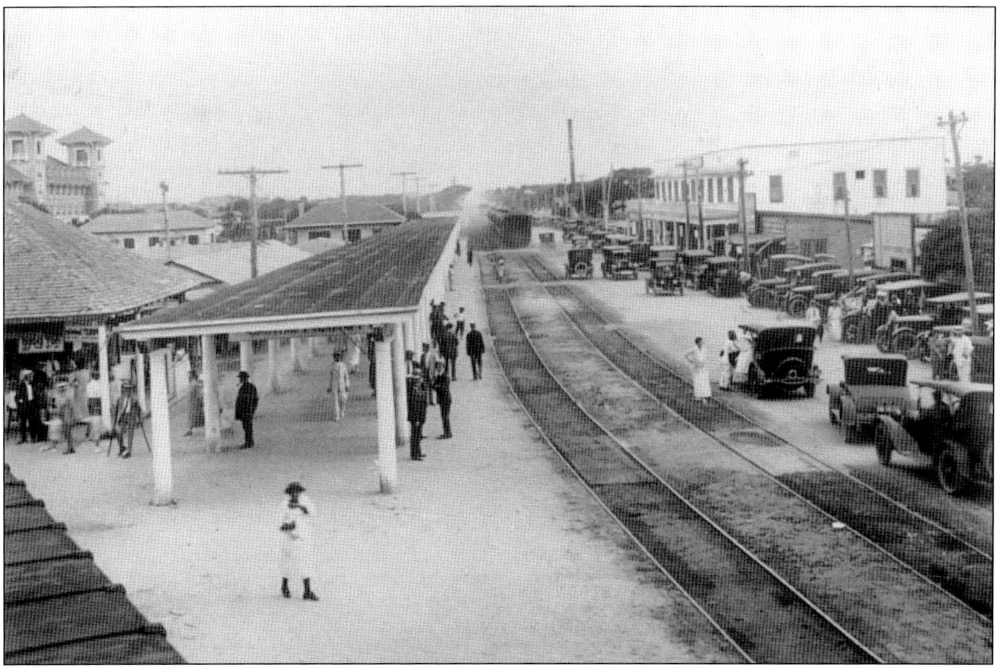

The train station at Tybee's south end was nothing more than a flat-roofed pavilion that protected waiting passengers from the rain and hot sun. In general, people were glad to be able to enjoy the convenience provided by the automobile, but many people missed, and later fondly recalled, when the trip to Tybee aboard the train was considered a social event.

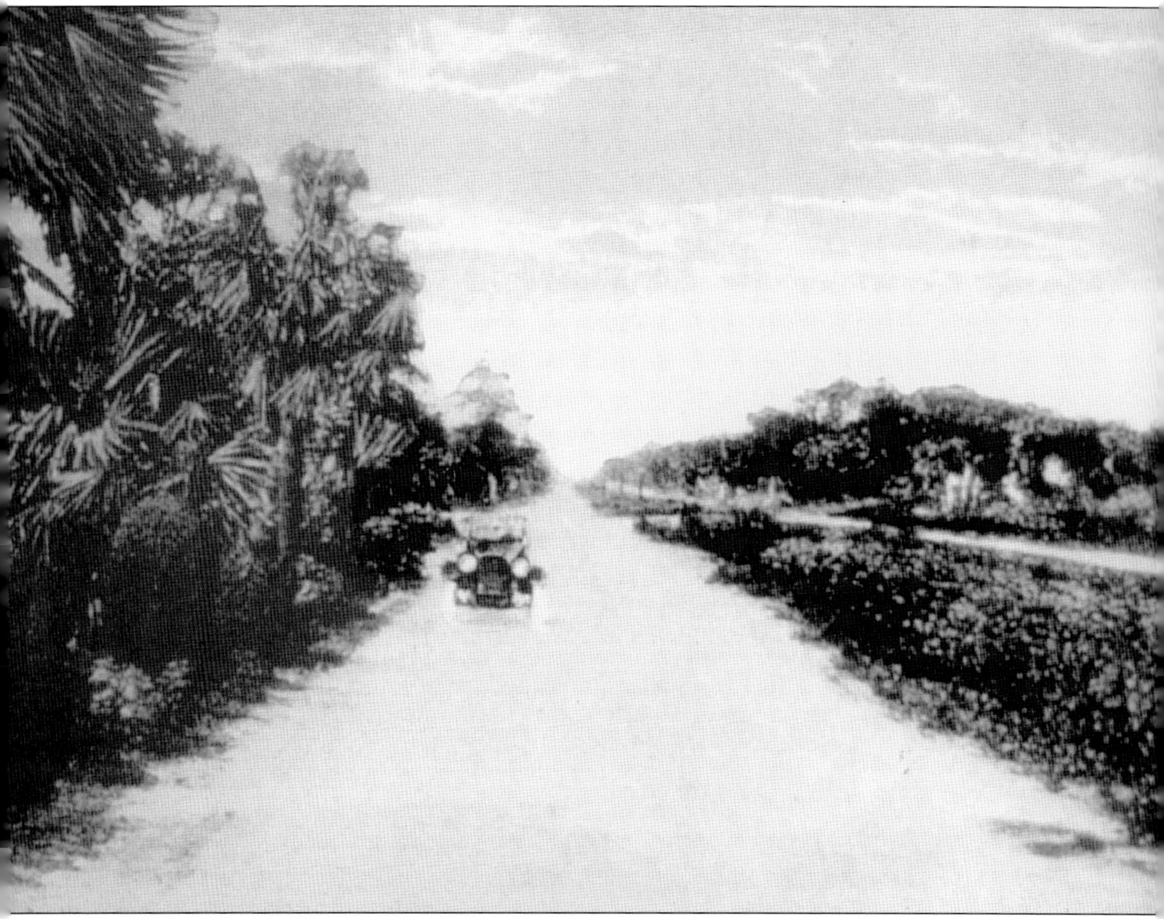

When the train was no longer available, people traveled to Tybee either by water or the Tybee Road. The above postcard photograph shows the road and railroad bed running parallel. After the Tybee train stopped running in 1933, the Central of Georgia Railway received permission from the Interstate Commerce Commission to abandon the line. The track was soon removed. The old railroad bed lay idle and overgrown until it became part of the National Rails to Trails program. It is now a biking and walking path.

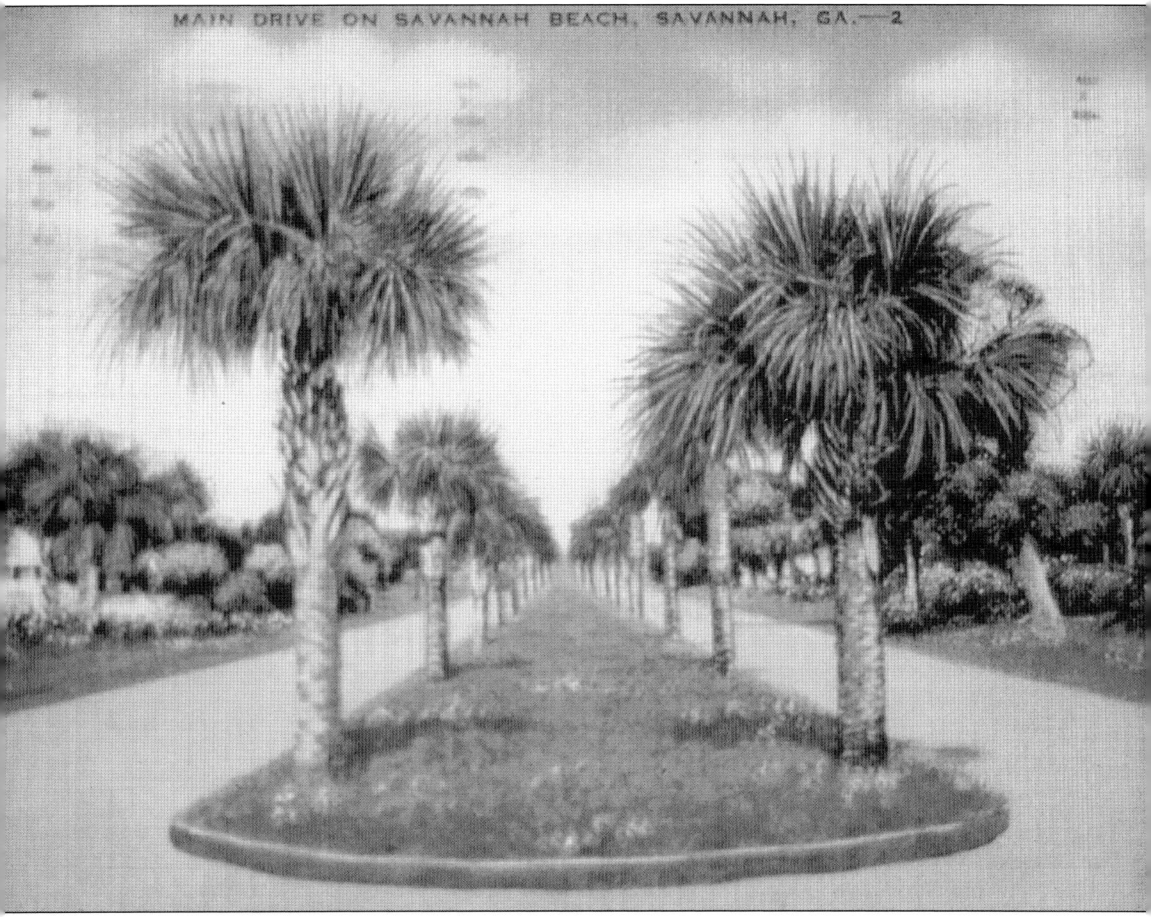

The highway to Tybee, U.S. Route 80, is a continuation of Savannah's Victory Drive, a palm and azalea-lined thoroughfare named as a memorial to Savannah soldiers who served in World War I. Extending eastward from Savannah and ending at the Atlantic Ocean on Tybee's south end, Victory Drive and the Tybee Road in conjunction were once known as the longest palm-lined drive in the United States. During those days, an island of palm trees ran the length of Tybee's Butler Avenue.

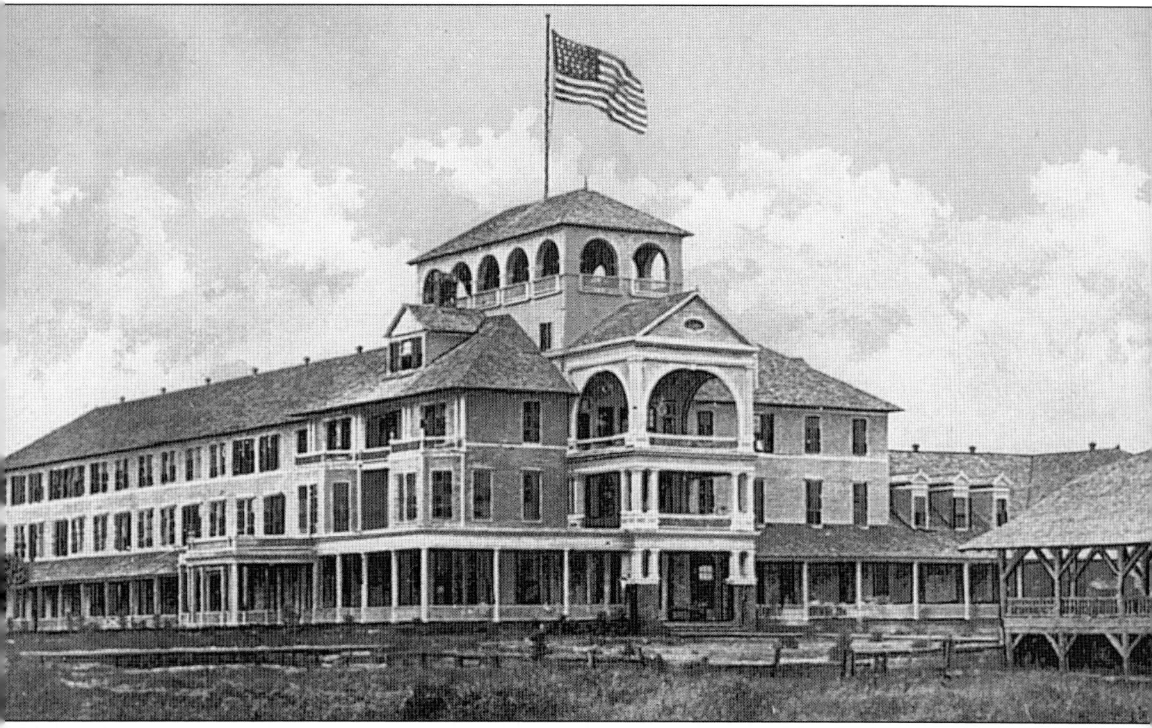

The completion of the first Hotel Tybee on the island's south end in 1891 soon elevated Tybee Island as a beach resort to the same level with older northern resorts. Summer cottages, clubs, dancing pavilions, bathhouses, boardinghouses, and other service-oriented businesses began to spring up around the new hotel. The Victorian style hostelry had piazzas stretching its entire length and breadth to catch every passing ocean breeze. The old Hotel Tybee was of wood construction and was destroyed by fire in 1908.

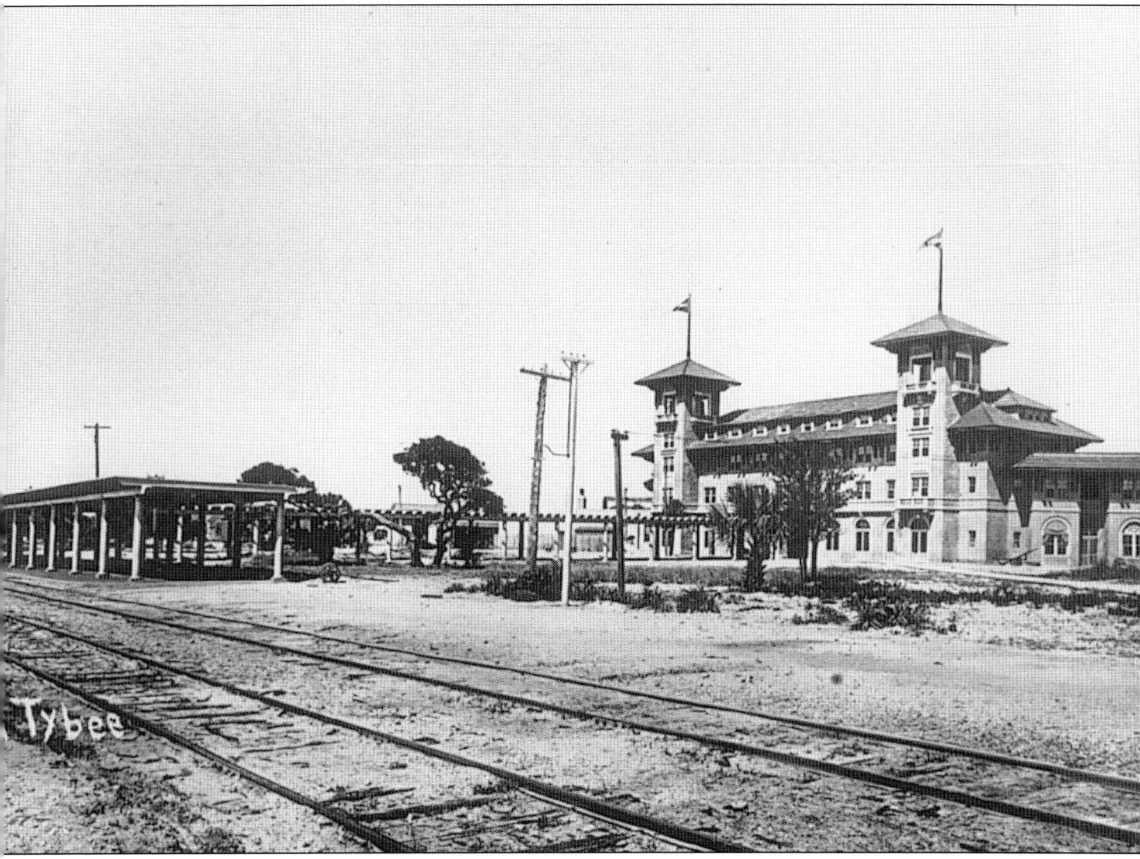

The old Hotel Tybee was replaced in 1911 by a new concrete building constructed on the same site. The new Hotel Tybee was built in the style of the Spanish Renaissance and was advertised as fireproof. It had 150 rooms, large verandas on the ocean side, two observation towers, bathing pavilions, dancing pavilions, and refreshment stands. The hotel's complex also included 12 cottages. A covered walkway led guests to a two-story pavilion with bathhouses, a dance floor, and a bandstand. Note in the photograph the close proximity of the Hotel Tybee to the railroad depot. The new Tybee Hotel was demolished in 1958 to make way for a newer hotel.

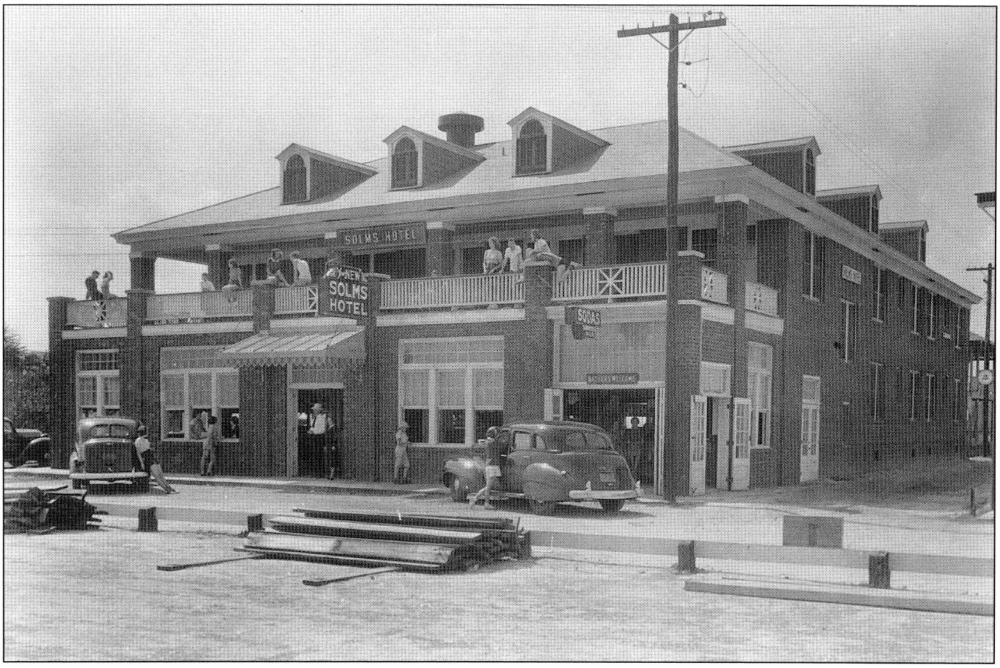

In addition to the major resort hotels, an assortment of smaller hotels and boardinghouses offered a less expensive alternative to tourists. Among the most popular of the smaller hotels was the Solms Hotel (*c.* 1930s), located on the corner of Izlar and Strand. A soda shop just off the lobby was a popular gathering place. This photograph of the Solms was taken in 1938. Some other small hotels of the day were the Sea Breeze Hotel (*c.* 1910s), Ocean View (*c.* 1910s), and the Beach View (*c.* 1910s). (Courtesy Georgia Historical Society.)

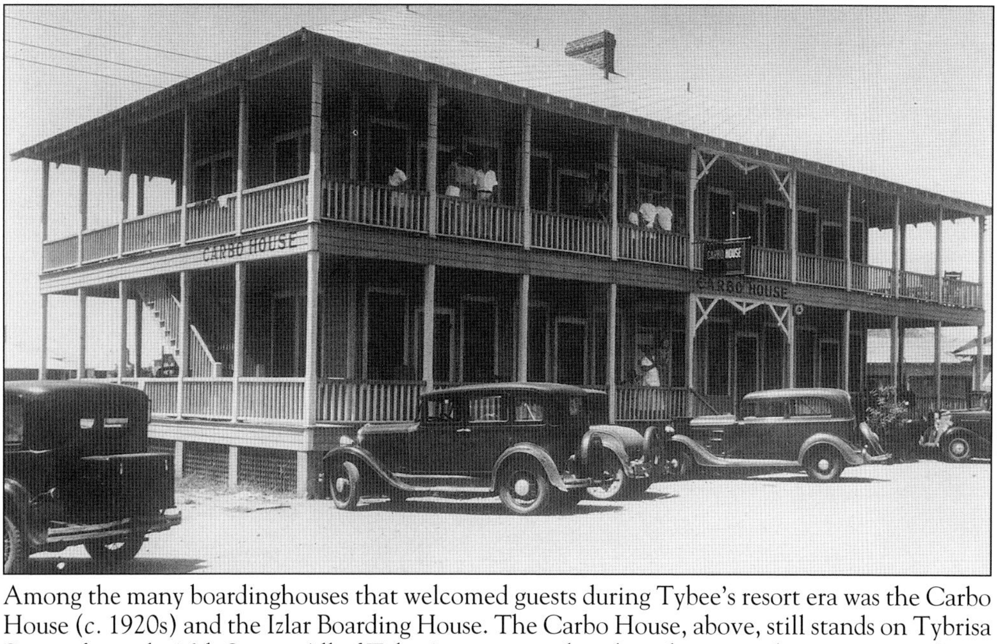

Among the many boardinghouses that welcomed guests during Tybee's resort era was the Carbo House (*c.* 1920s) and the Izlar Boarding House. The Carbo House, above, still stands on Tybrisa Street, formerly 16th Street. All of Tybee's resort area hotels and rooming houses were within a short walk to "The Front," as the main resort area was called.

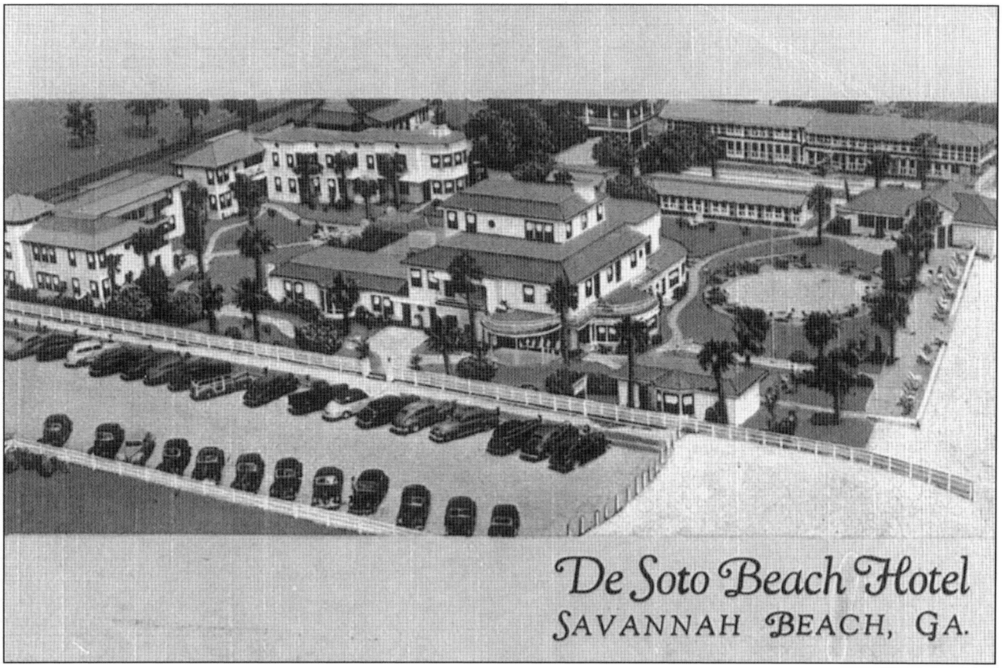

Despite the lean years brought on by the Great Depression of the early 1930s, Savannah Beach (Tybee) remained a popular regional summer resort throughout the 1940s and 1950s. The DeSoto Beach Hotel was built in 1940 to serve as a private beach club. The hotel complex was composed of Mediterranean-style villas with a pavilion and recreation area. The hotel hosted some of the delegates attending the International Monetary Conference meeting in Savannah in 1947. The DeSoto Beach later became a popular social retreat for islanders. It was demolished in 1999 to make way for a condominium development.

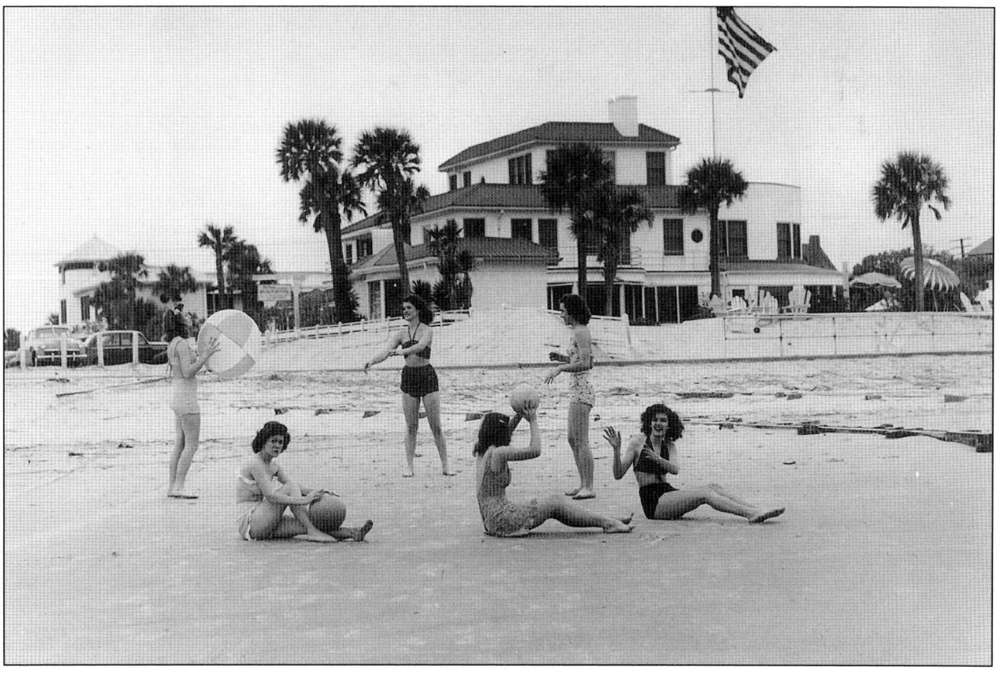

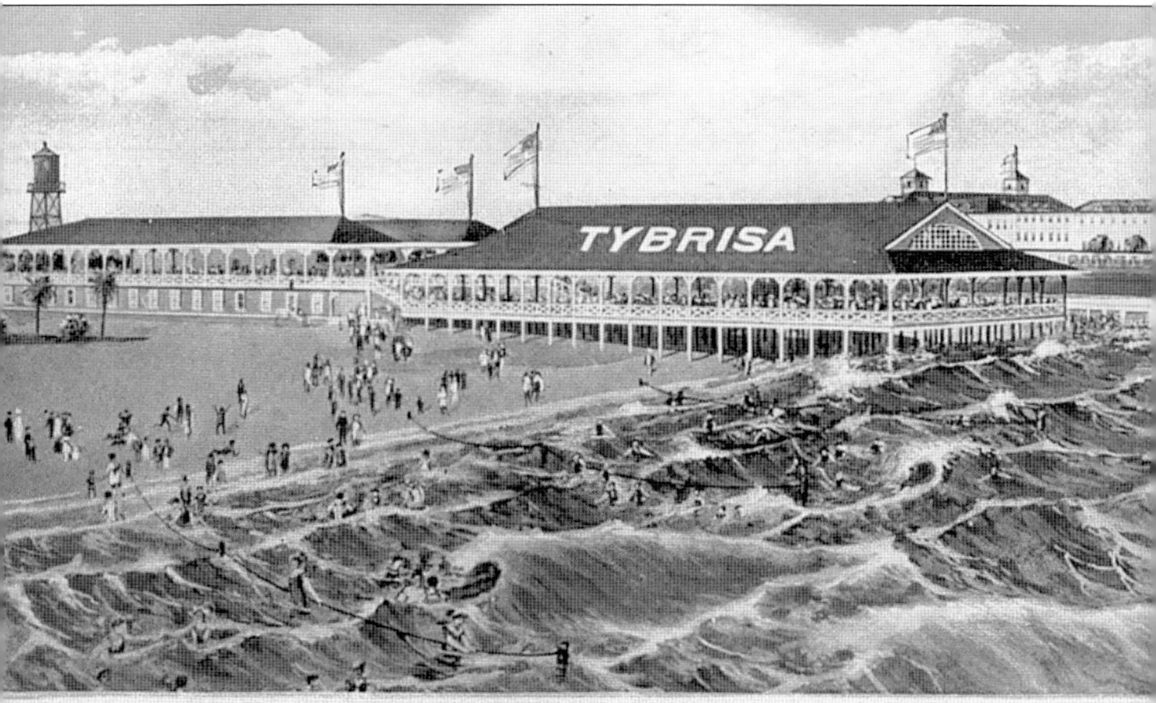

"TYBRISA COMPANY, INC., PAVILIONS AND BATH HOUSES".
TYBEE, GEORGIA.

The railroad had a tremendous influence on the development of Tybee Island as a beach resort. In the early 1900s, the Central of Georgia Railway erected an enormous pavilion, named the Tybrisa, to entice people to come to the resort by way of their railroad system. The Tybrisa became the entertainment anchor of the resort district during Tybee's golden era as a resort in the 1920s. Located on the corner of 16th and Strand, the Tybrisa was Tybee's largest and most well-known pavilion. The wooden piers of the large, hip-roof structure stretched out over the beach beyond the high water mark. The dance floor with its famous crystal ball and bandstand were located in the center of the pavilion, and the wrap-around veranda was lined with rocking chairs where one could sit and watch the dancers. (Courtesy Jane South Lindner.)

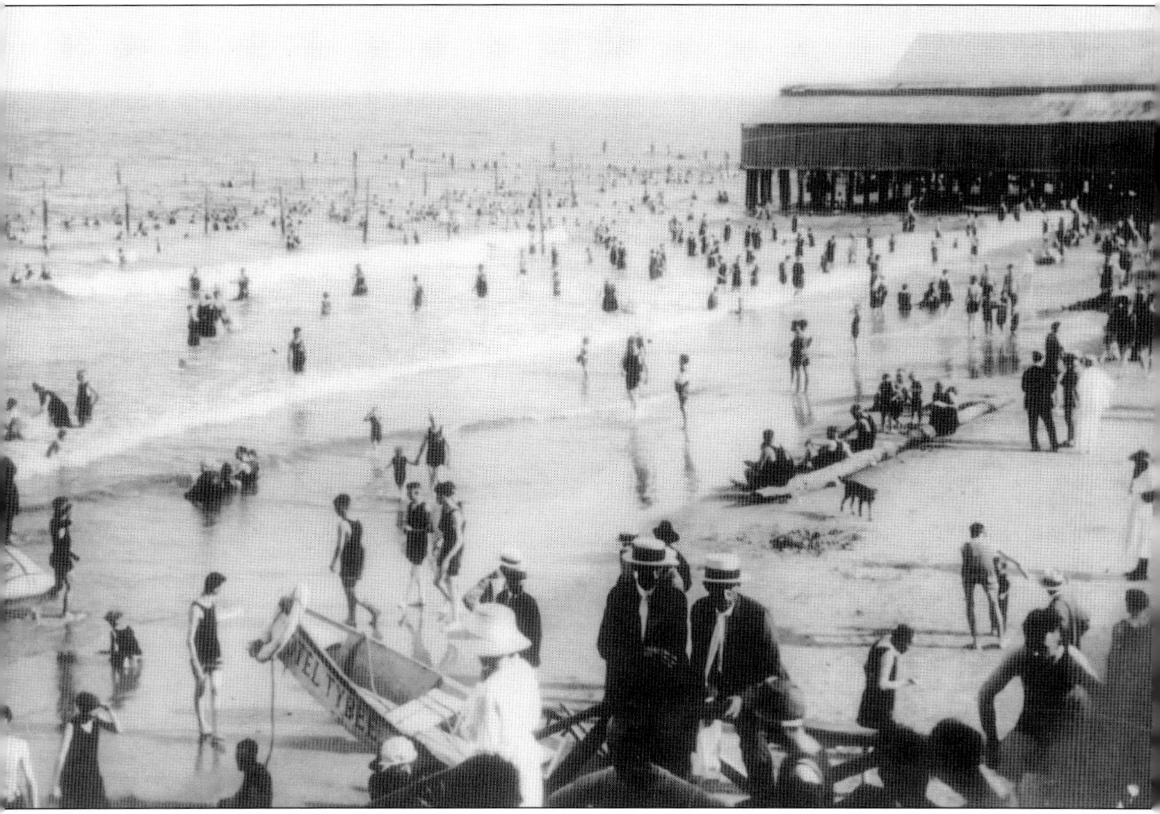

This is a typical beach scene from the 1930s, with a part of the Tybrisa pictured in the top right corner. In the early days, the Tybrisa's bathhouses were situated on the beach. During the 1920s, a large two-story building was constructed in back of the pavilion. The new structure, called The Breakers, housed bathhouses on the bottom floor. A dance floor and bowling alley were located on the top floor. Many of the men's bathing suits look alike because they were rented. The Hotel Tybee complex, The Breakers, and the Tybrisa Pavilion became the center of resort activity on Tybee.

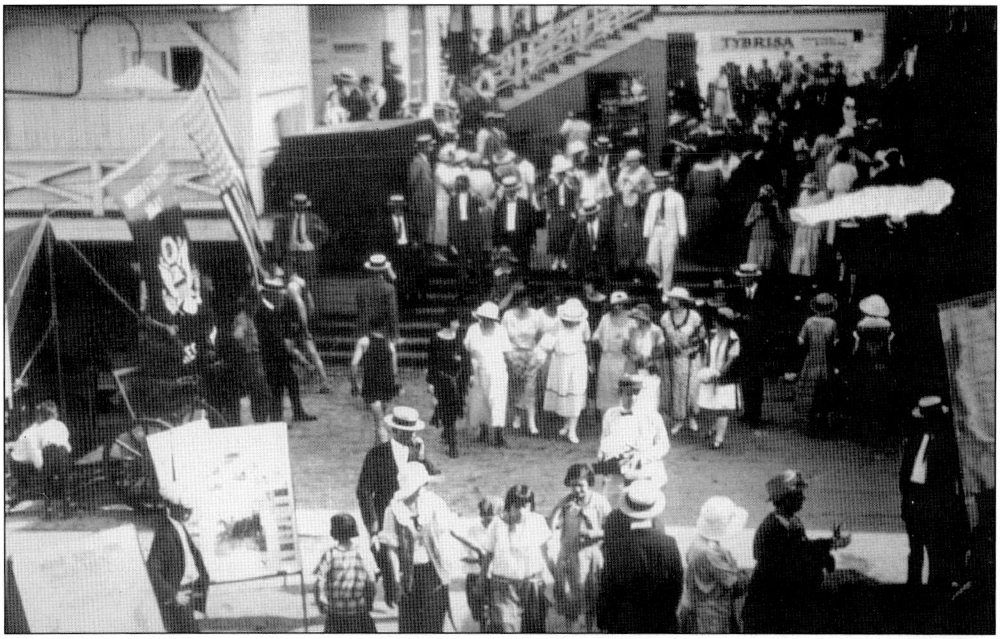

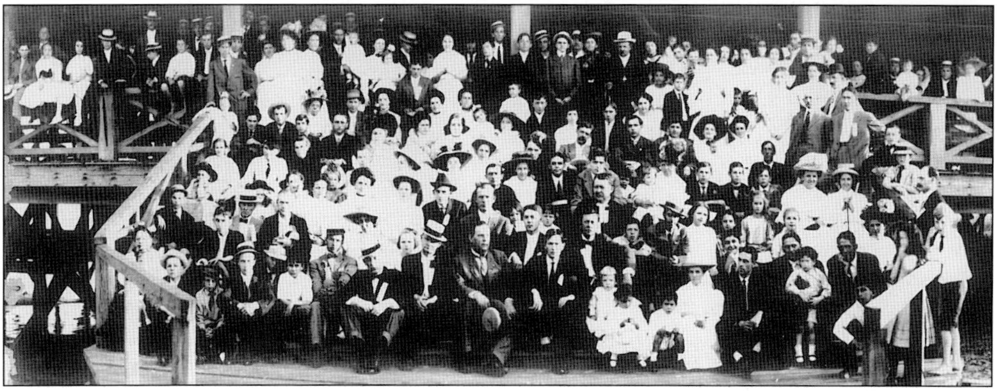

The two photographs above, taken at the Tybrisa in the early 1900s, illustrate the social atmosphere of a day at the beach. It is interesting to note how people dressed to go to the beach then as compared to today. Women wore long dresses and hats and men were often attired in coats, ties, and boaters (round, flat-crowned straw hats).

Opposite: To some beachgoers, a vacation at Tybee would not have been complete without a personalized picture postcard to send to friends and relatives, or just to keep as a remembrance. Swimmers who desired to take a cool dip in the ocean waves but did not have their own bathing costumes could rent them. The three young men in the inset invited a canine friend to pose with them. Ida Virden, the woman in the main photograph, is dressed in typical ladies' fashion of the day.

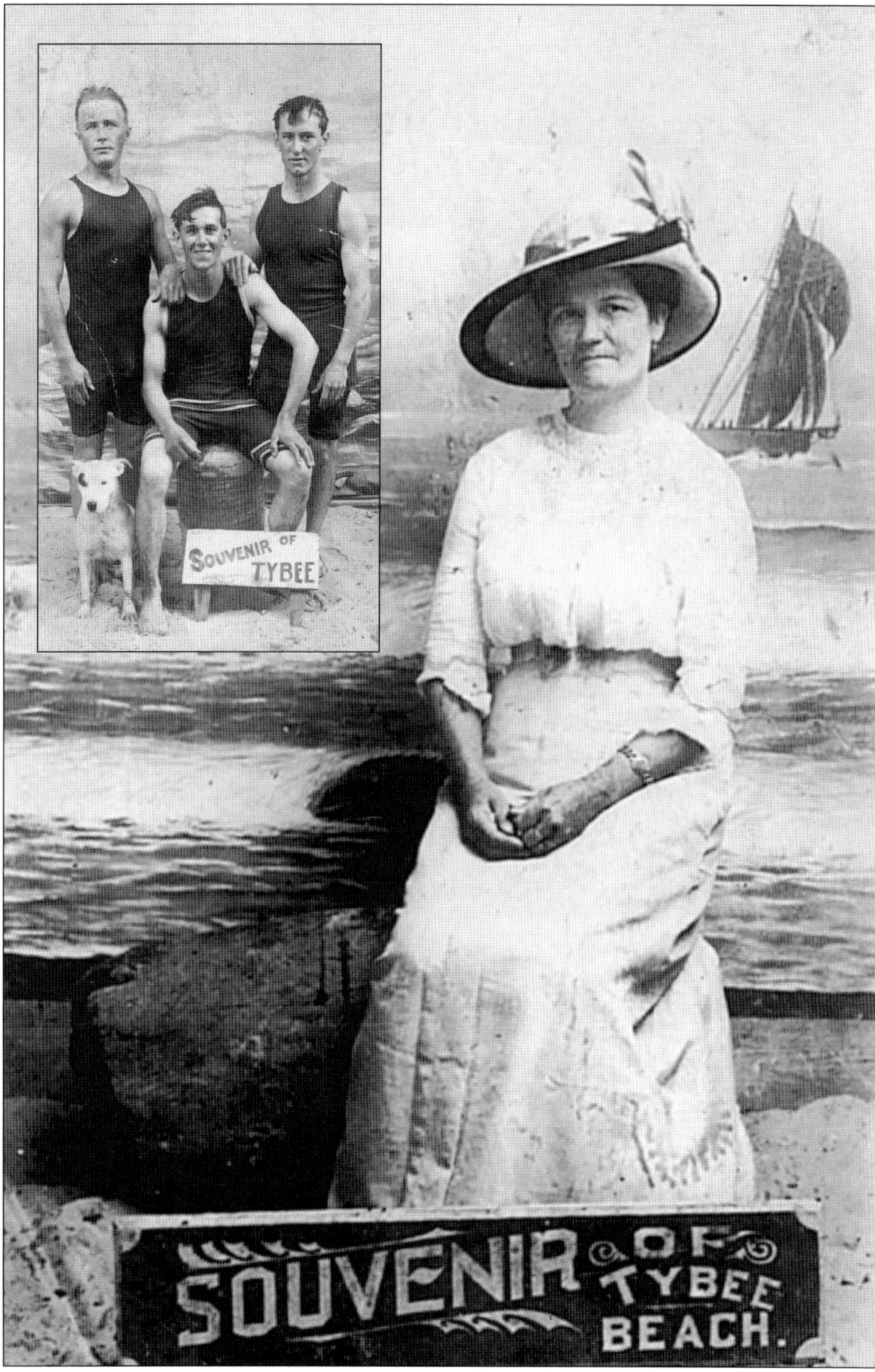
SOUVENIR OF TYBEE
SOUVENIR OF TYBEE BEACH.

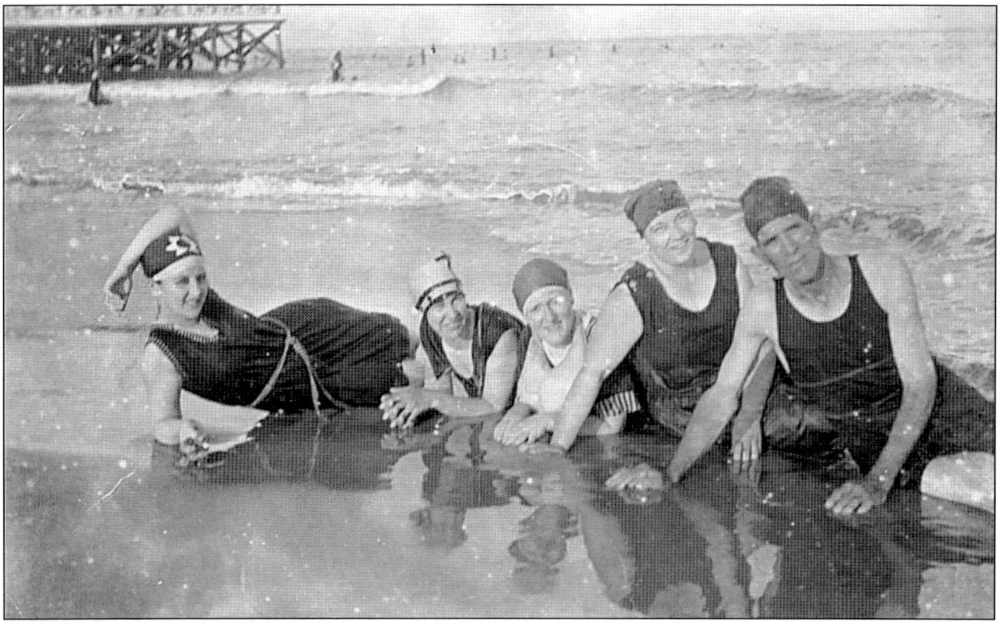

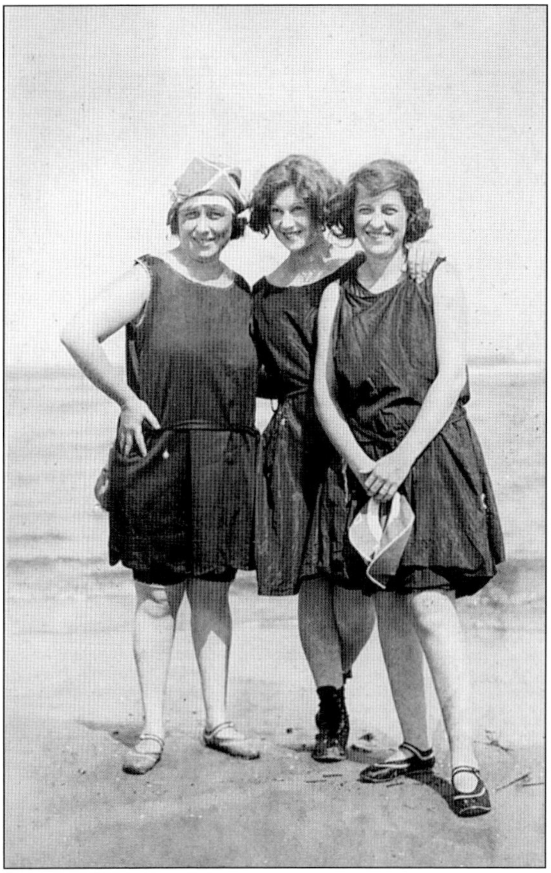

Whether lounging at the edge of the surf or just posing with friends for a photograph, these unidentified bathers from the turn of the 20th century seem to be enjoying themselves. The early bathing costumes, sometimes made of wool, did not bare much skin to the Georgia sun. Note that bathing caps of varying styles were in vogue.

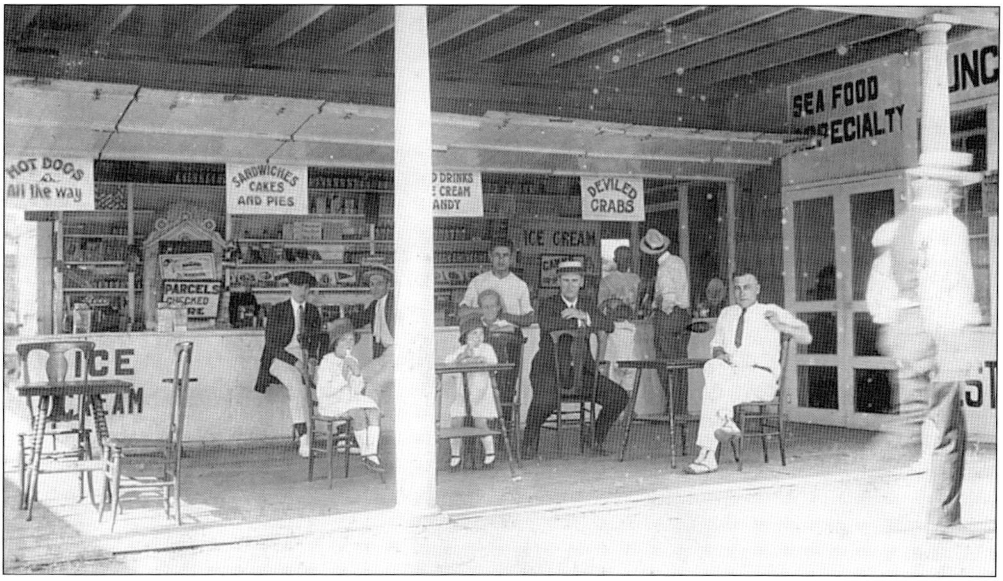

Not everyone came to Tybee's beach to swim. Some took time out from the beach to enjoy a light meal or cold drink at one of the indoor or outdoor eating establishments. Others passed the time taking in the ocean breezes from the veranda of their hotel, while enjoying the view of the beach and Atlantic Ocean. This veranda scene is at the Solms Hotel on The Strand.

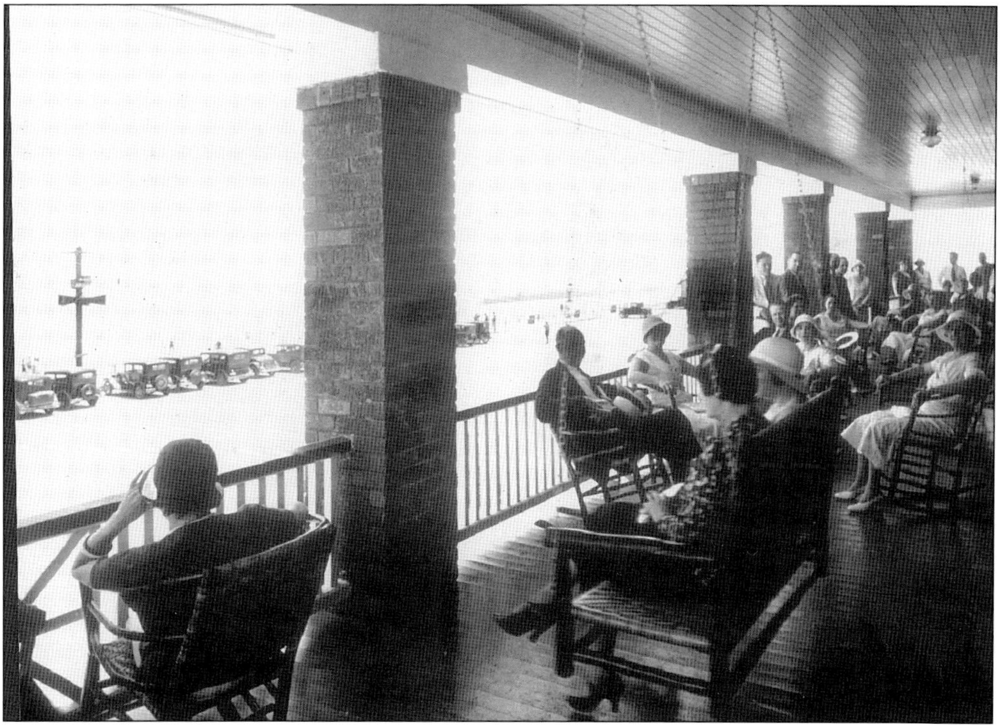

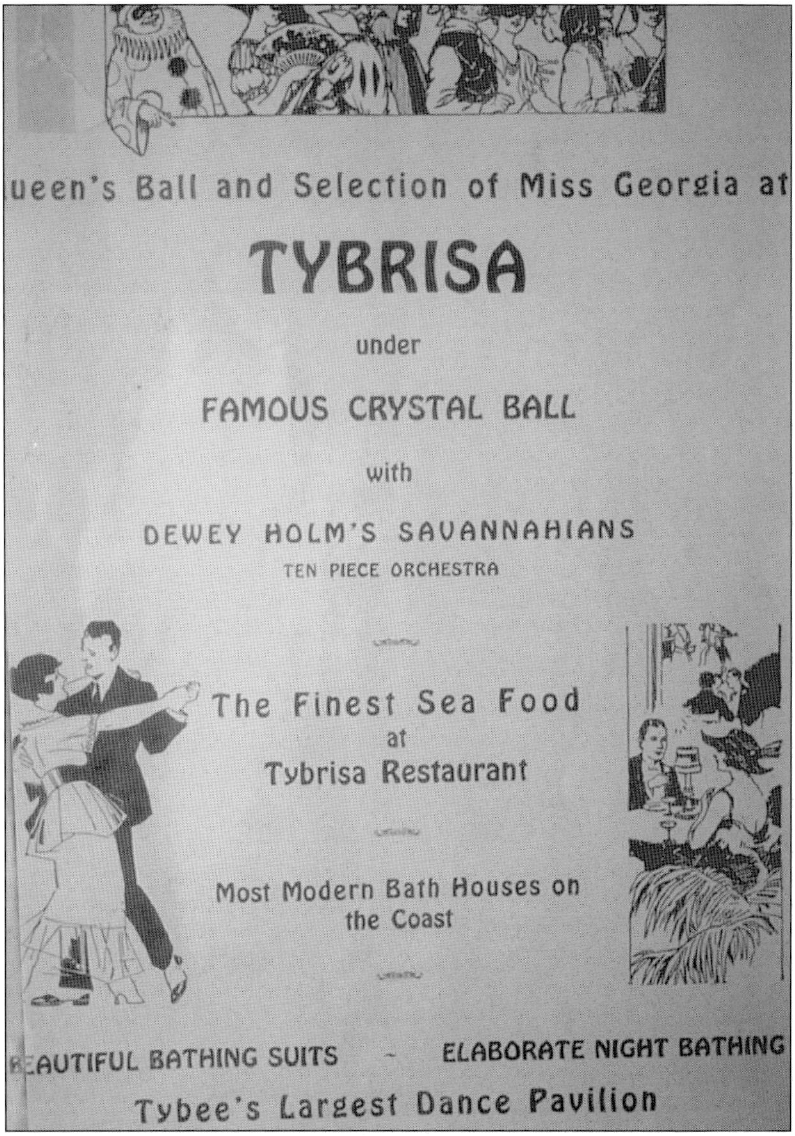

Tybee's popularity as a seaside resort was never greater than during the 1920s and early 1930s. Those were the days that have been labeled musically as the jazz and big band era. Tybee's ocean breezes carried the orchestral sounds of Bob Crosby, Tommy Dorsey, Glen Gray, Cab Calloway, Louis Armstrong, Ted Weems, Duke Ellington, and Blue Steele. Note that the above poster advertises "elaborate night bathing." Lighting on the beach enabled tourists to take an after dark dip in the ocean. Tybee was one of the earliest coastal resorts to offer night swimming. Also notice that bathing suit rentals are advertised.

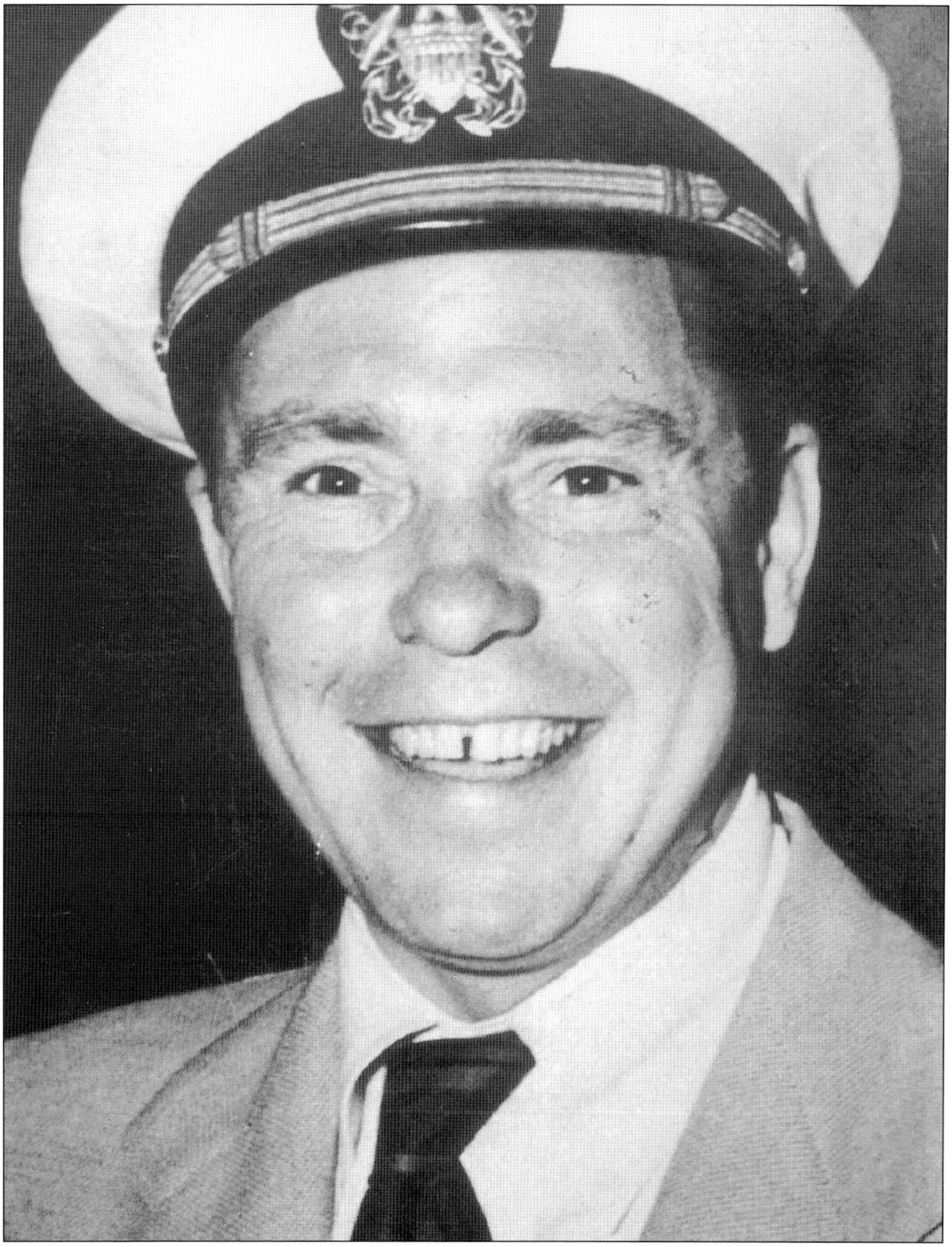

Tybee's golden years as a beach resort were captured in song and story. In 1926, songwriter Samuel B. Miller wrote a dance tune entitled, "Tybee Where the Georgia Peaches Go." The song became a regional hit and was played nightly at the Tybrisa by Dewey Holm's Savannahians. Also published in 1926 was Savannah poet Conrad Aiken's short story, "Strange Moonlight," in which he wrote about his experiences on the train to Tybee. Famous songwriter and Savannah native Johnny Mercer (above) liked to attend dances at the Tybrisa and the Tybee Hotel Pavilion during his vacations from school. He later included Tybee among the islands mentioned in his recording of "The Thousand Islands."

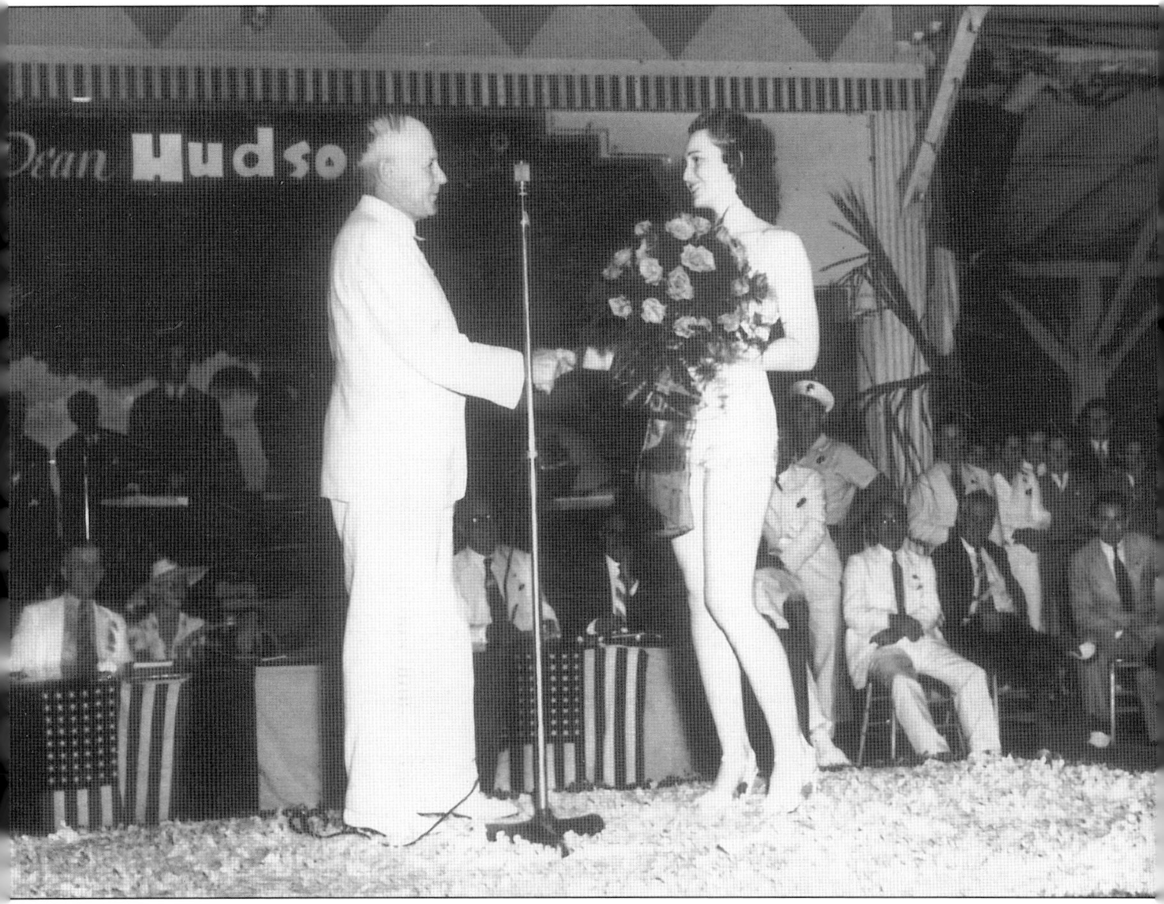

The Tybrisa was the setting for three early Miss Georgia beauty pageants. The first Miss Georgia pageant was held at the Tybrisa on July 26, 1926. There was no talent competition or contestant interviews, and the contestants were forbidden to wear bathing suits. The next Miss Georgia competition at the Tybrisa took place in 1939 and the final pageant at Tybee was in 1941. In the above 1939 photograph taken at the Tybrisa, the new Miss Georgia receives a bouquet and congratulations.

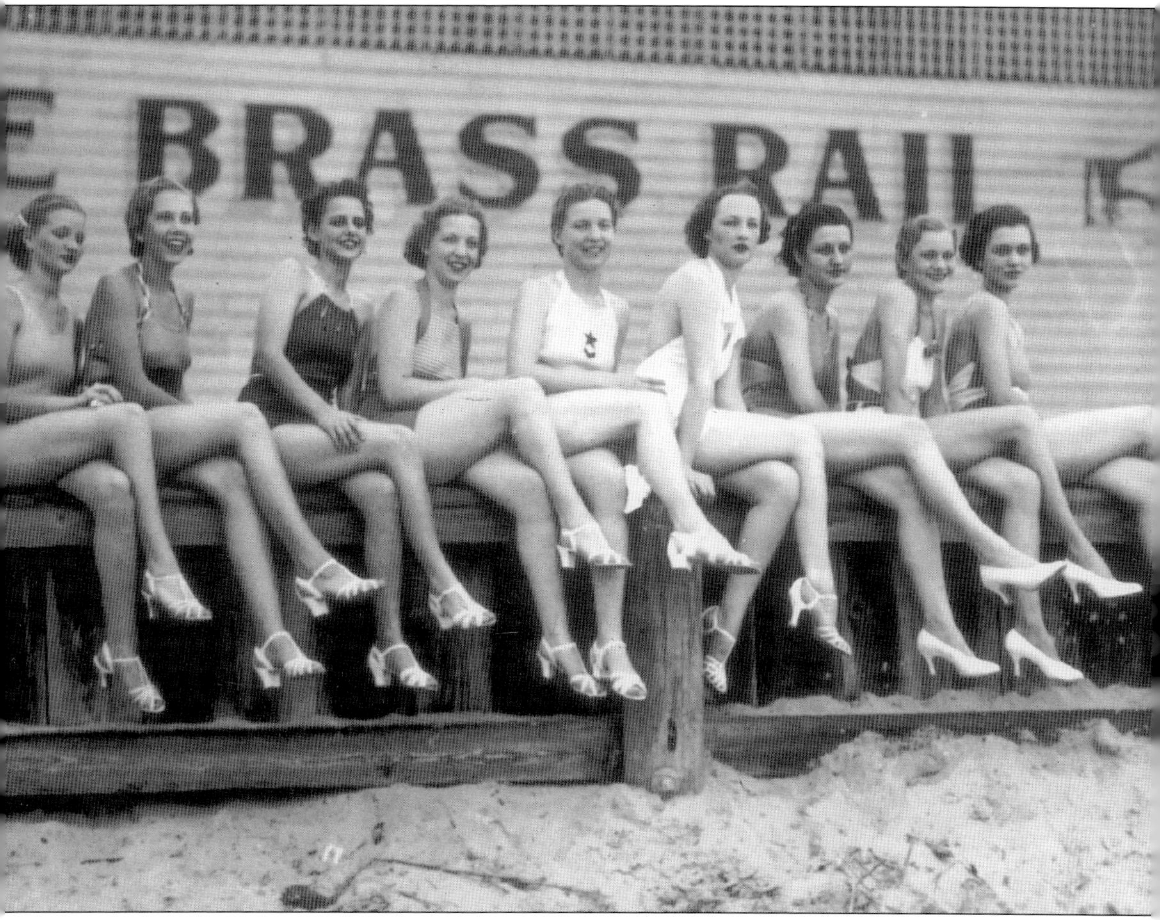

These young beauty contestants participating in the 1939 Miss Georgia pageant pose near the entrance to the Brass Rail, a popular Tybee night club that opened in 1939 on the corner of 15th Street and Strand. The Tybrisa Pavilion, The Breakers, and the Brass Rail were burned to the ground by a devastating fire in 1967. Tybee's resort complex lost its main attractions.

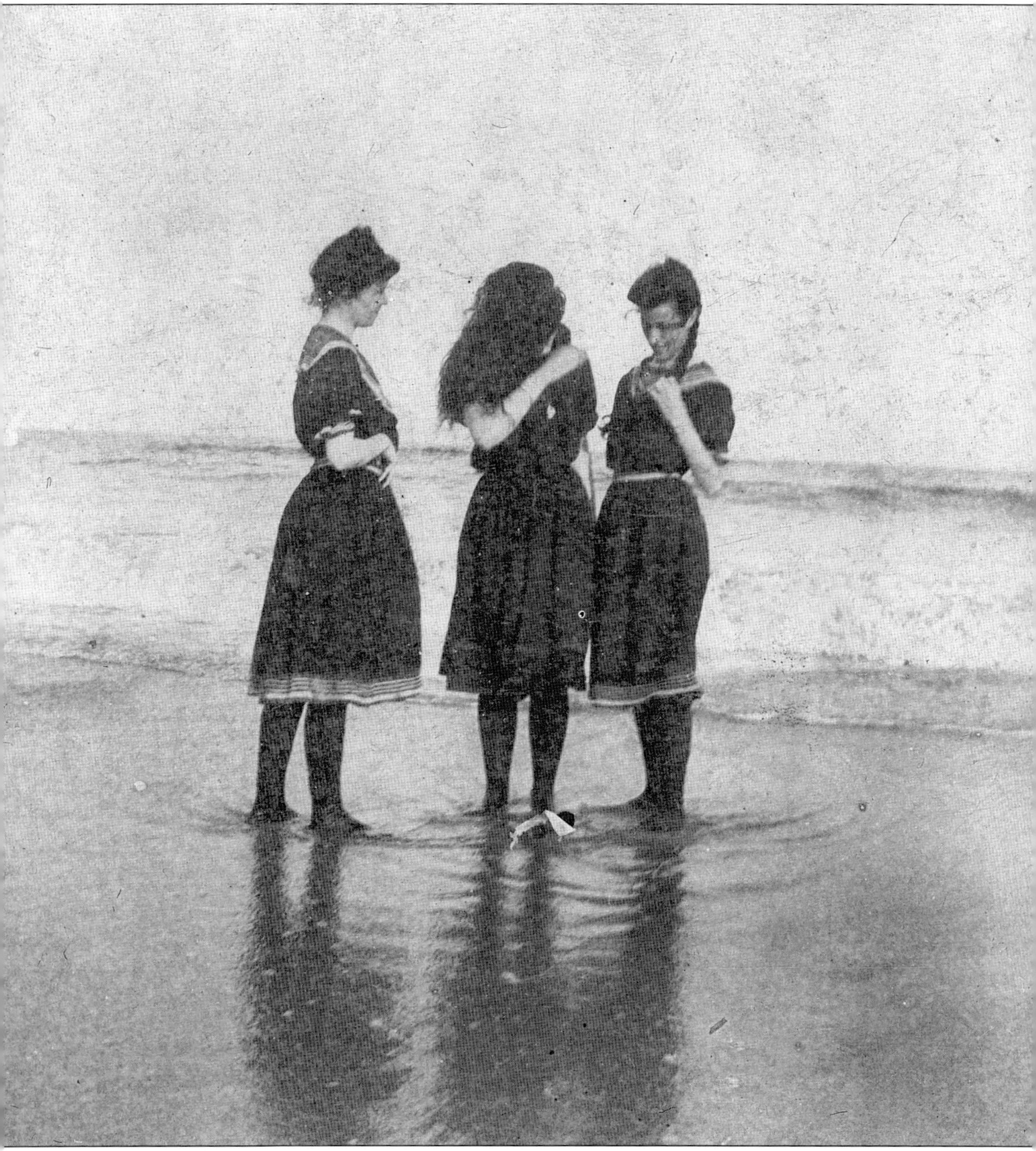

The beach attire of the three young ladies in this photograph taken on Tybee Beach in 1903 is in sharp contrast from that worn by the young ladies shown on the previous page. When ladies went into the ocean for a swim in the early 1900s, they wore black stockings and bloomers. Their voluminous bathing suits had wide skirts that came below the knees. Small weights were sewn into the hems of the skirts so that no matter how the lady moved, her skirt would go down, never revealing the thighs. Earlier bathing costumes had high necks and long sleeves. Writing on the back of the above photograph identified the three young ladies only as "The Three Graces . . . Faith, Hope, Charity."

Six

Island Life

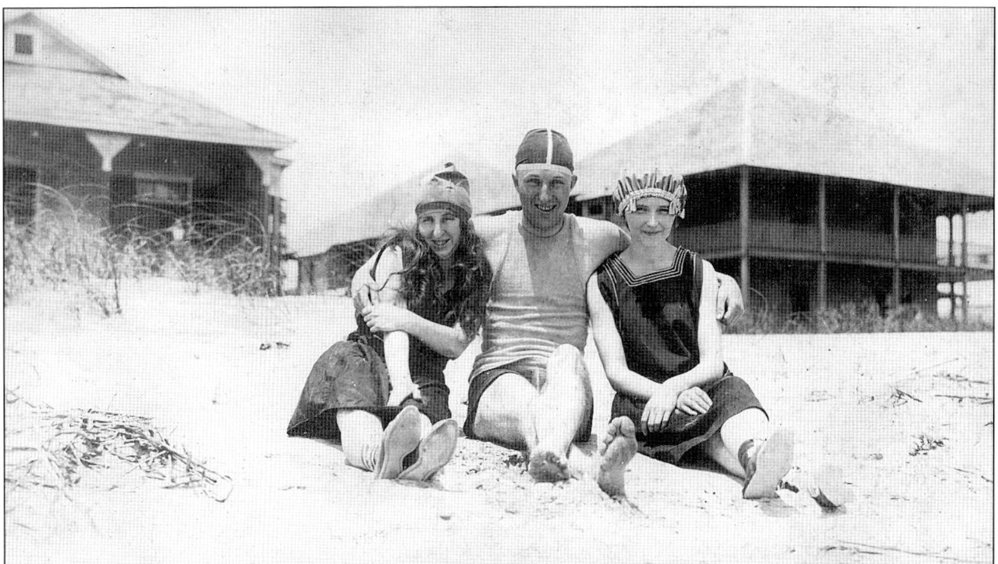

Better accessibility to Tybee Island as a result of the opening of the Tybee Road enabled more people to establish both summer homes and year-round residences on the island. This scene shows typical beach cottages in the background.

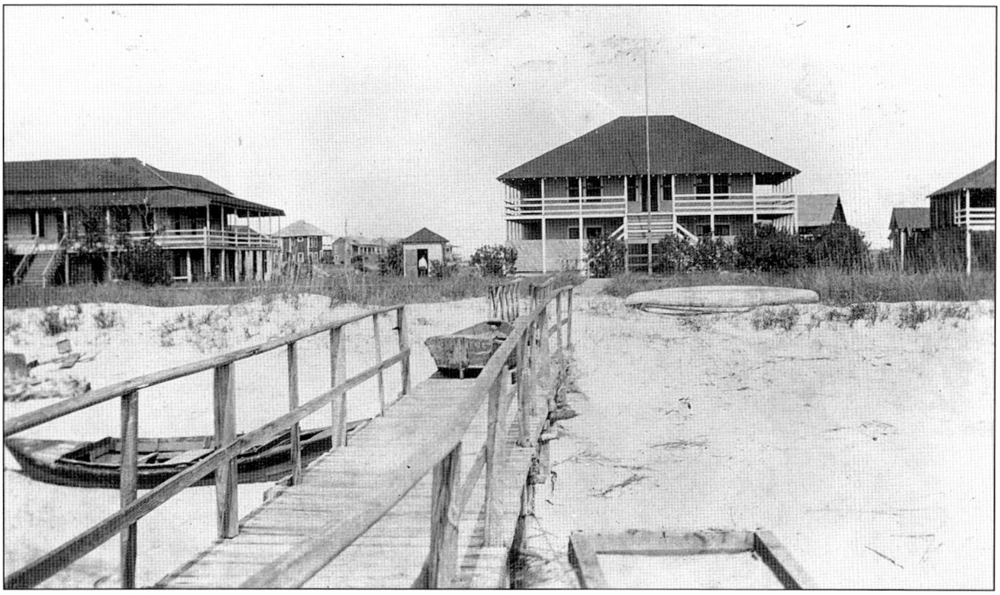

During the late 1800s and early 1900s, part-time residents seeking an escape from the summer heat of the city built beach cottages along Tybee's shore line. The cottages were designed by their owners to take full advantage of the ocean breezes, and also to survive the often brutal forces of nature that are typical of Tybee and other low-lying coastal areas.

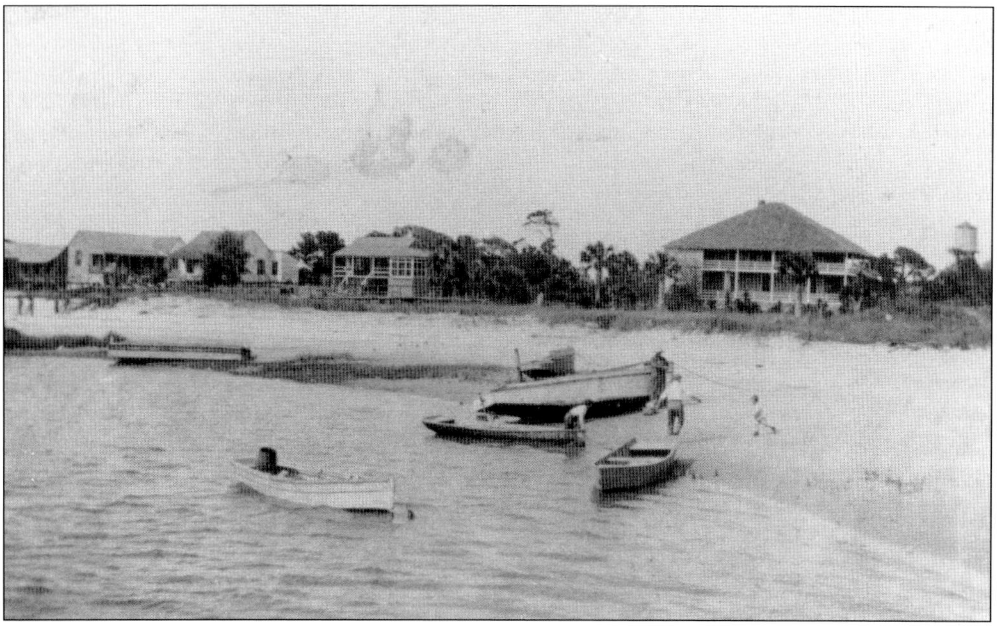

The elevated design of the typical beach cottage protected it from rising flood waters and tides. The design also improved air circulation that cooled the home. The air circulation also had a drying effect that deterred rotting of the wood structure. Heart pine was a favorite building material because it was hard and dense and filled with sap. These characteristics were said to be an impediment to termites.

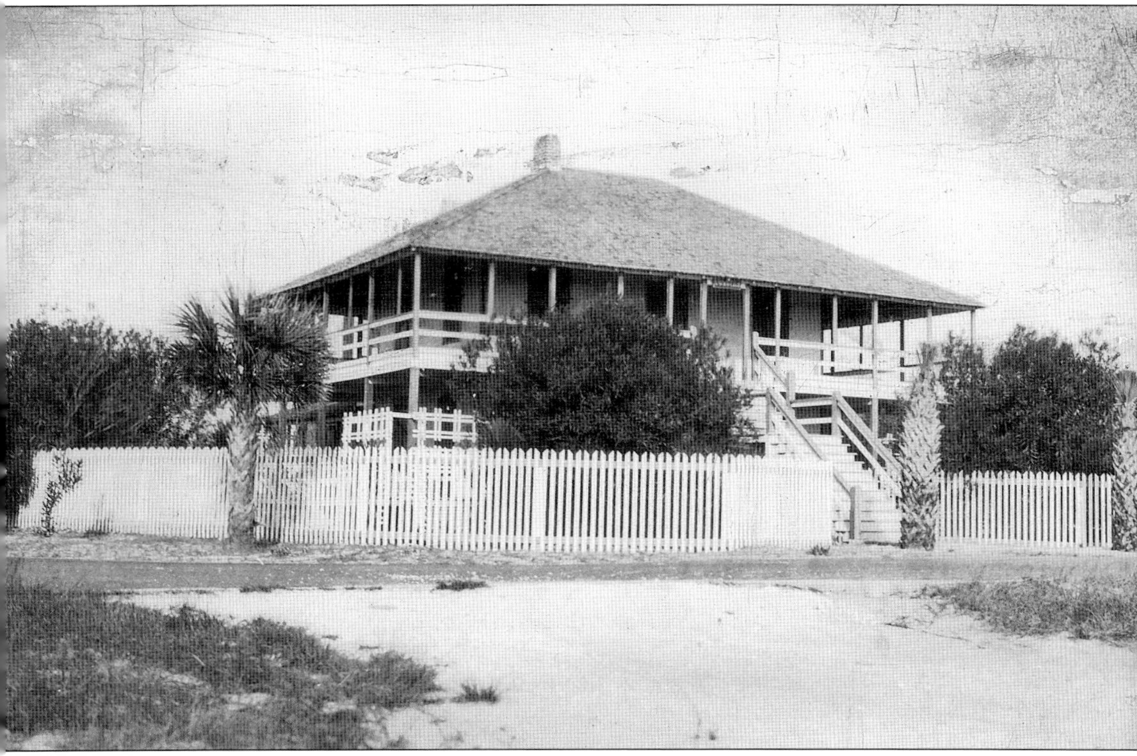

Some recognizable architectural features of a typical Tybee beach cottage are its wraparound porches and large windows and doors that work together to provide natural air conditioning. Louvered shutters on the windows could be closed to protect against the elements, while still providing for air flow about the house. The high pitch of the hipped roof also played a role in cooling the home's interior. Historic preservationists have pointed out that this beach cottage architecture may no longer exist anywhere but Tybee Island. Several of the unique beach cottages have been restored and continue to echo back to Tybee's early days as a residential island.

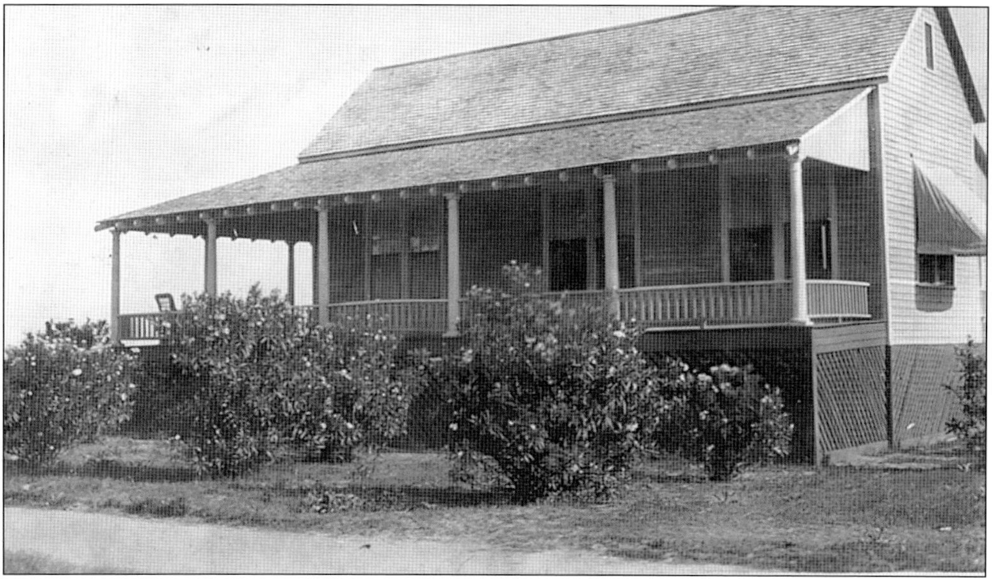

These photographs illustrate two examples of other types of beach architecture that could be found on Tybee Island during the early 1900s. Examples of early island architecture still exist on Tybee, but many of the older homes have been replaced by more modern single or multi-family dwellings.

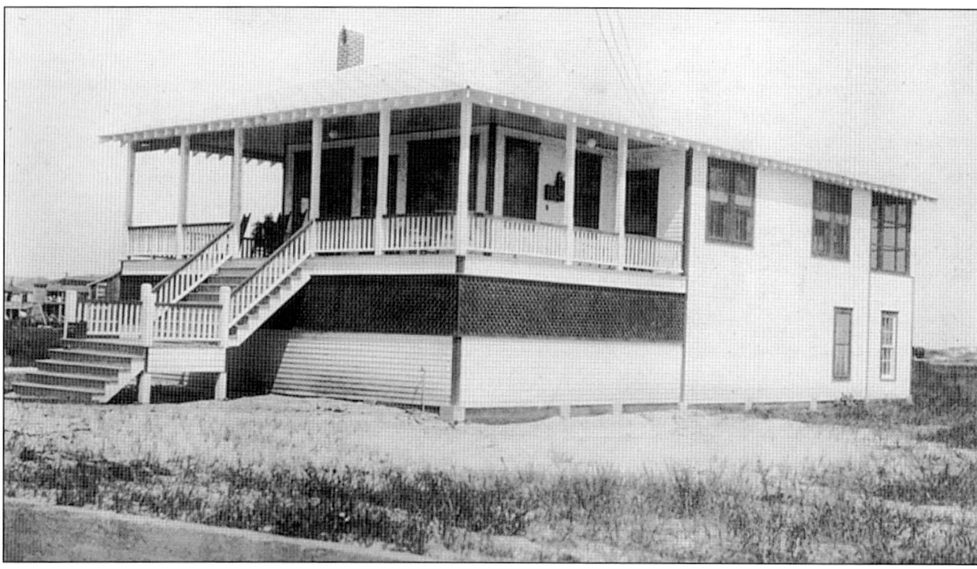

A popular commercial and pleasure activity for Tybee residents is fishing in the ocean or the many rivers and creeks that border the island. A large sea bass was caught by this lucky angler from the early 1900s while fishing off the sea wall.

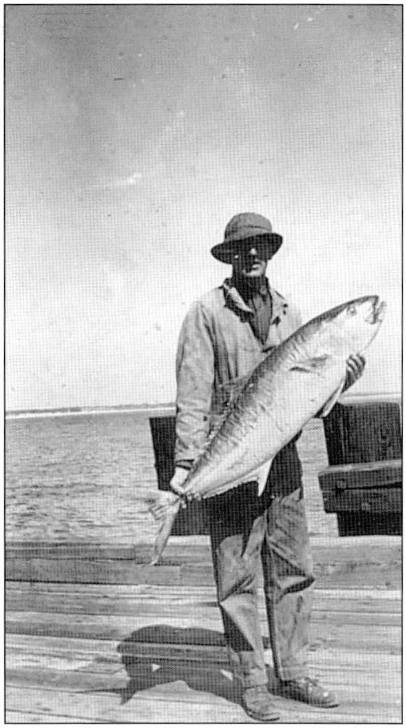

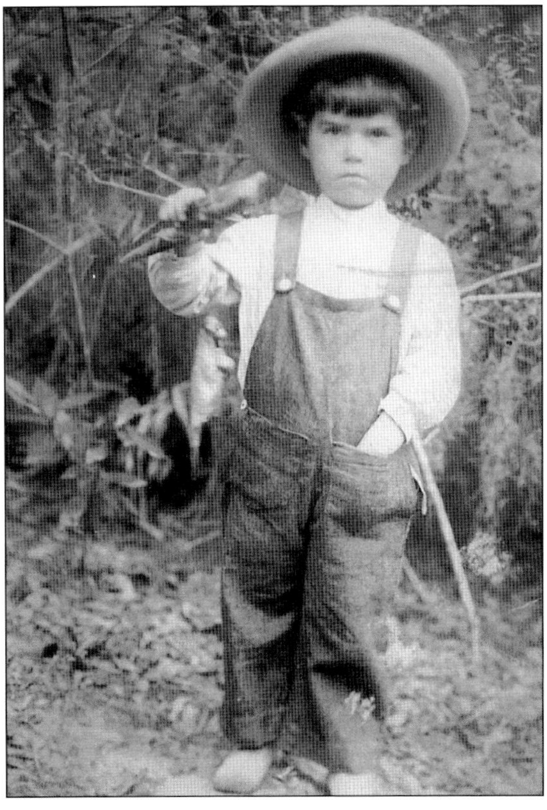

Fishing success is all a matter of perspective. Young David Doyle is shown here displaying his catch. Could that be a look of disappointment and not pride on his face? Perhaps he was a little unhappy about being photographed. David later served at Fort Screven in the 72nd Co. CAC.

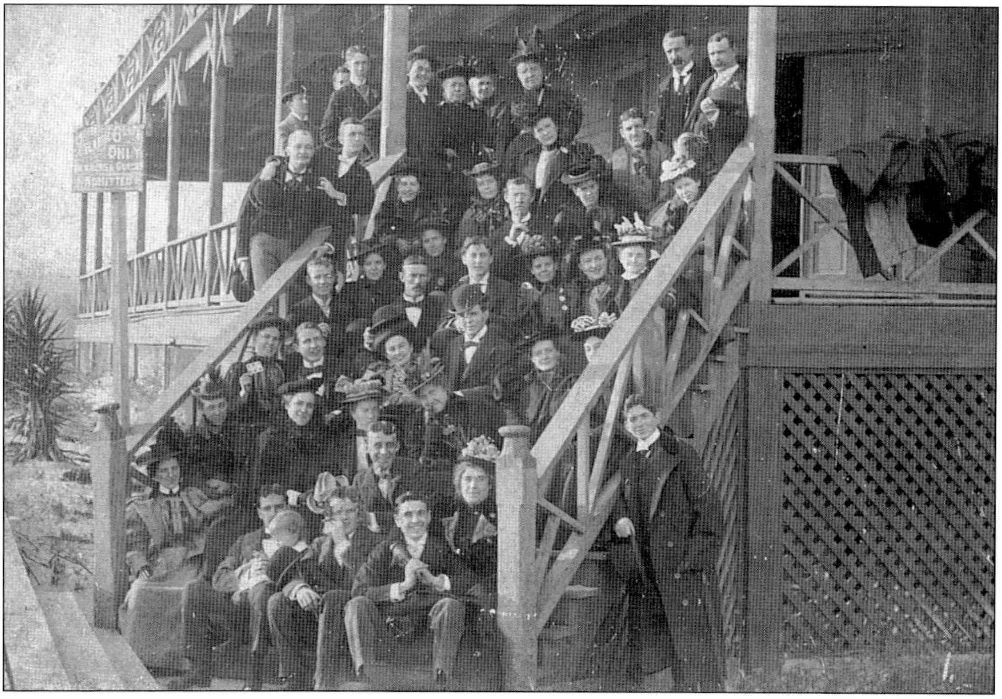

The early 20th century saw the establishment of several private clubs on Tybee Island. Two of the most popular were the Atlantic Club and the Amfico Club. The two photographs on this page are of the members and clubhouse of the Atlantic Club. As the sign indicates, the private clubs were open to members and guests only, and undoubtedly offered to their members some amenities that were not available to the average resident or weekend visitor. The heavier clothing worn by some of the people indicate the photos may have been taken during the late fall or winter. (Courtesy Margaret Trexler.)

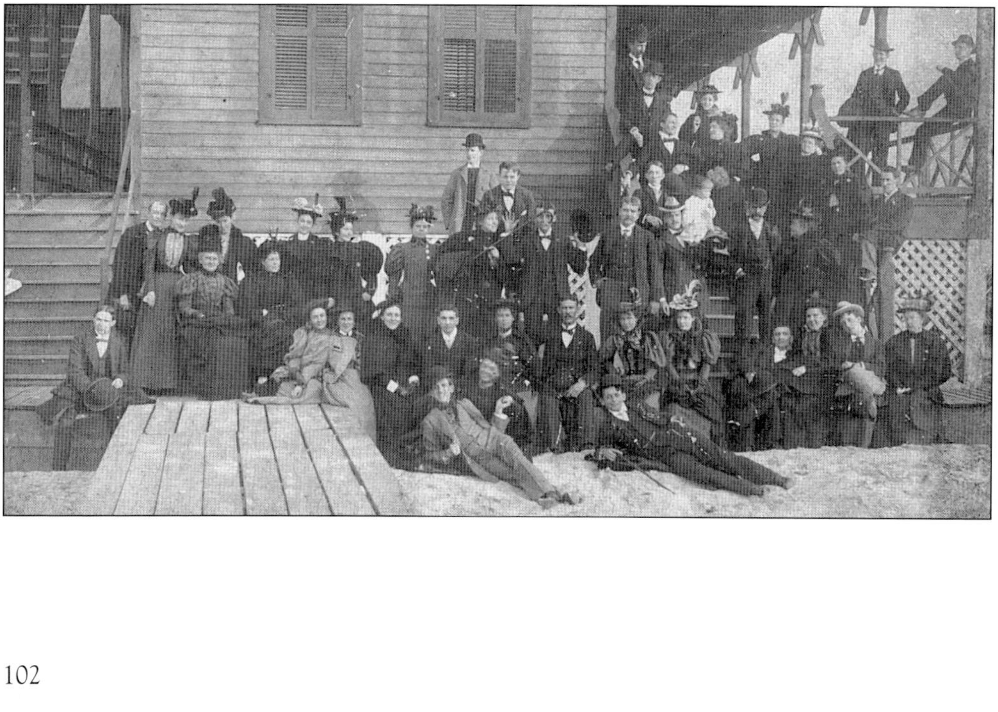

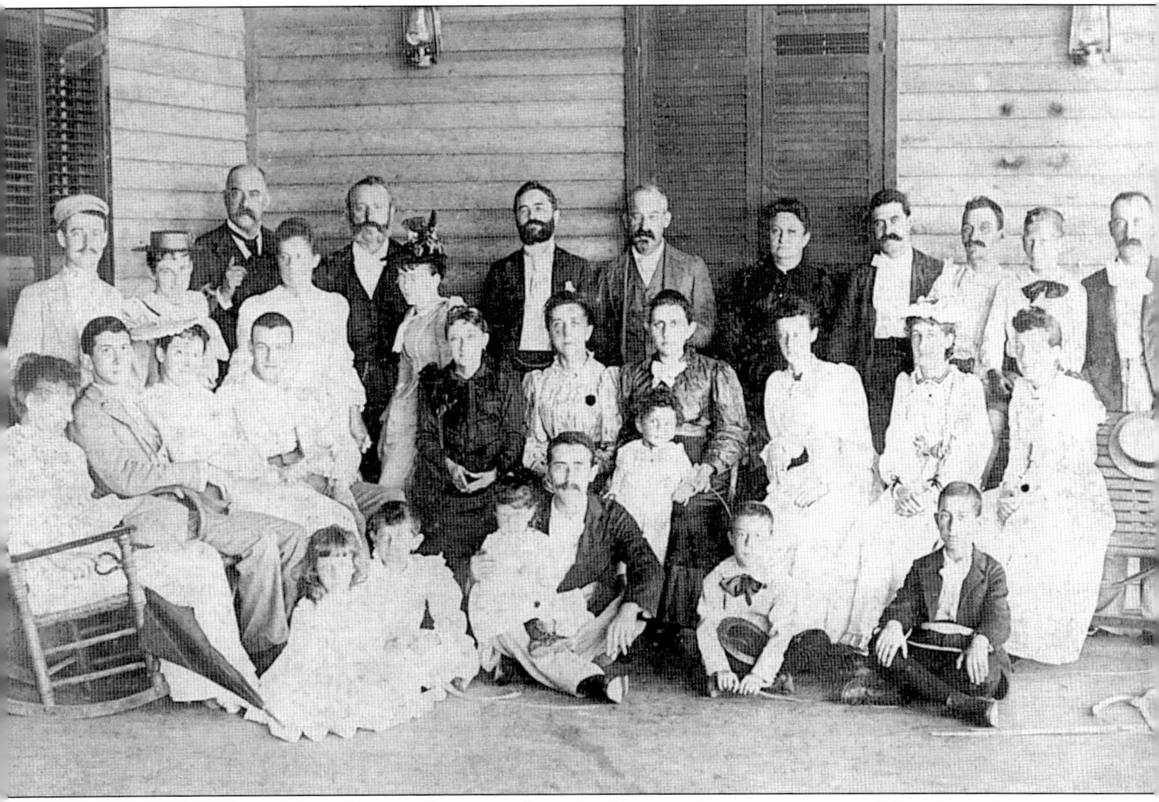

Tybee Island has always been a favorite place for hosting house parties and family gatherings, traditions that continue to the present day. The saying is that if you have a house at the beach, you will surely have a lot of house guests. This 1890 photograph is typical of a family reunion of the time. A family day or weekend at a Tybee home might include a picnic or cookout, fishing, boating, a walk on the beach, or perhaps a swim in the surf. And, of course, it was a treat in itself to escape the hustle and bustle of city life for a more relaxing beach atmosphere.

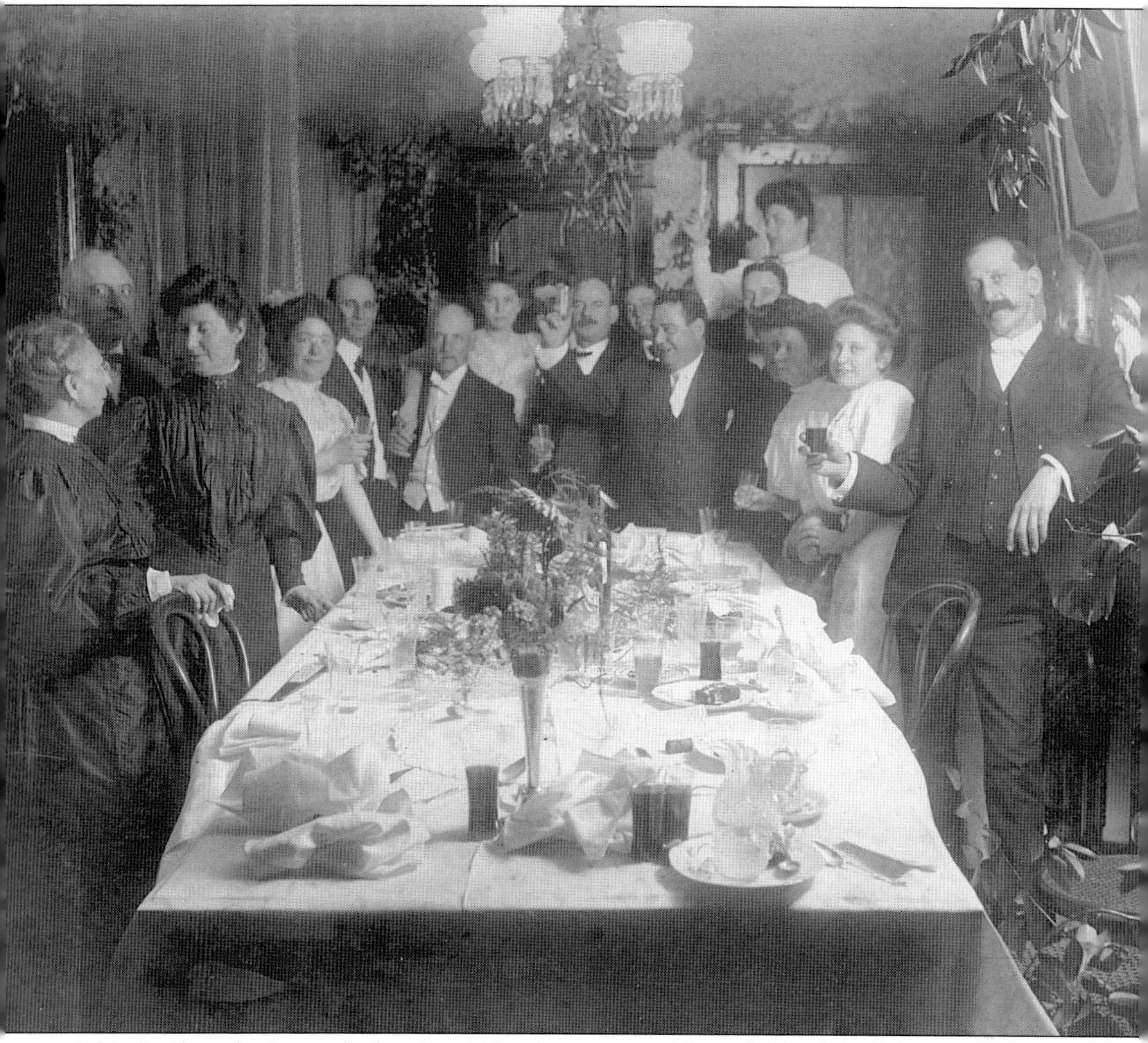

This family gathering took place in 1906 at the home of Mr. and Mrs. A.P. Solomon on West Liberty Street in Savannah. The Solomons purchased a summer home on Tybee in 1918 and became one of the island's most prominent families. Two years after buying his home at Savannah Beach (Tybee), A.P. Solomon was operating the town's water works. According to the memories of one early Tybee part-time resident, "If you wanted water to your house, you had to have Mr. Solomon turn it on." Solomon organized the Savannah Beach Volunteer Fire Department in 1924 and made one of the first efforts to construct jetties to deter beach erosion.

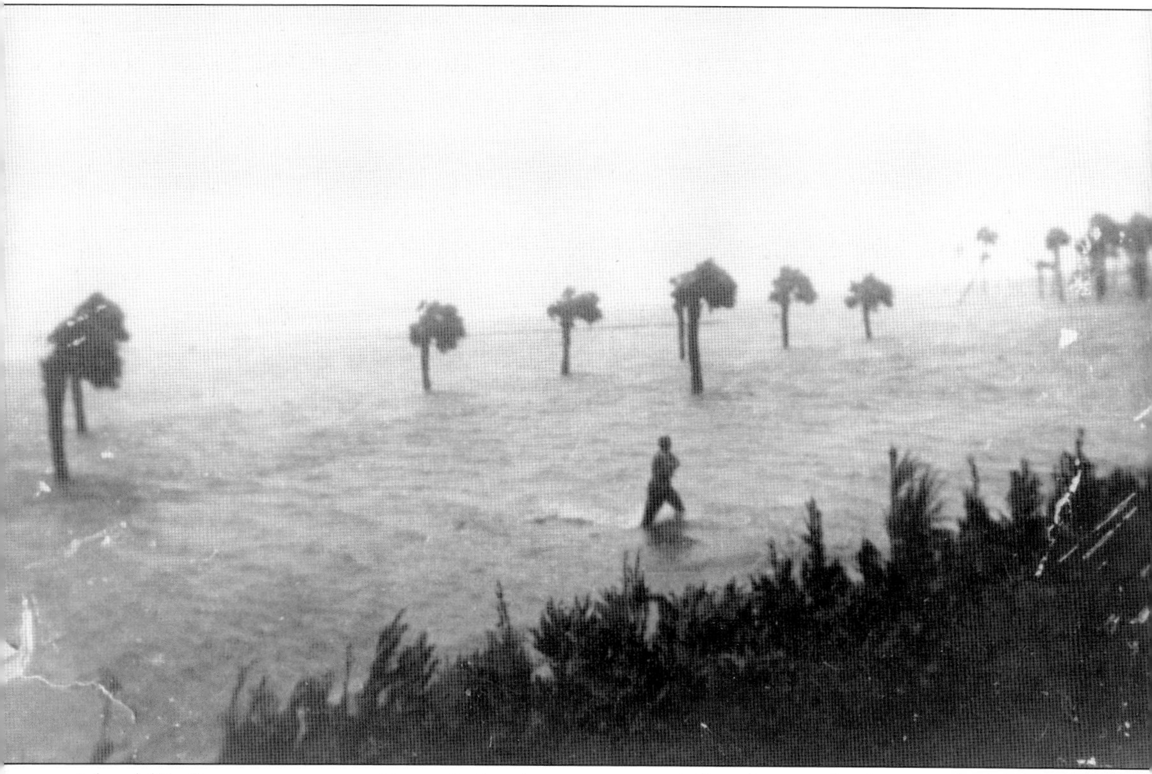

Island life for permanent residents is for the most part idyllic. It can also be very frightening at times when Mother Nature goes on a rampage. Coastal barrier islands, such as Tybee, are subject to Nor'easters and hurricanes that can result in high winds, storm surges, and possible resulting damage. The hurricane season is a time of some stress for islanders, especially newer residents who have never experienced a severe coastal storm. The date of this photograph is unknown, but it demonstrates the high winds and tides that can accompany a storm. Notice that the palm trees are standing in water, indicating coastal flooding. One hardy individual seems intent on defying nature.

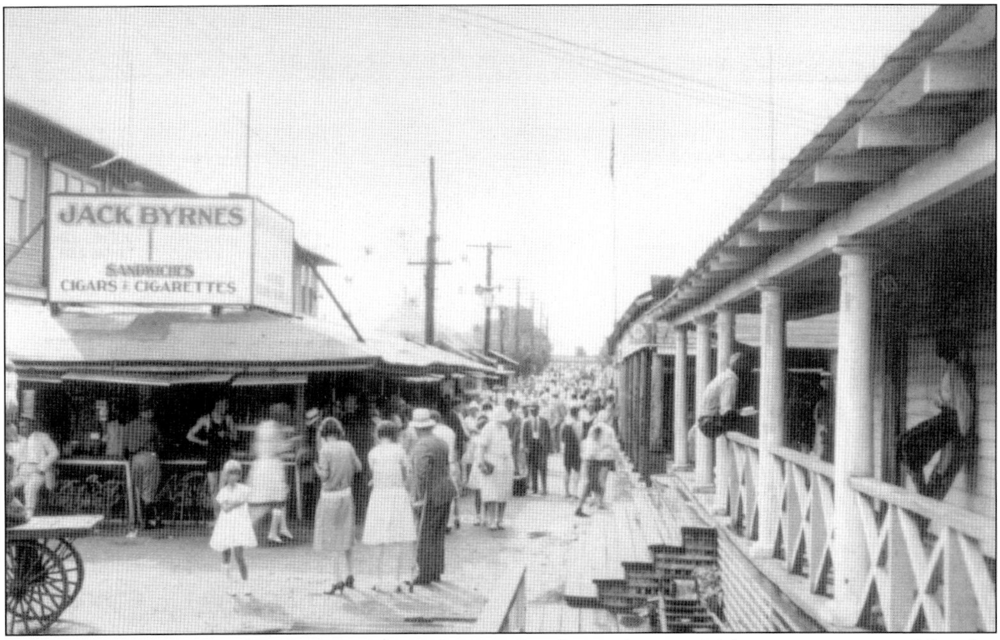

During the early decades of the 1900s, the crush of people in a Tybee street scene like the one above would probably have included tourists, part-time residents, permanent residents, and perhaps soldiers from Fort Screven, all enjoying the social atmosphere of the island. Jack Byrnes place, located near the Tybrisa, was a popular source for sandwiches and drinks. Fort Screven's soldiers were considered a vital part of the community. The men in the photograph below are members of a soldiers' bowling team that competed in the Savannah Beach city league in 1915. Dressed in their civilian clothes, these dapper gentlemen look more like residents or tourists than soldiers.

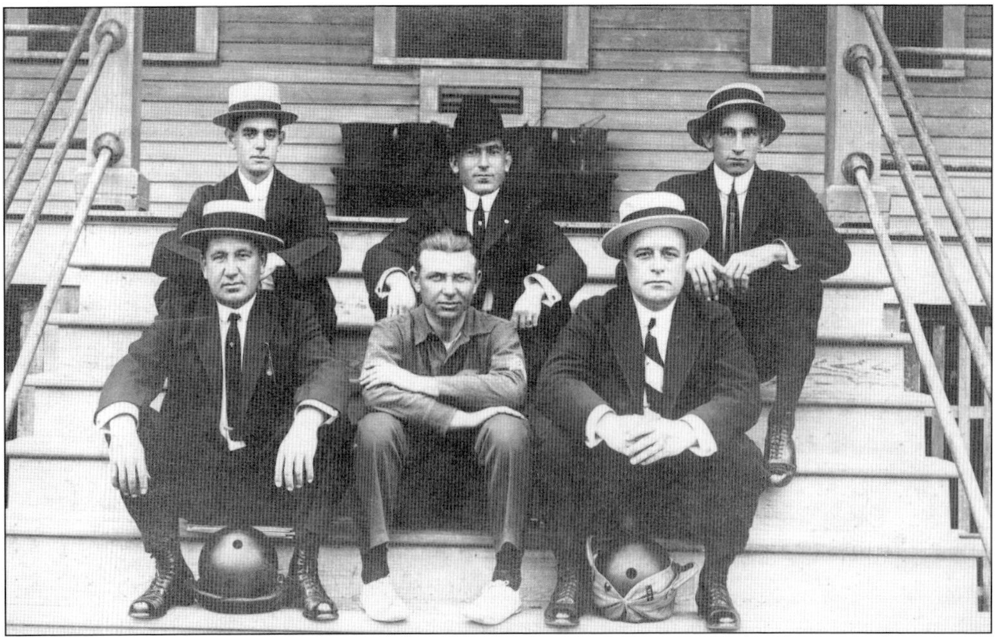

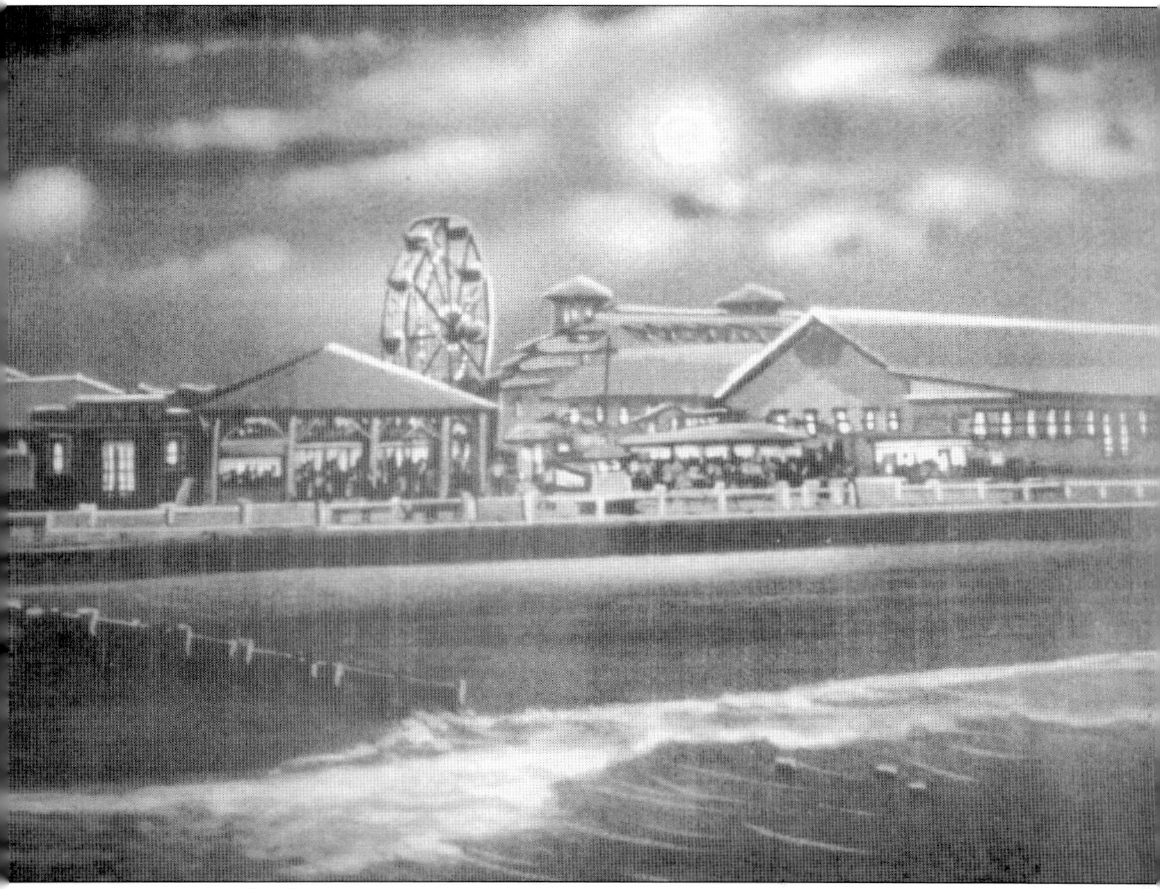

During much of Tybee's resort years, an amusement park was available on the south end for both visitors and residents. This postcard image of a portion of the The Strand shows a Ferris wheel. A later amusement park, the Tybee Amusement Park, opened during the 1950s at a location on 16th Street, now Tybrisa Street. The Tybee Amusement Park was closed in 1999 and the rides and other equipment sold at auction. A hotel now occupies the site.

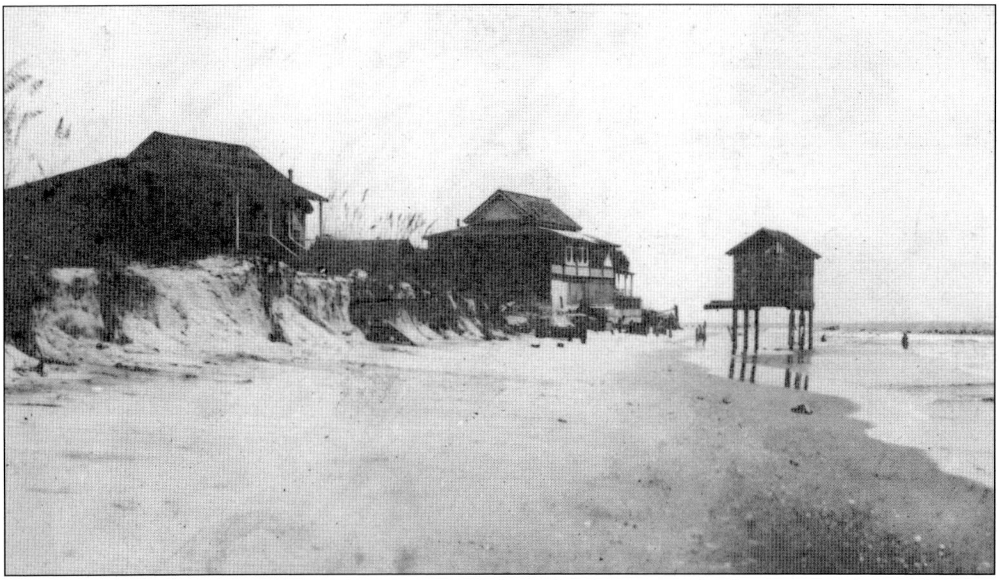

Since Tybee's south end was where most of the island's resort facilities were located, early residential cottages were concentrated along the south beach and the Back River. Beach homes were also built on the northern end of the island. These photographs from 1921 are examples of homes that were constructed on Tybee's north beach area.

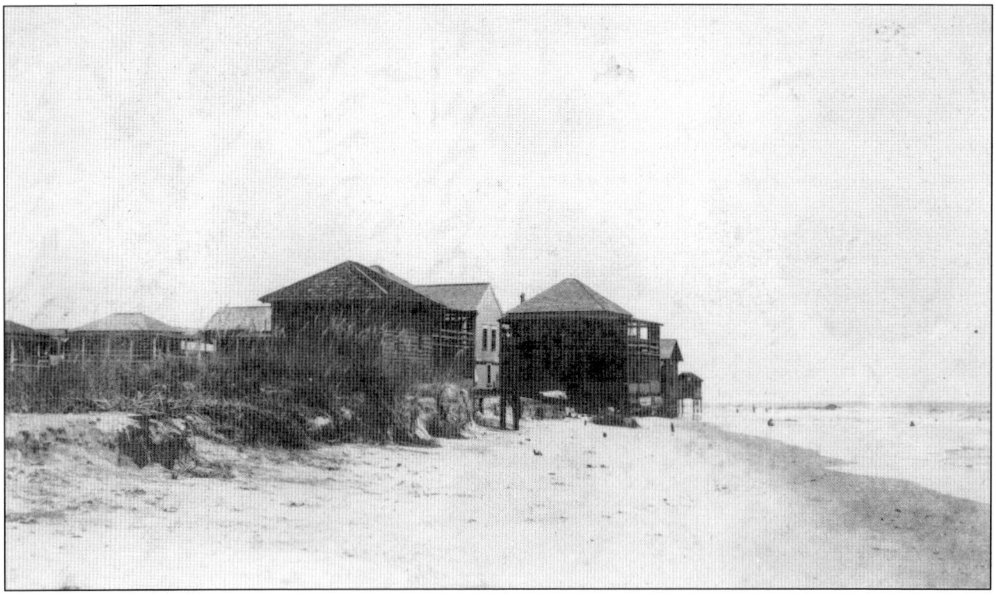

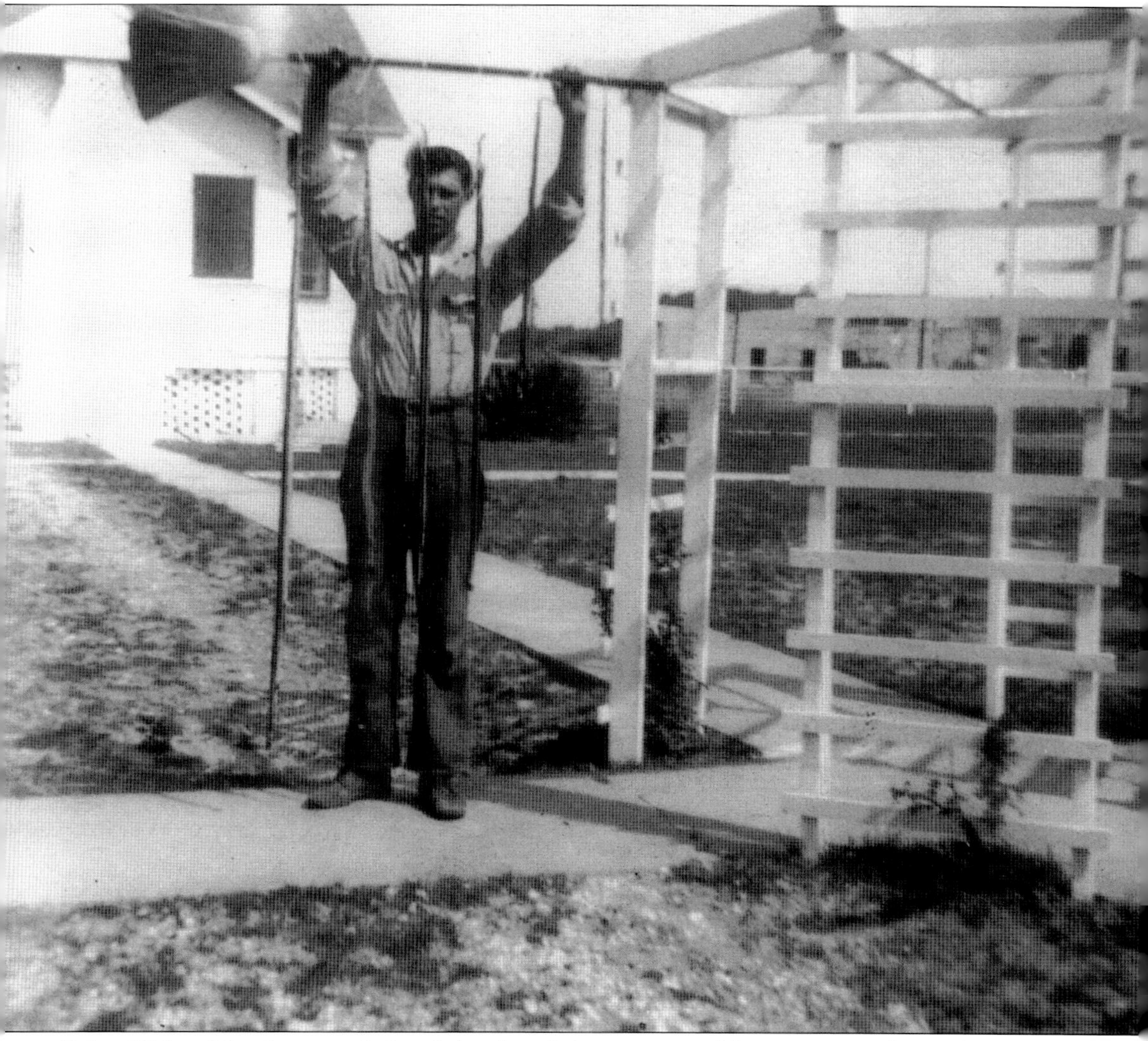

Before Tybee Island was settled and developed, it was covered by a maritime forest. It was a natural habitat for a diversity of birds, animals, and reptiles. The island still hosts a variety of sea birds and other species, small animals such as raccoons and opossums, and reptiles. In this photograph, a Coast Guard sailor displays a collection of snakes killed around the area of the Tybee Lighthouse. (Courtesy Charles and Carolyn Baker.)

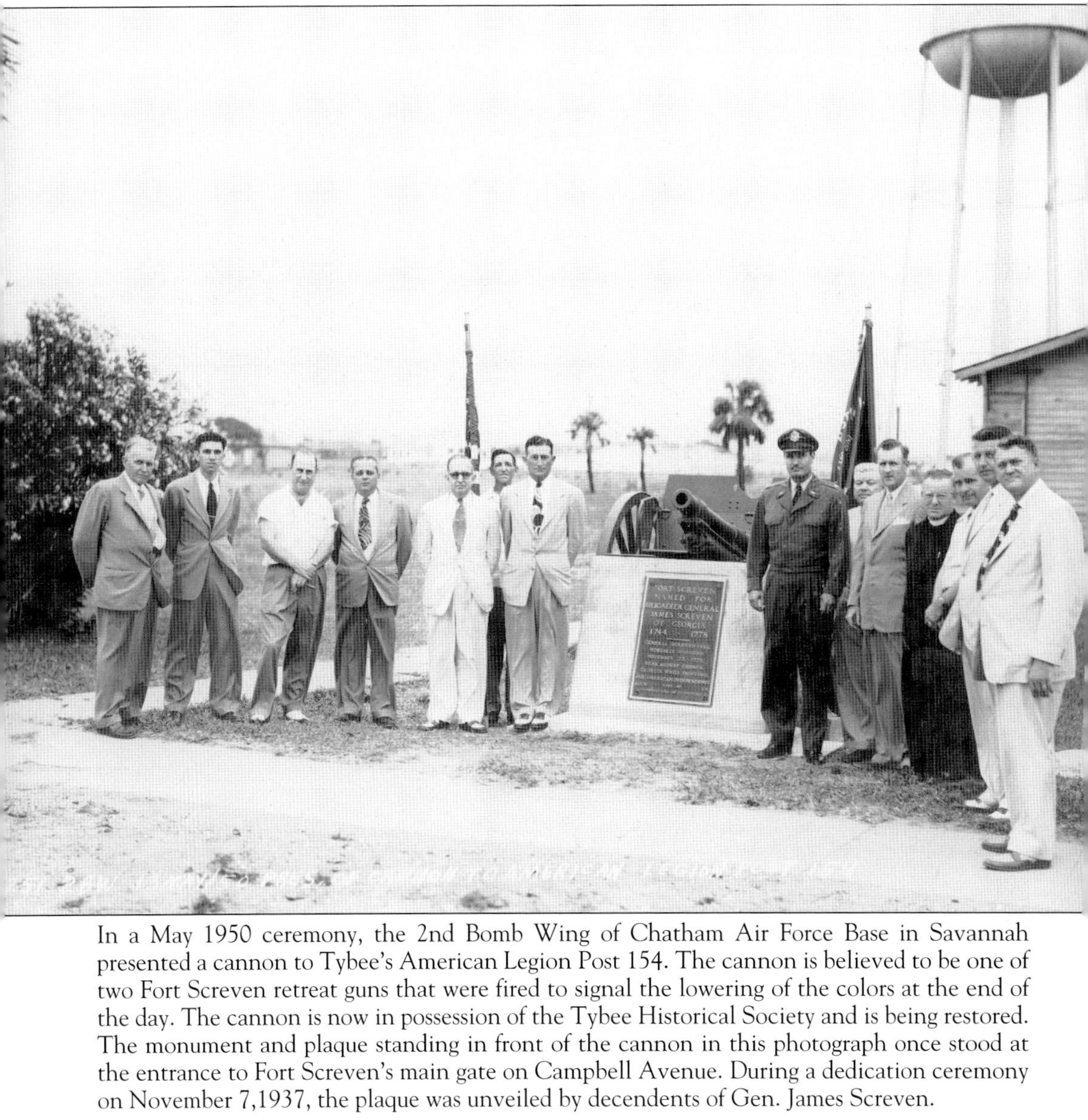

In a May 1950 ceremony, the 2nd Bomb Wing of Chatham Air Force Base in Savannah presented a cannon to Tybee's American Legion Post 154. The cannon is believed to be one of two Fort Screven retreat guns that were fired to signal the lowering of the colors at the end of the day. The cannon is now in possession of the Tybee Historical Society and is being restored. The monument and plaque standing in front of the cannon in this photograph once stood at the entrance to Fort Screven's main gate on Campbell Avenue. During a dedication ceremony on November 7,1937, the plaque was unveiled by decendents of Gen. James Screven.

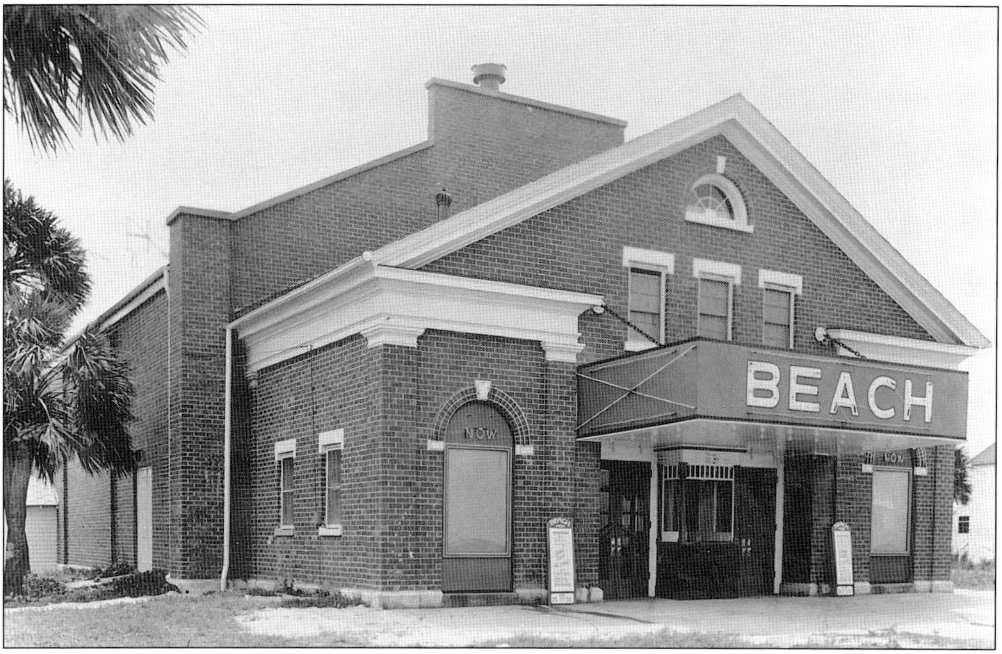

After Fort Screven was closed at the end of World War II, the old post theater continued to operate for several years under private ownership. Attending movies at the Beach Theater remained a favorite evening entertainment for island residents. According to older residents, it was a great place to take a date. The exterior view of the Beach was taken in 1946. The interior view of the theater auditorium was probably taken about the same time. (Courtesy Georgia Historical Society.)

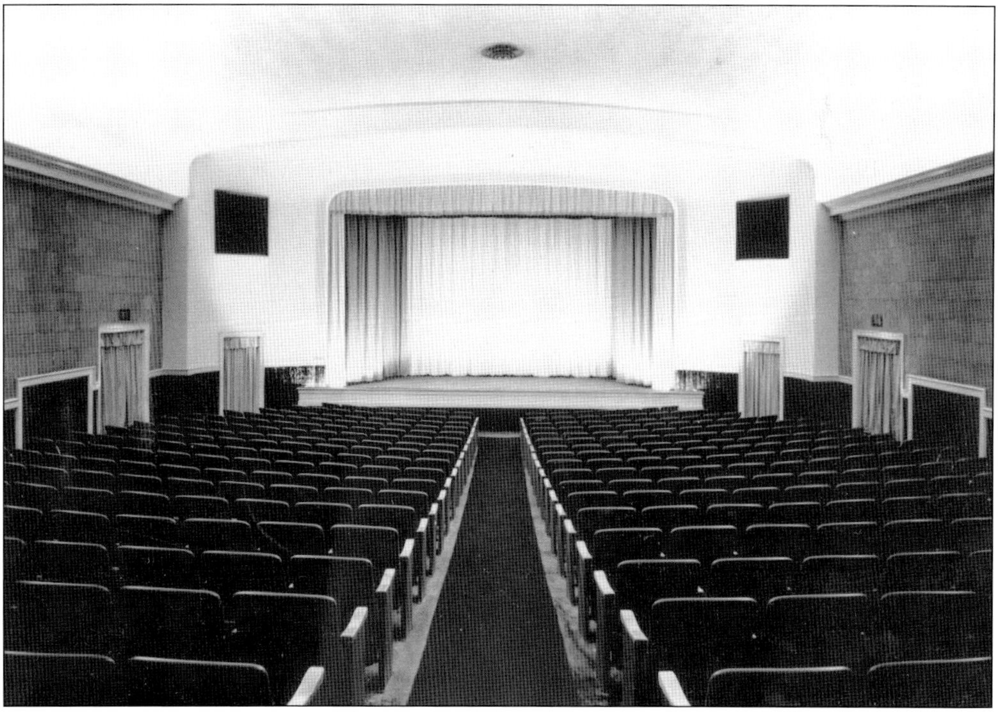

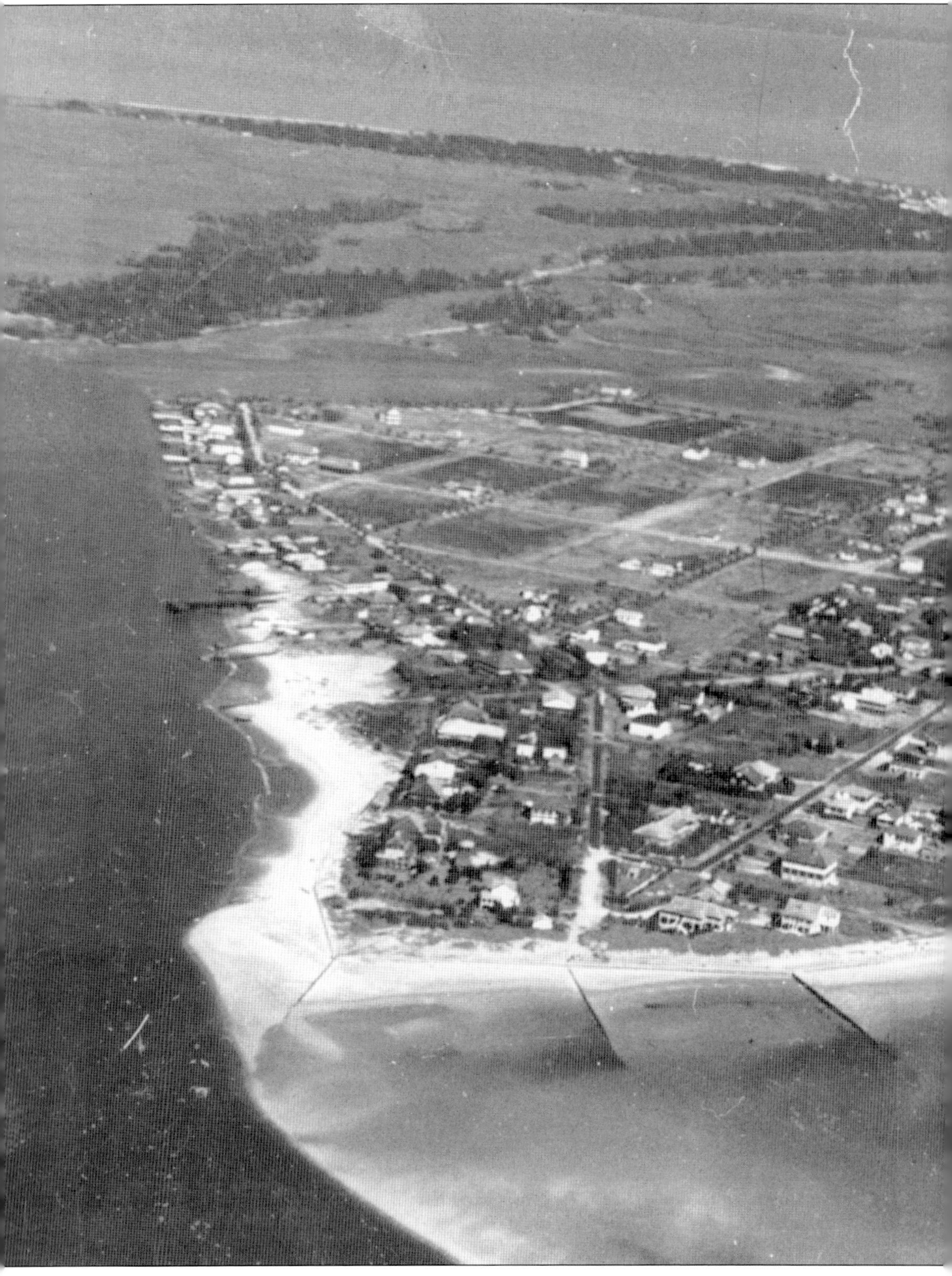

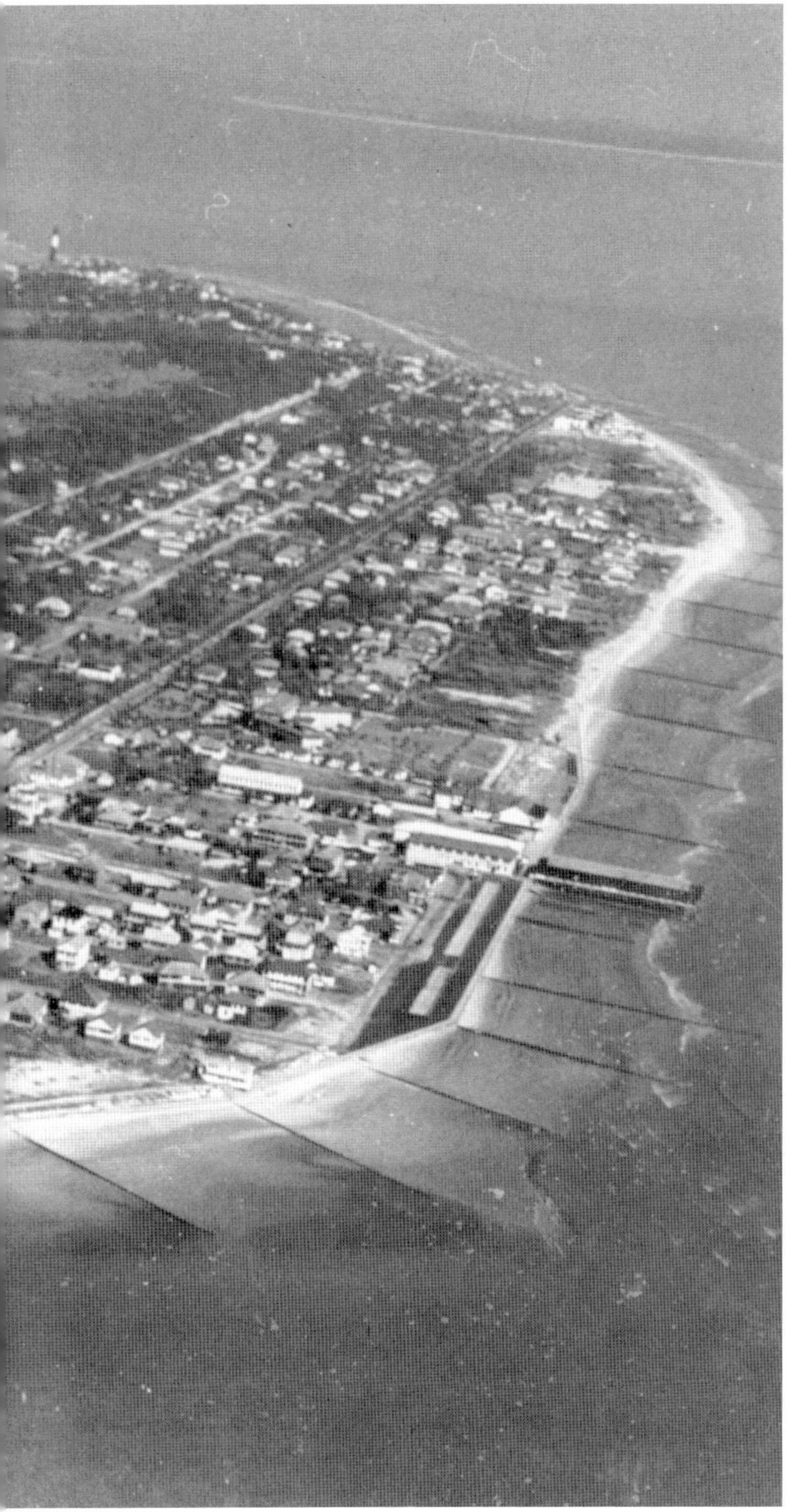

This aerial view of Tybee Island was taken sometime in the 1950s. The Tybrisa Pier and Pavilion can be seen jutting out over the south beach. The Tybrisa and several surrounding structures burned in 1967. The lighthouse is standing on the north shore. At the time this picture was taken, Tybee's early resort boom was coming to an end and the island began to take on its much-publicized laid back, residential ambience.

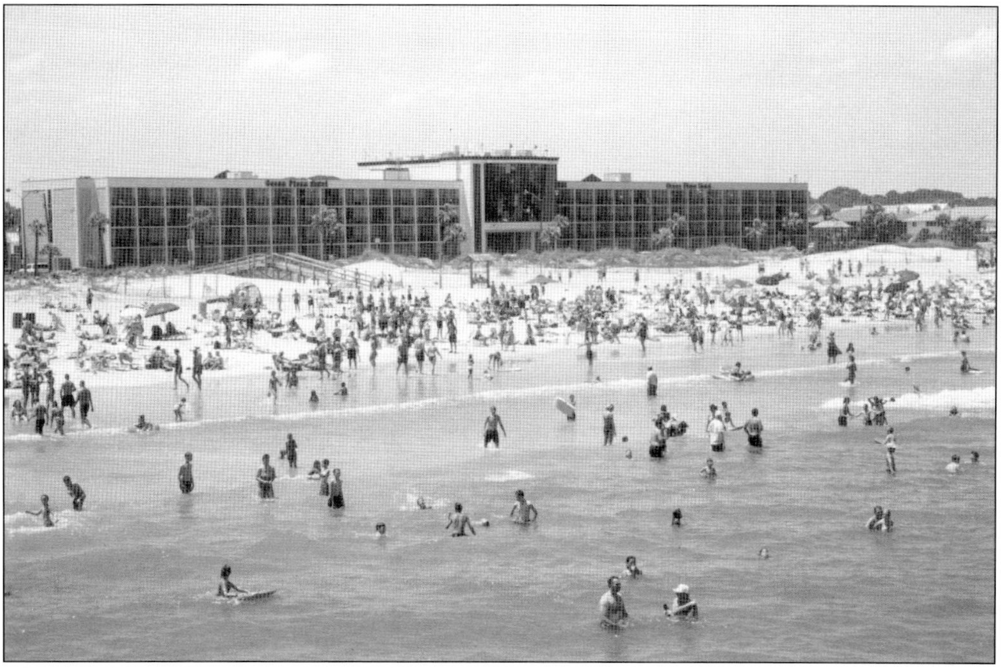

This beach scene from a busy holiday weekend in the year 2000 illustrates Tybee Island's resurgence as a beach resort during the decade of the 1990s. New hotels, rental properties, and beach renourishments are contributing to the revival of tourism.

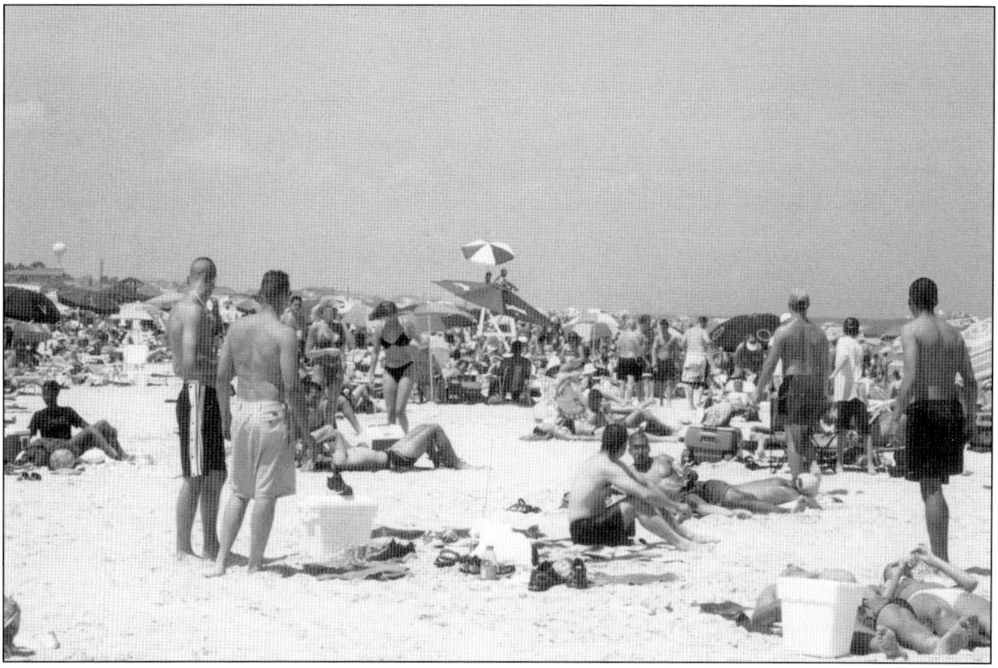

The more things change, the more they remain the same. The "bathing costumes" are now quite briefer and the automobiles that bring people to the beach are more modern, but a visit to Tybee Island has not otherwise changed since 1900. Now as it was then, tourists and daytrippers enjoy the sun, sand, and surf, the beachfront hotels, and the many dining establishments.

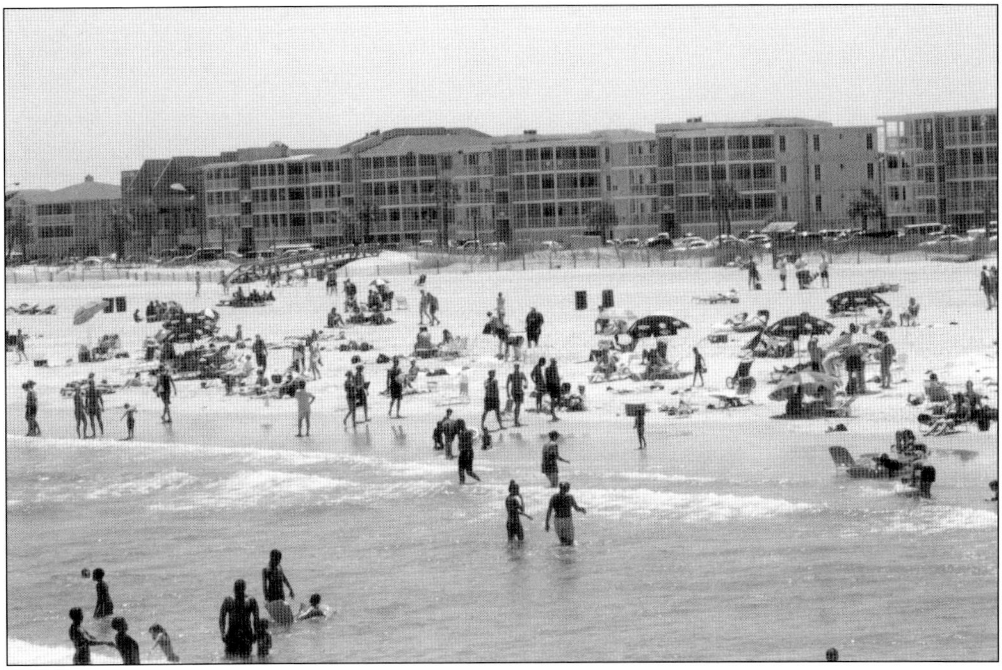

Most of the older buildings that lined The Strand and the Boardwalk during Tybee's early resort days of the 1900s have been replaced by oceanfront condominiums, as shown in this photo from 2000.

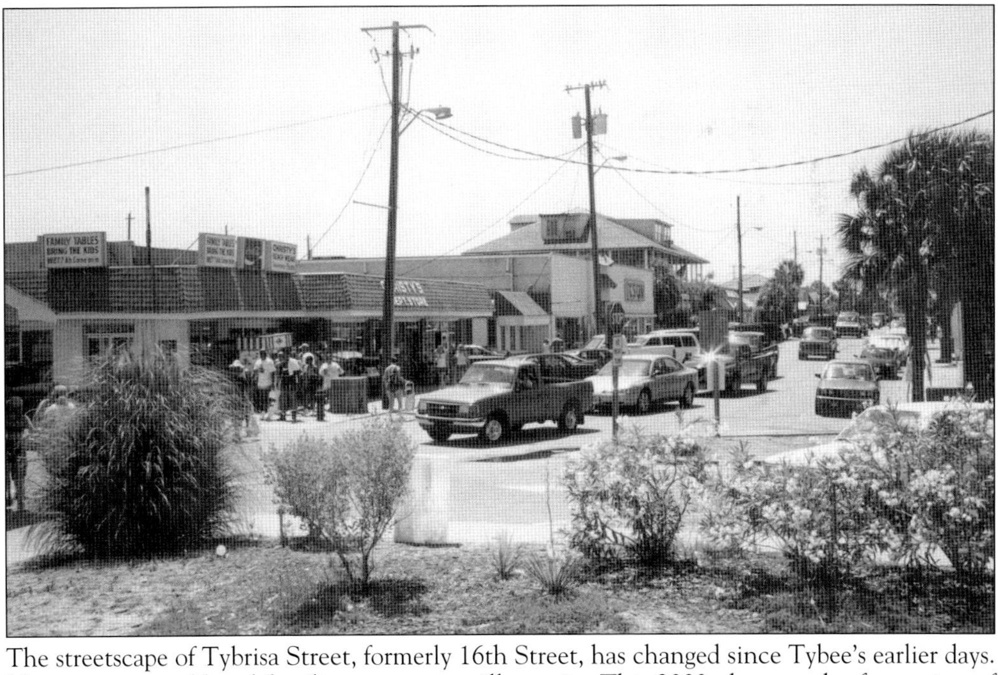

The streetscape of Tybrisa Street, formerly 16th Street, has changed since Tybee's earlier days. However, some old and familiar structures still remain. This 2000 photograph of a section of Tybrisa Street near The Strand shows Christy's Department Store (est. 1944), T.S. Chu and Co. Department Store (est. 1933), and the Carbo House (*c*. 1920s). For many years, the Tybee Amusement Park occupied an area on the opposite side of the street.

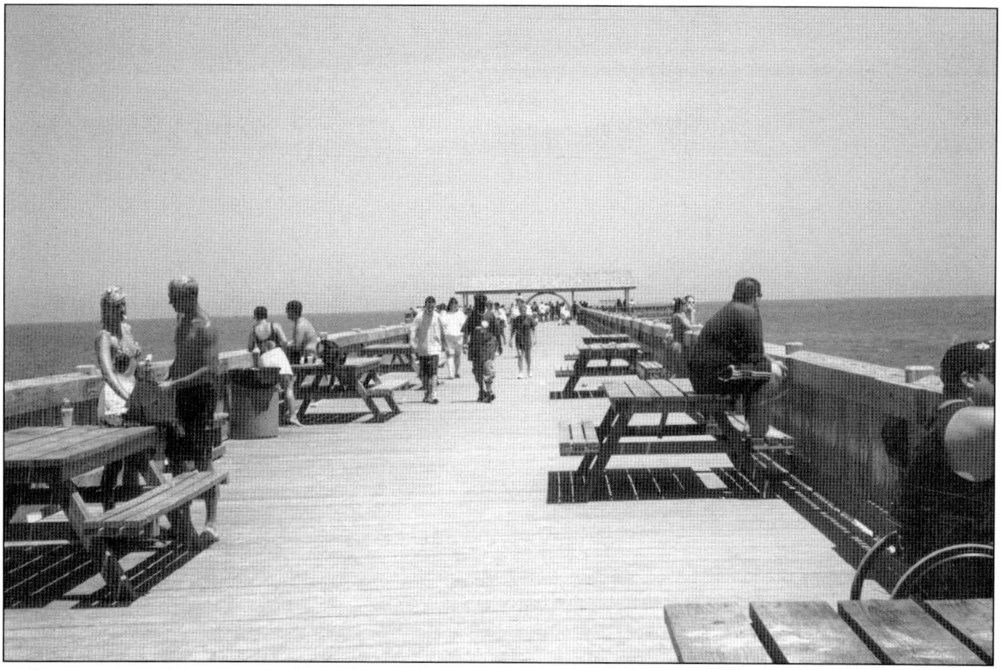

Tybee's new public pier and pavilion occupies the same location as the historic Tybrisa. The pier stretches out over the beach and into the surf. It is a popular spot for fishing enthusiasts and for those who simply want to watch the never-ceasing activity of the beach and the Atlantic Ocean. The pavilion area is used for concerts, dances, festivals, and other community and private functions.

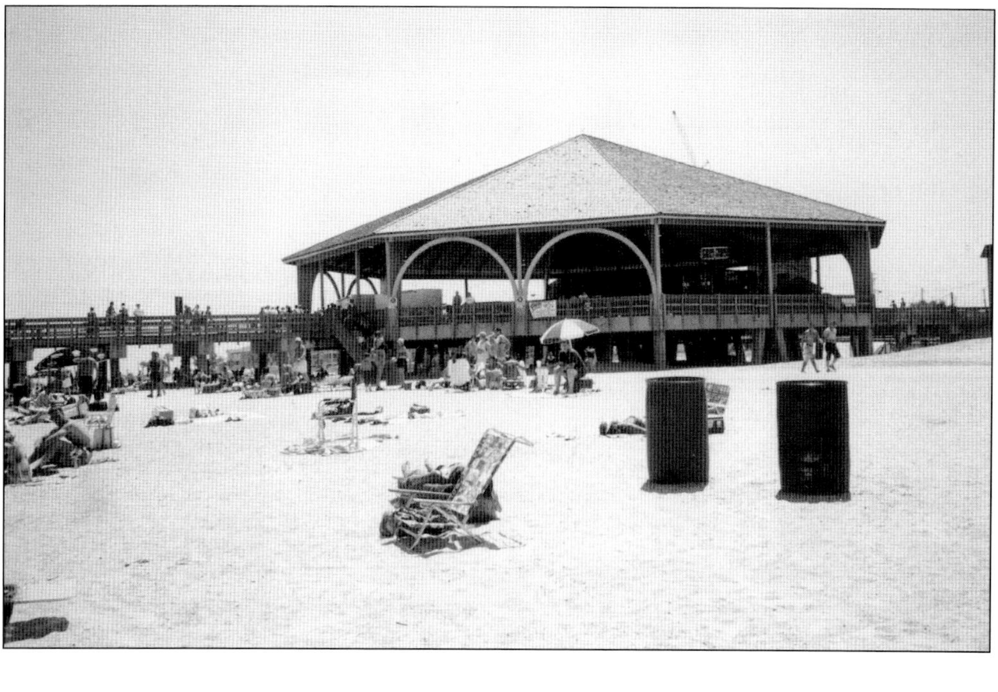

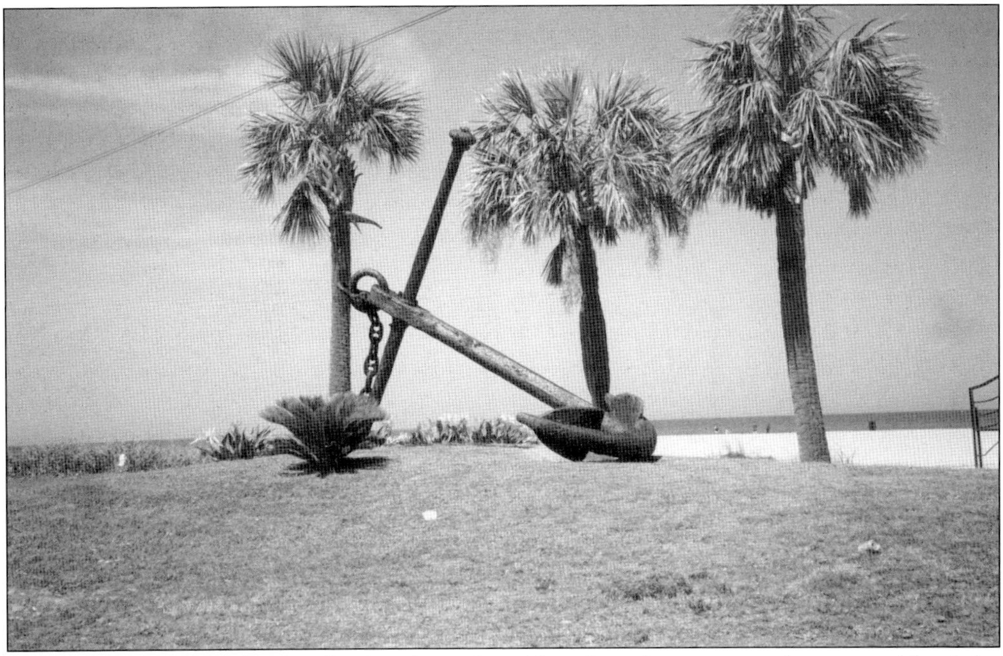

One of Tybee's most familiar landmarks is the old anchor that rests on the ocean side of the big curve of Butler Avenue. The anchor was salvaged from the sunken wreck of an old wooden sailing ship discovered several miles off the island's north shore. The anchor was recovered in 1989 by Capt. Bill Walsh Sr. of Tybee Island and donated to the city. It is a favorite picture-taking spot for tourists.

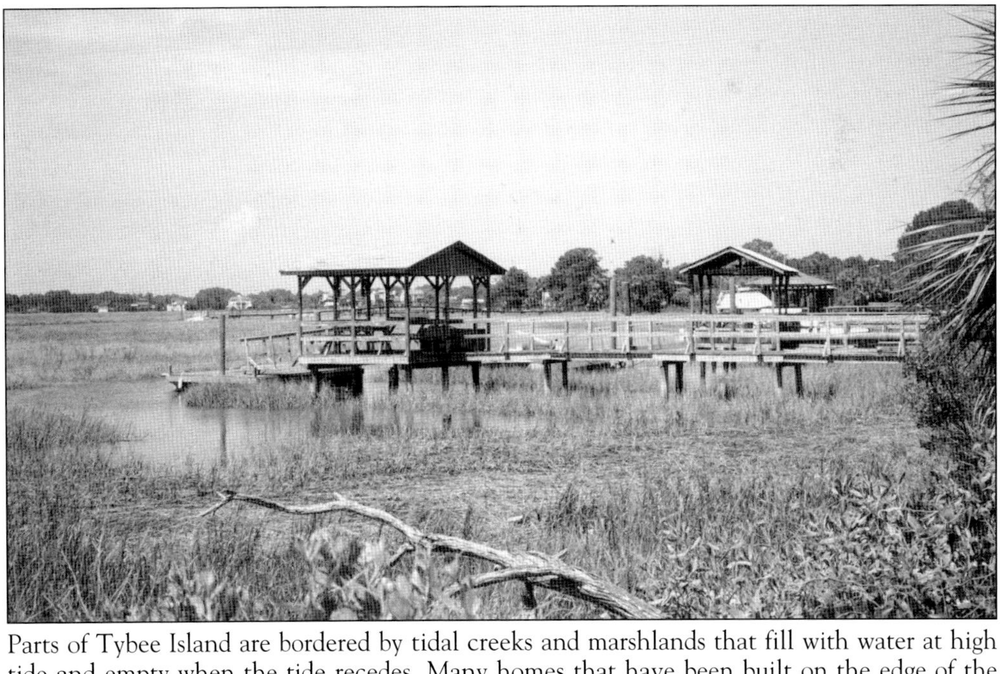

Parts of Tybee Island are bordered by tidal creeks and marshlands that fill with water at high tide and empty when the tide recedes. Many homes that have been built on the edge of the marshlands have docks and small pavilions for fishing, or for sitting and watching the sunset. Watercraft can only move in and out of some marsh areas during times of high tide.

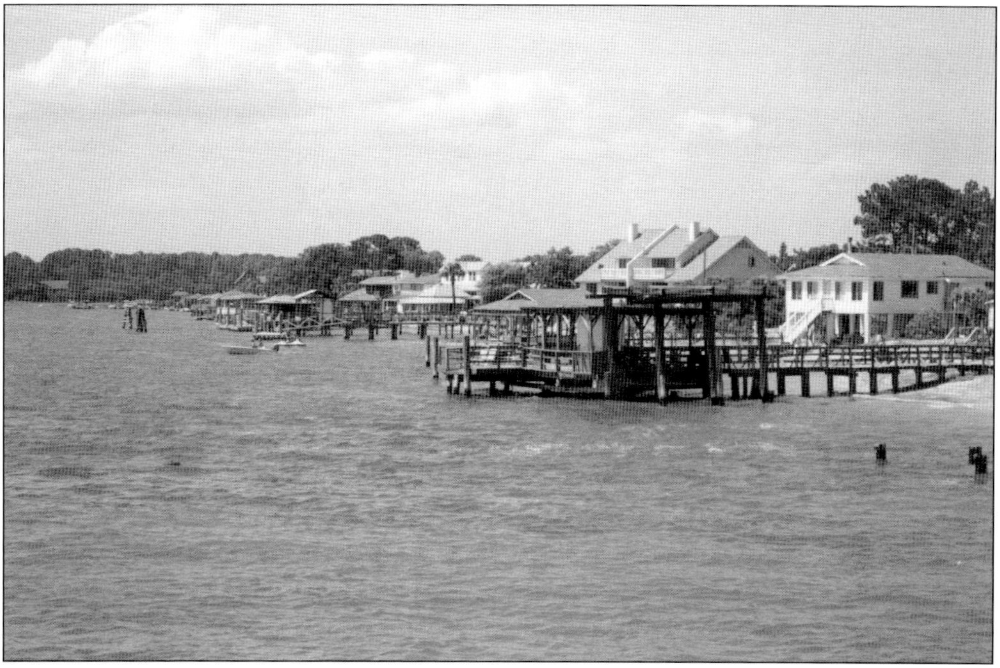

This is a photograph of part of an expanse of beach along the Back River. Because of its proximity to Tybee's old resort complex, the Back River was one of the earliest residential areas to develop. It is now a mix of old and new residences. Many of the homes have docks and pavilions.

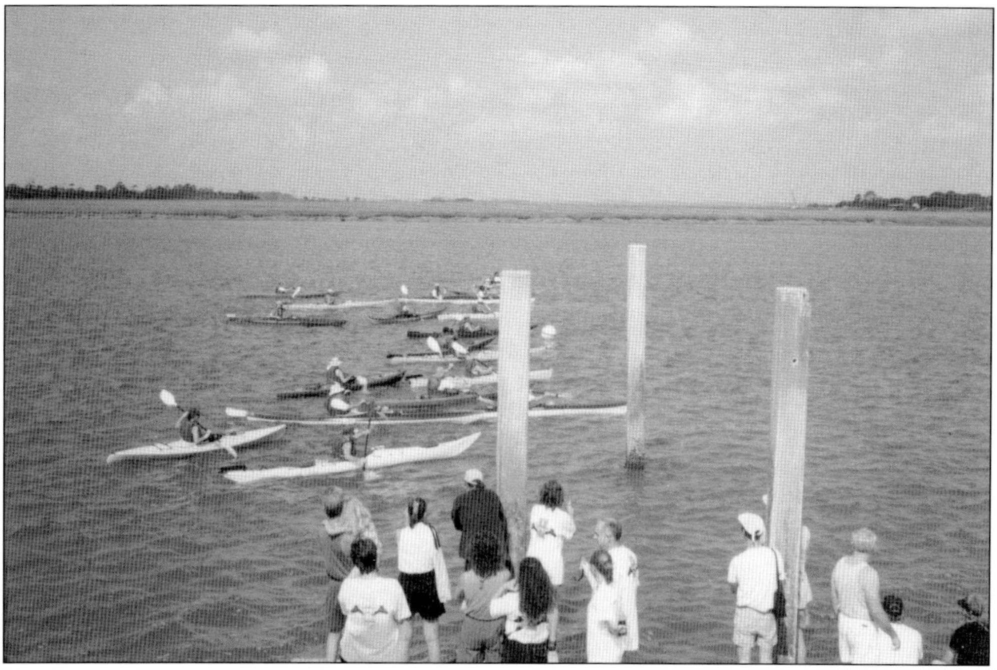

Kayaking is becoming a popular water sport on Tybee's rivers and creeks. This photograph is of one of the popular kayak races that are run on the Back River. The event draws many competitors as well as many observers. (Courtesy J.R. Roseberry.)

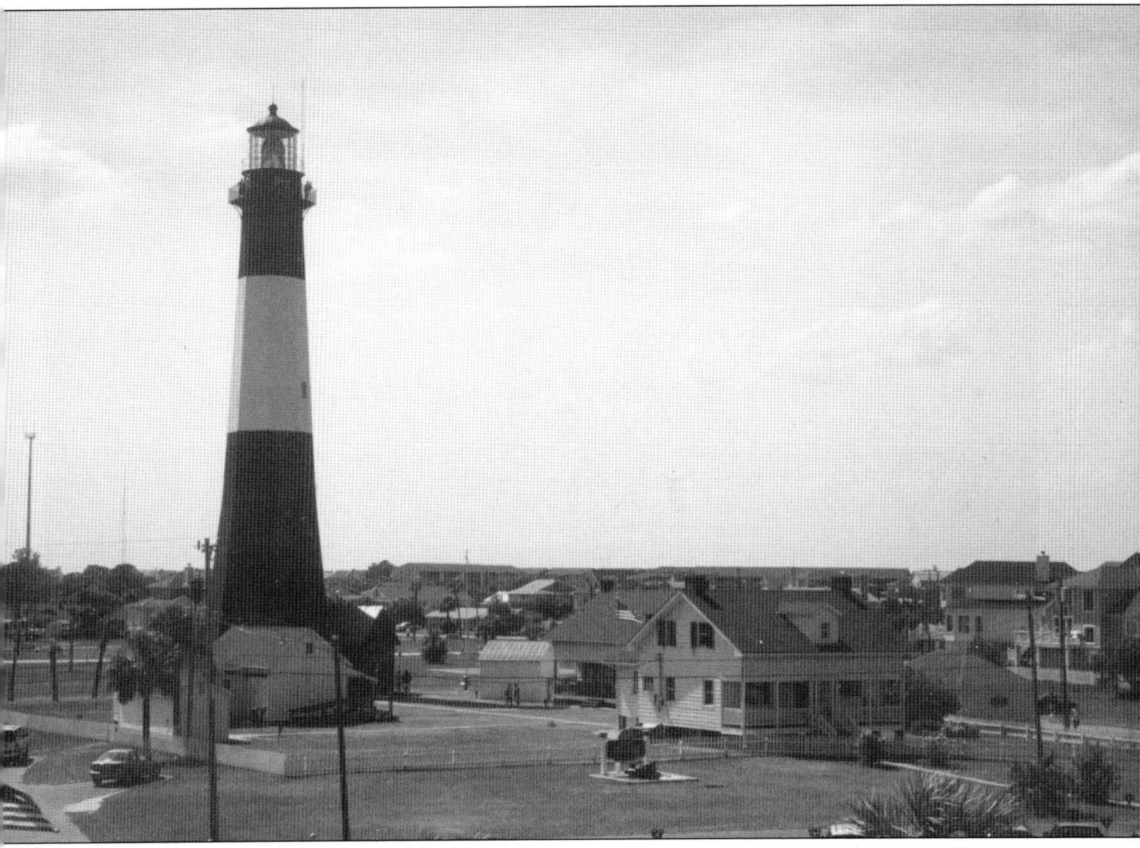

This photograph of the Tybee Island Lighthouse and Lightstation was taken in 2000. An extensive restoration of the historic lighthouse, the oldest and tallest in Georgia, was completed in 1999. The Tybee Lightstation is one of only a few in the country that has all of its support buildings intact. The exterior paint pattern, or daymark, of the lighthouse is the only one of its kind in the country. The site is visited by over 70,000 people a year. Notice the new residential development that surrounds the light station complex.

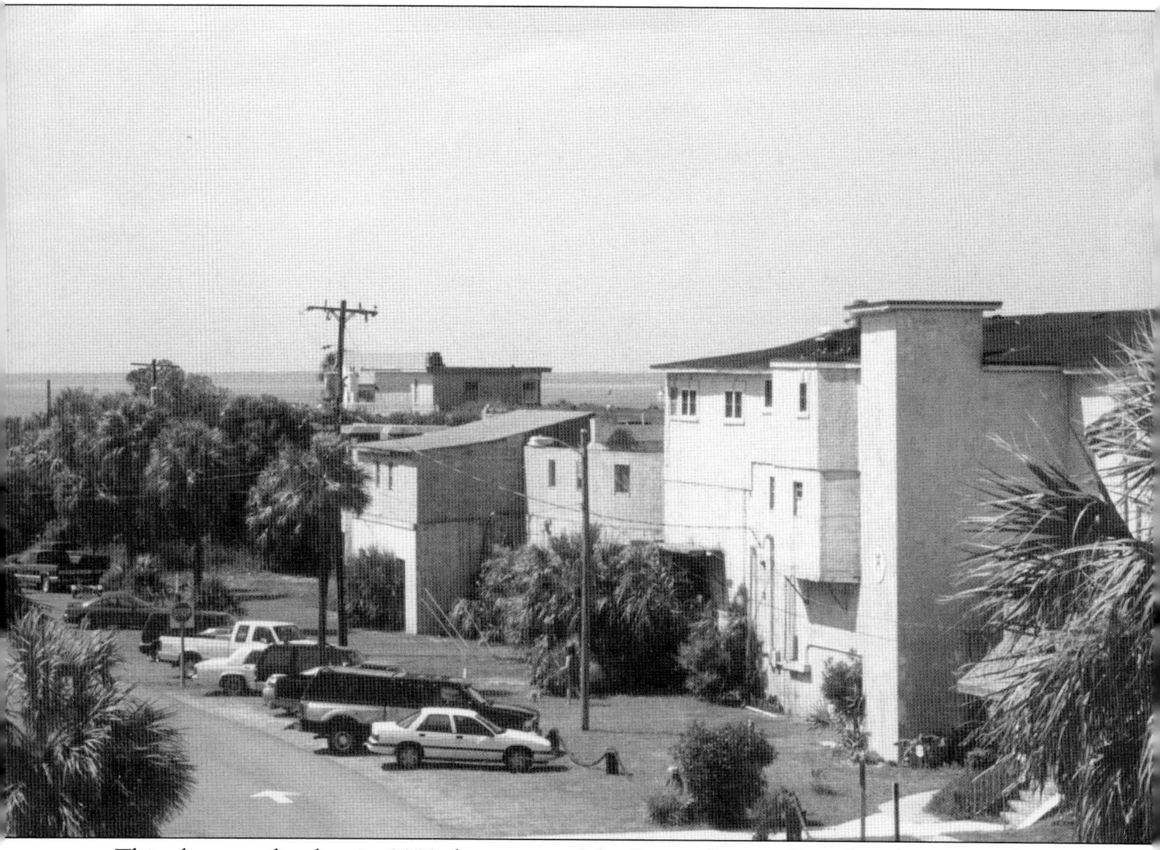

This photograph taken in 2000 shows part of the former Battery Brumby of Fort Screven. Most of the old concrete fortifications have come under private ownership since the city of Savannah Beach sold the fort property to private investors after World War II. The house to the far left sits atop one of the former gun positions. The complex to the far right houses the Tybee Lite Shrine Club. The small section in the middle is what remains of gun position #3.

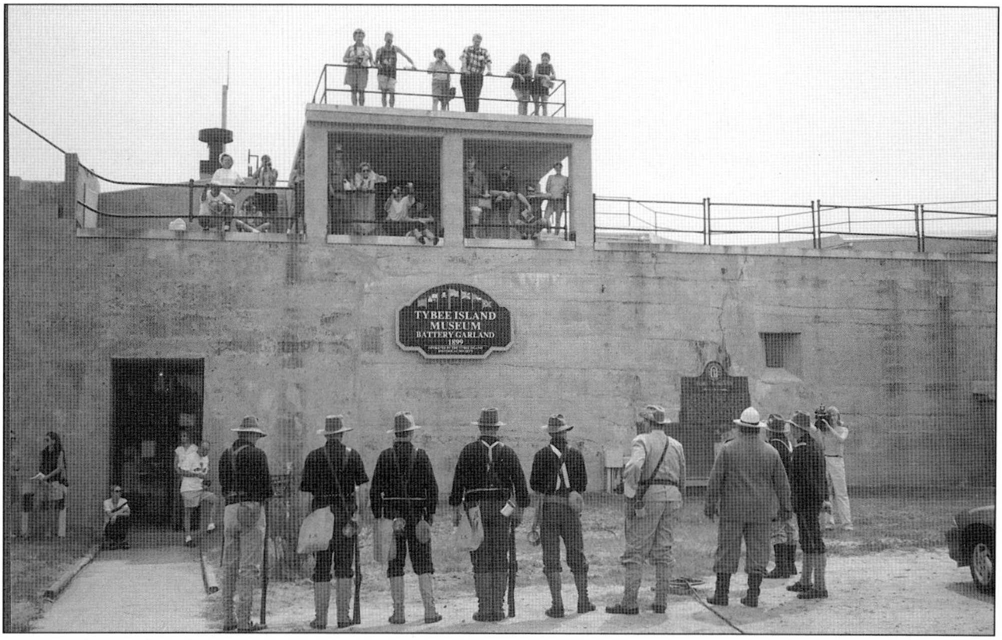

The Tybee Island Historical Society frequently sponsors festivals and reenactments that give islanders and visitors a chance to relive some of Tybee's past. A major part of the festivals is the appearance of uniformed military history interpreters representing all of the nation's wars in which Tybee was directly involved. In the above photograph, taken during an observance of the 1998 Spanish-American War Centennial, a group of uniformed reenactors gave demonstrations for visitors to the Tybee Island Museum, formerly Battery Garland. Alex Solera of Tampa, FL, below, portrayed a Army officer of the Spanish-American War era.

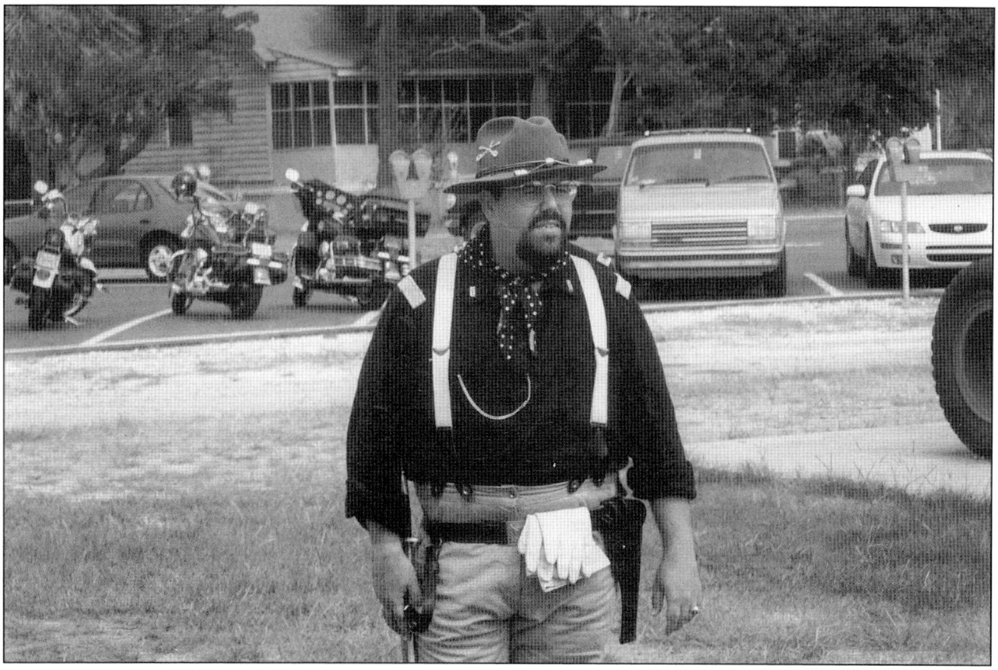

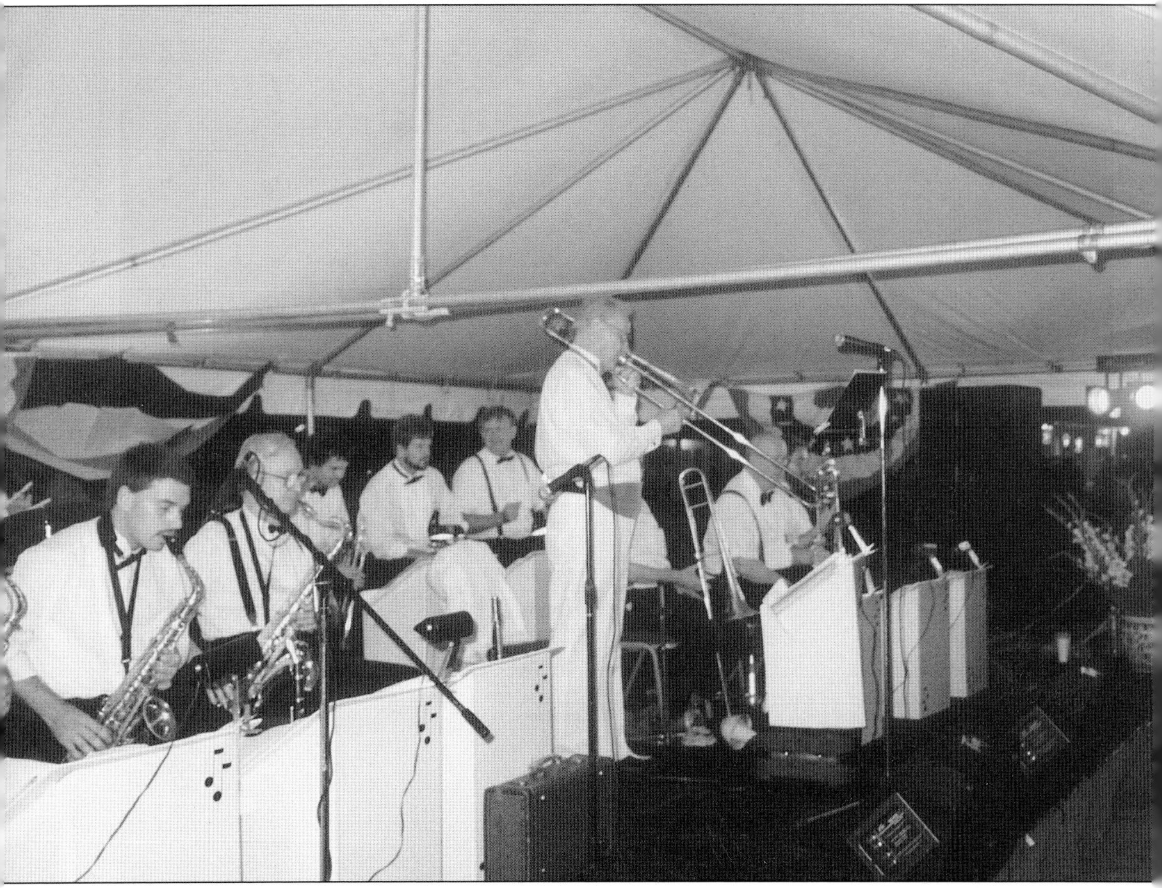

Many Tybee Island and Savannah residents still have fond memories of dancing under the reflecting ball at the Tybrisa or under the stars on the beach to the sweet and swinging sounds of the big bands. For a few hours one evening in the 1990s, they were given a chance to relive those good times of their youth when Warren Covington brought his big band to play for a dance under a huge tent that was erected on the beach. Covington and his band made a return engagement to help celebrate the opening of the new Tybee Pier and Pavilion. Crowds now pack the new Tybee Pavilion to listen to all kinds of music, from classical to big band, from country to beach music, and from jazz to rock and roll.

The skies over Tybee's beaches are decorated each summer with colorful displays of kites of different sizes and configurations, each controlled by talented kite flying enthusiasts. The annual Gone With the Wind kite festivals are attended by expert flyers from Georgia and surrounding states. The festivals include contests, displays, demonstrations, and free instruction for the novice kite flier. (Courtesy Carl Looper.)

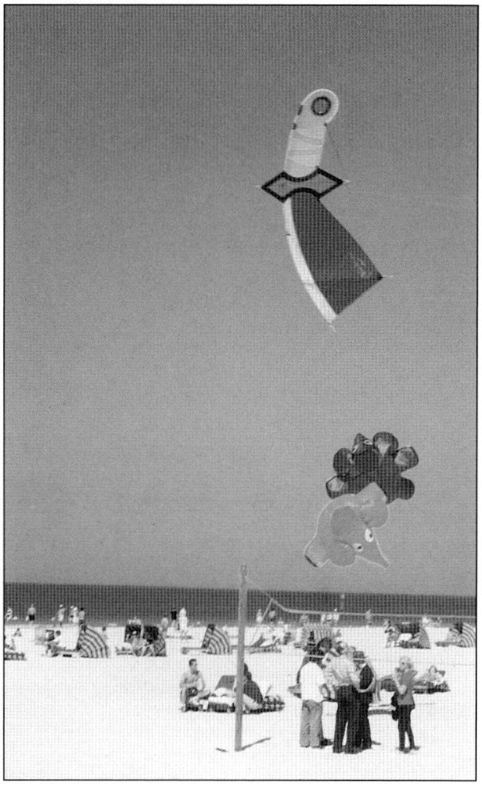

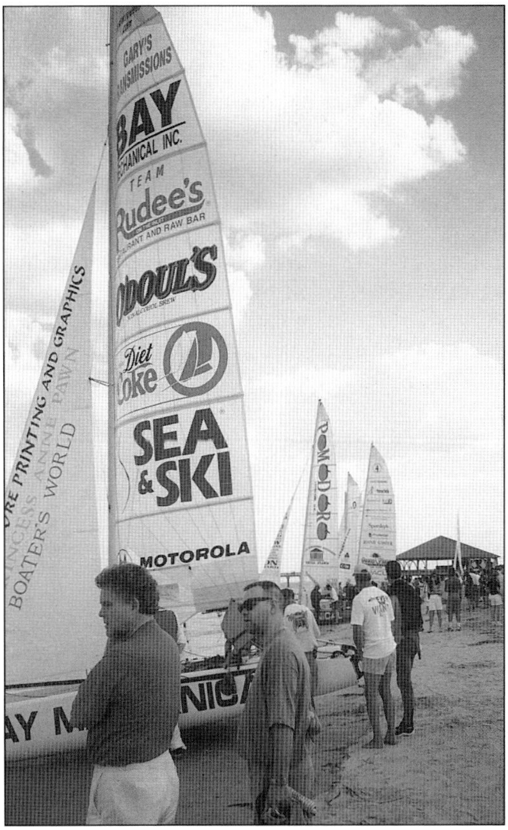

Tybee Island is one of the original stopovers and check points for the annual Worrell 1000 boat race that begins in Fort Lauderdale, FL, and ends at Virginia Beach, VA. Tybee marks the approximate halfway point of the approximate 1,000-mile race up the East Coast. A Tybee sailing team obtained sponsorships and began competing in the Worrell 1000 in 1999. (Courtesy J.R. Roseberry.)

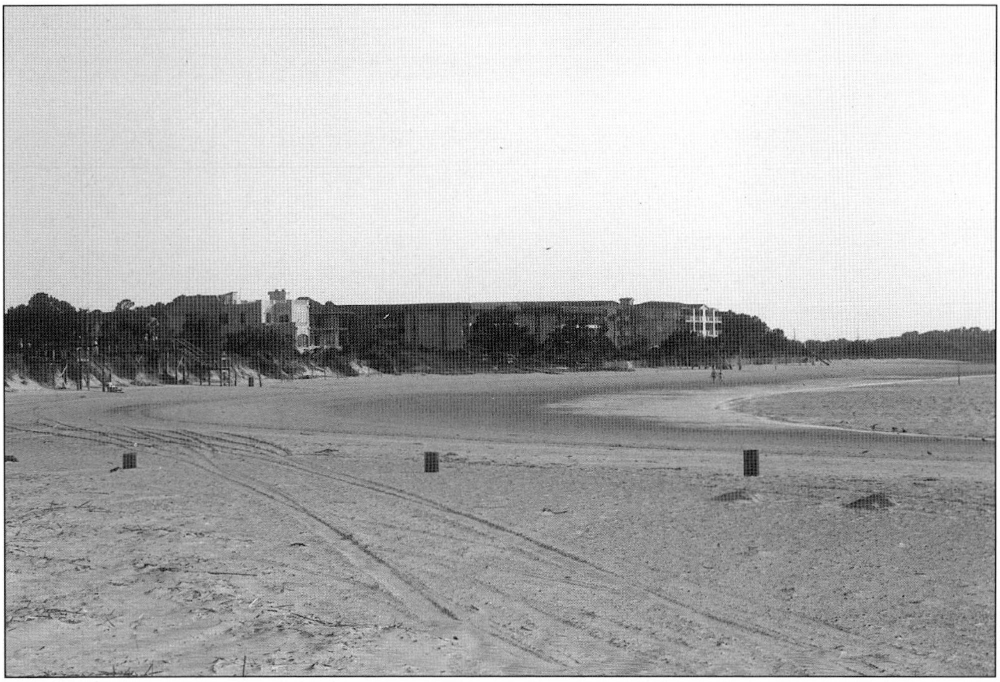

As these photographs so vividly indicate, Tybee Island is no longer the "best kept secret on the east coast." The word has spread and the close of the 20th century and beginning of the 21st century has seen an unprecedented growth in the number of single and multi-family homes on the small island. The beach homes and condominiums shown in these photographs are on the north beach area. Tybee Island's full-time resident population is approaching 3,500. There are also many part-time residents who have chosen the island to establish their second homes.

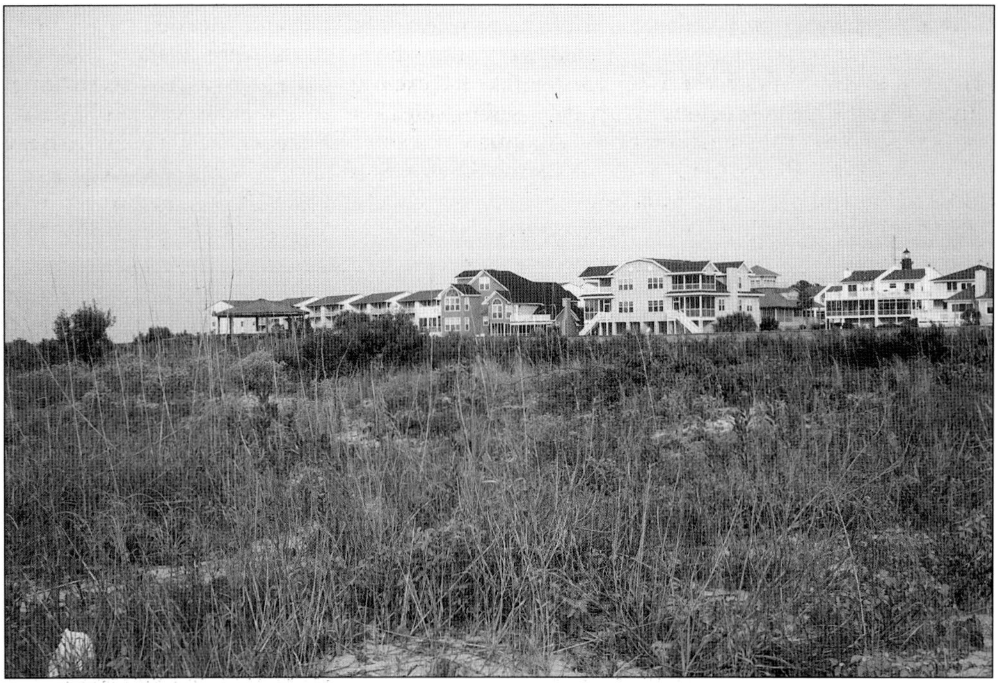

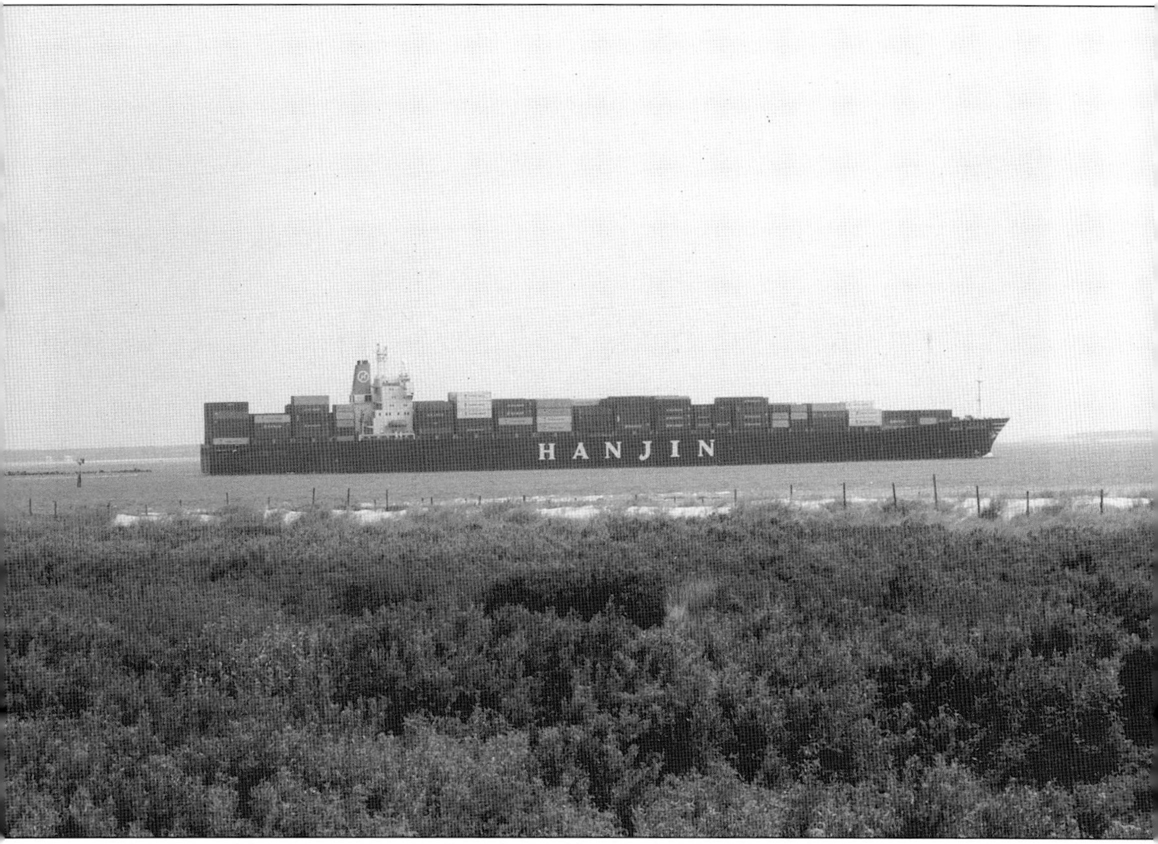

Every day several large oceangoing ships from all over the world pass by Tybee as they enter and leave the Port of Savannah, one of the east coast's busiest ports. Residents view this as a normal part of living on Tybee Island. To visitors, however, the sight of these large ships gliding smoothly through the water is unfamiliar and exciting. Tybee Island has a long maritime history. In the Georgia colony's early days, sailing ships entered and left Savannah by passing through an area at the junction of the Atlantic Ocean and Savannah River called the Bay of Shoals, or Tybee Roads. On May 11, 1819, the S.S. *Savannah*, the first steam-powered vessel to cross the Atlantic, steamed from Savannah to Tybee and returned. Its honored passenger for that short voyage was visiting President James Monroe.

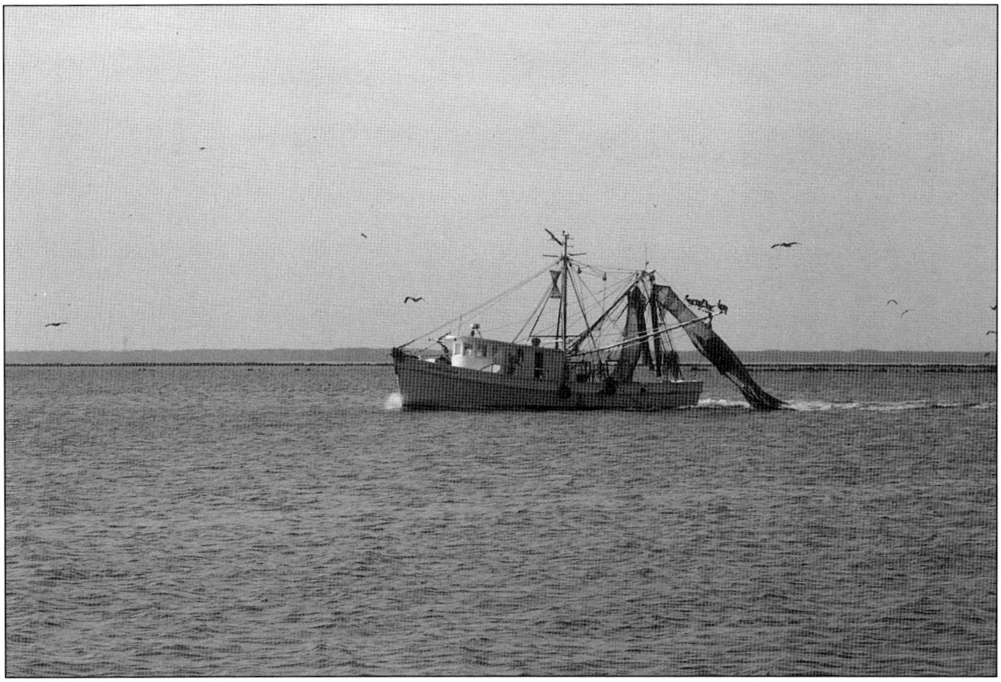

Georgia's shrimping season is a busy time on the waters around Tybee and all along the Georgia coast. From early morning to late evening, Tybee's shrimp boats can be seen casting their nets to capture the favorite seafood delicacy of the region. In the above photograph, a shrimp boat passes the north beach on its way to its home port. The bottom photograph is of shrimp boats tied up at their Lazaretto Creek docks. The bridge spanning the river in the background is a section of the Tybee Road.

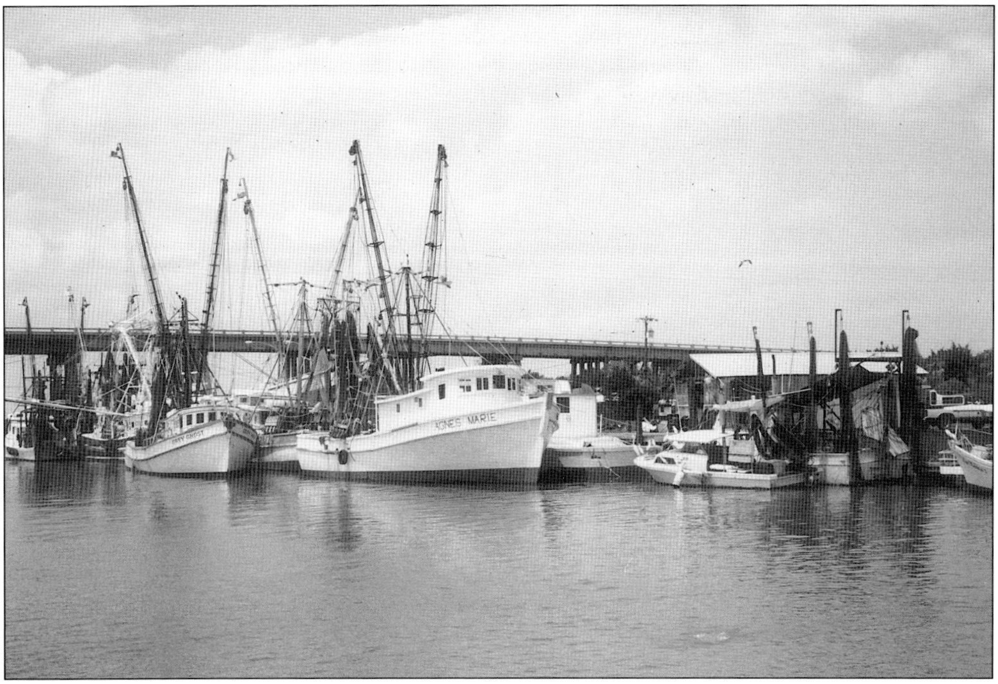

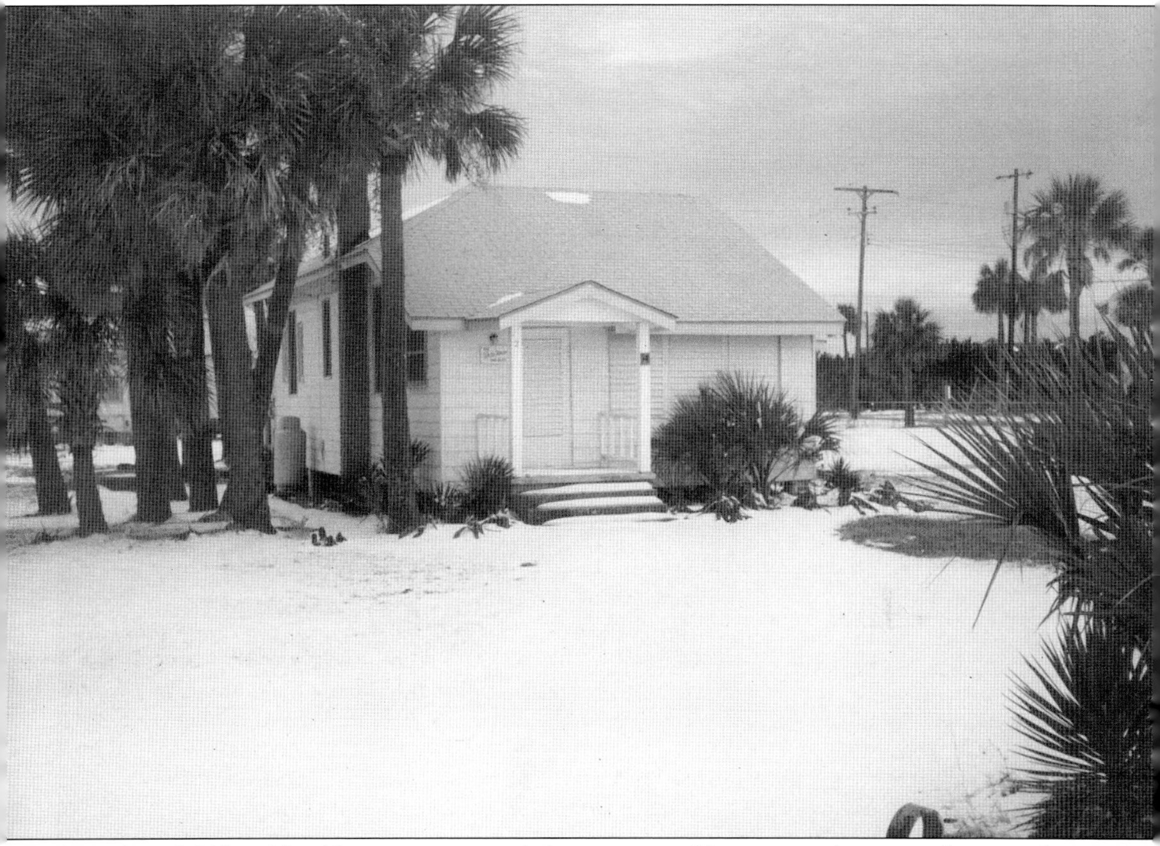

Even though Tybee Island has a semi-tropical climate most of the time, and snow on the ground is an unfamiliar sight, the island enjoyed at least one white Christmas in recent years. This photograph of the White cottage, located in the Fort Screven area, was taken on Christmas Day, 1989. (Courtesy Louise White.)

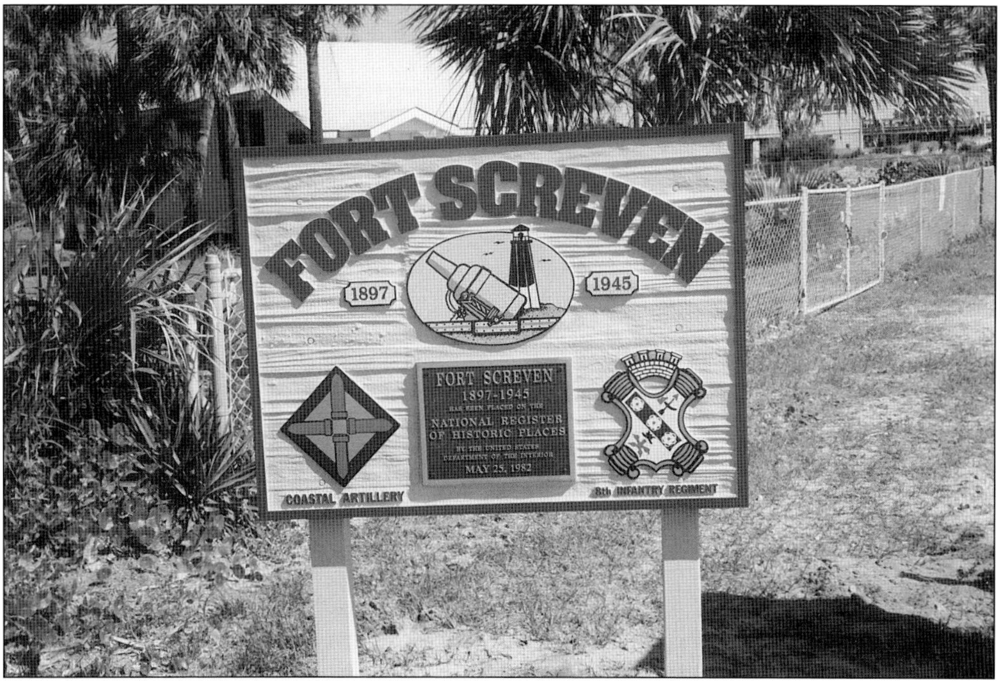

As the Tybee Island that older residents remember continues to change with the times, many islanders are involved in projects designed to promote awareness of their island's colorful past. Interpretive signs placed at two of the former Fort Screven reservation gates inform readers that the Fort Screven area is listed on the prestigious National Register of Historic Places. Tybee has three National Historic districts.

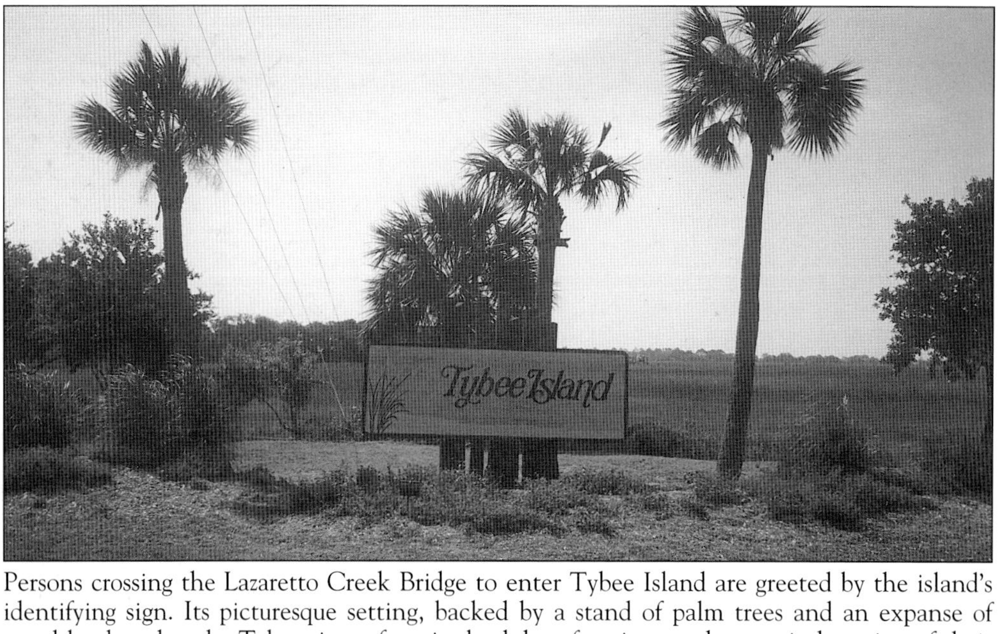

Persons crossing the Lazaretto Creek Bridge to enter Tybee Island are greeted by the island's identifying sign. Its picturesque setting, backed by a stand of palm trees and an expanse of marshland, makes the Tybee sign a favorite backdrop for pictures that remind tourists of their island vacation and invite them back. A familiar island saying warns visitors that once they get Tybee sand between their toes, they will forever have an urge to return.